KURT HARTWIG

Modern Czech Theatre

Modern

STUDIES IN

THEATRE HISTORY

& CULTURE

Edited by Thomas Postlewait

JARKA M. BURIAN

Czech Theatre

REFLECTOR AND CONSCIENCE OF A NATION

UNIVERSITY OF IOWA PRESS ⚘ IOWA CITY

University of Iowa Press, Iowa City 52242
Copyright © 2000 by Jarka M. Burian
All rights reserved
Printed in the United States of America
http://www.uiowa.edu/~uipress
No part of this book may be reproduced or used in any form or by
any means, electronic or mechanical, including photocopying
and recording, without permission in writing from the publisher.
All reasonable steps have been taken to contact copyright holders
of material used in this book. The publisher would be pleased to
make suitable arrangements with any whom it has not been possible to reach.

The publication of this book was generously supported by the
University of Iowa Foundation.

Printed on acid-free paper

Library of Congress Cataloging-in-Publication Data
Burian, Jarka, 1927–
Modern Czech theatre: reflector and conscience of a nation /
by Jarka M. Burian.
    p.   cm. — (Studies in theatre history and culture)
Includes bibliographical references and index.
ISBN 0-87745-711-5 (cloth), ISBN 0-87745-722-0 (paper)
1. Theater — Czech Republic — History — 20th century.
2. Czech drama — 20th century — History and criticism.
I. Title. II. Series.
PN2859.C9 B84   2000
792'.094371'0904–dc21   99-058328

00 01 02 03 04 C 5 4 3 2 1
00 01 02 03 04 P 5 4 3 2 1

This book is dedicated to the memory of my parents, Jaroslav Valerian Burian and Olga Marsano Burian, who fostered my interest in Czech culture and in the theatre.

CONTENTS

Preface, ix

Acknowledgments, xi

Introduction, 1

1   1780–1900: Some Exposition before the Main Action, 9
2   1900–1938: From the Turn of the Century to Munich, 20
3   Theatre during the Occupation and War Years, 57
4   The Postwar Years and the 1950s, 67
5   The Dynamic 1960s, Part One: Significant New Plays, 93
6   The Dynamic 1960s, Part Two: Key Productions in New Studio Theatres and Elsewhere, 111
7   August 1968: The Trauma and Its Aftermath, 137
8   A Gradual Thawing in the 1980s, 153
9   1989: Annus Mirabilis for the Czechs and Their Theatre, 181
10 Liberation and Its Pains: The First Year after the November Revolution, 189
11 Czech Theatre of the 1990s, 199

Notes, 231

Selected Bibliography, 245

Index, 251

PREFACE

Although the achievements of Czech theatre and its leading individuals have been noted abroad throughout the century in reviews, articles, and even textbooks and encyclopedias, such foreign attention for the most part has been sporadic and fragmentary. A few books in English have been devoted to the work of individuals like Karel Čapek or Josef Svoboda or to Czech playwrights of the mid-century, but a book-length study of Czech theatre has yet to appear in English. I have attempted to remedy that unwarranted omission with this book, which focuses on twentieth-century Czech theatre after tracing its roots in the previous century.

A first-generation American of Czech parents, I grew up in New Jersey, with Czech as my first language before starting regular public school. My first contacts with Czech theatre were vivid but only intermittent. As a ten-year-old in 1937, I spent the summer in Czechoslovakia with my mother; among my memories were not only the funeral procession of Thomas G. Masaryk (founding father and first president of Czechoslovakia), but a few visits to the National Theatre in Prague, including one to see the Czech version of George S. Kaufman and Moss Hart's *You Can't Take It with You*. I also recall seeing my father in several amateur productions of Czech plays in the Czech quarter of New York in the mid- and late 1930s, including František Langer's *The Mounted Patrol* (Jízdní hlídka). In January 1939 in New York City I attended the first émigré performance of the masterful comic duo of Jiří Voskovec and Jan Werich, who had been forced to close their unique theatre in Prague the previous fall after the debacle at Munich. On leave from duty with the Army of Occupation in Germany in 1947, I visited Prague again and saw several major productions, even though I was not aware of those responsible for them: Jiří Frejka's production of *Macbeth*, starring Otomar Krejča, designed by František Tröster; and Jindřich Honzl's production of the Čapek brothers' *The Insect Comedy*, designed by Josef Svoboda. The names (other than the authors') meant nothing to me then, but they already were, or were to become, decisive figures in the history of modern Czech theatre, and the specific productions were postwar landmarks. Such were the seeds and the soil for my eventual serious interest in Czech theatre. In graduate school and then when teaching I occasionally translated and directed a Czech play, including Viktor Dyk's *The Coming to Wisdom of Don Quixote*, the Čapeks' *Insect Comedy*, and the American premiere of Václav Havel's *The Memorandum* (December 1966 at the University at Albany, New York).

The primary impulse for my later, formal studies of Czech theatre derived from my numerous on-site experiences as an audience member, theatre researcher, and even theatre practitioner in what is now the Czech Republic. These visits occurred between 1965 and 1997 while I was on leave from the Department of Theatre at the University at Albany. In addition to research in archives during those visits abroad, I had the opportunity for direct observation of the Czech theatre and its audiences during literally hundreds of performances, many of which occurred in critical, highly charged times for both the Czechs and their theatre. Over the years, I also met and interviewed many leading artists, critics, and scholars, some of whose theatre experiences dated back to the 1920s.

Moreover, during my first postwar visit, in 1965, after lecturing on American theatre to university students in Prague, Brno, and Bratislava, I had the rare experience of directing a professional production (in Czech) of Tennessee Williams' *The Glass Menagerie* in the professional repertory theatre in Kladno, some twenty miles east of Prague center. The involvement was invaluable. It acquainted me directly with the personnel, structure, and daily operations of Czech repertory practice from within its working spaces.

From such varied encounters with the Czech stage and those creating it, as well as from my research in written materials, I developed and published numerous studies to call attention to this distinctive theatre in relation to its sociopolitical context. The present book is an edited and supplemented selection of those publications, along with substantial new material.

ACKNOWLEDGMENTS

It is a pleasure to acknowledge my indebtedness and thanks to a variety of organizations and individuals.

For granting me permission to reprint parts of articles originally appearing in their journals and periodicals, I am grateful to the editors of *American Theatre*, the *Drama Review, Drama Survey, Educational Theatre Journal, Modern Drama, Plays and Players, Slavic and East European Performance, Theatre Design and Technology, Theatre History Studies, Theatre Journal, Theatre Survey*, and the *Village Voice*.

I am equally indebted to the liberal kindness of numerous photographic artists in granting permission for their works to be used as enhancements of the following study. Above all I wish to acknowledge the contribution made to my writings by the photographs of the late Jaromír Svoboda, and to thank his widow, Zdena Svobodová, for her authorization to use a selection of his photos here. Others whose photographic artistry is to be found in the following pages are Jaroslav Krejčí, Alexandr Paul, Oldřich Pernica, Vojtěch Pisařík, Martin Poš, Jaroslav Prokop, Josef Ptáček, Lubomír Rohan, Vilém Sochůrek, Martin Špelda, Josef Svoboda, and Vladislav Vaňák. I also wish to thank the Czech National Theatre and its archive, headed by Zdena Benešová; the Prague Theatre Institute; and other Prague theatres for a few uncredited photographs, as noted in their respective captions.

My research and subsequent publications relating to Czech theatre were encouraged and facilitated by the generous support of others. I am deeply grateful to the administrations, committees, and councils of the following institutions.

The U.S. State Department Specialist's Grant supported my stay in Czechoslovakia in the fall of 1965, when I lectured at several universities and became seriously involved in Czech theatre. The Inter-University Committee on Travel Grants supported my research in Czechoslovakia in 1968–1969; the International Research Exchanges Board (IREX) underwrote two of my extended research visits to Prague (1974–1975, 1993–1994); the Council for International Exchange of Scholars (Fulbright Program) funded my research visit to Prague in the spring of

1988. My gratitude extends to several offices and ministries of the Czechoslovak Socialist Republic and its successor, the Czech Republic, for sharing in the support of these international cooperative grants. The National Endowment for the Humanities awarded me a valuable summer research grant in the 1970s; and from 1965 onward the State University of New York and the administration of the University at Albany provided me with a variety of grants and leaves of absence for my research and publications in Czech theatre.

Several specific institutions and archives in Prague provided me with cordial and sustained assistance in my studies.

Since 1965, the Prague Theatre Institute (Divadelní ústav) has been instrumental in my liaison with Czech theatres and their artists and has also granted me access to its own library and archives. I am especially grateful to its directors and other personnel, in particular the following: Eva Soukupová, director from the 1960s until the late 1980s, and subsequent directors Helena Albertová and Ondřej Černý. Jarmila Gabrielová, head of the institute's international liaison section, has for four decades continued to be a friendly counselor and guide. Others who provided generous help over the years include Blanka Calábková, Alena Kulhanková, Jaroslav Máchek, Květoslava Marková, Ladislava Petišková, Miroslava Potučková, Věra Ptáčková, and the personnel of the institute's archives.

The Theatre Section of the National Museum was a rich source of materials, especially those concerning Czech theatre from its beginnings to the mid-twentieth century. Some of its key personnel who provided me with valuable guidance were Jiří Hilmera, Vilemína Pecharová, and Jaroslav Janů.

The Cabinet for the Study of Czech Theatre, of the Czech Academy of Science, comprises specialist scholars dedicated to ongoing projects and publications in the history of Czech theatre. My work in Czech theatre owes a great deal to their scholarship and friendly counsel. Those with whom I had the most communication included František Černý (for long its guiding spirit), Adolf Scherl, Eva Šormová, Evžen Turnovský, and Milan Obst.

The Department of Theatre and Film Studies of Charles University often was a source of supplemental information from its store of graduate dissertations and its audio library and also provided valuable assistance from its faculty and staff, among whom I would particularly like to mention Jan Hyvnar, Josef Herman, and Eva Kolárová, in addition to the already cited František Černý, dean of Czech theatre scholars.

Czech theatre artists were not only a constant source of pleasure when I observed their work as a member of the audience, but also a unique fountain of information and insight when I met with them on one or more occasions to converse about their work and associations in the past as well as the present.

They belonged to several generations, and several were creative in more than one area of theatre. Here I should like to mention them with regard to their primary activity.

Actors included Bohumil Bezouška, Ladislav Boháč, Pavel Landovský, Martin Liška, Radovan Lukavský, Marie Málková, Miloš Nedbal, Ladislav Pešek, Luba Skořepová, Vladimír Šmeral, Jiřina Stránská, Jiří Voskovec, and Jan Werich.

Directors or choreographers generous with their time were Hana Burešová, Lída Engelová, Jan Grossman, Miloš Hynšt, Nina Jirsíková, Jan Kačer, Zdeněk Kaloč, Petr Kracik, Otomar Krejča, Karel Kříž, František Laurin, Petr Lébl, Miroslav Macháček, Ota Ornest, Karel Palouš, Luboš Pistorius, Jaromír Pleskot, Alfred Radok, Ivan Rajmont, Jan Schmid, Evald Schorm, Ladislav Smoček, Vladimír Strnisko, and Jaroslav Vostrý.

Designers who shared insights concerning not only their distinctive art but their broader awareness of Czech theatre were Jan Dušek, Jaroslav Malina, Miroslav Melena, Marta Rozskopová, Josef Svoboda, Ladislav Vychodil, Jana Zbořilová, and Ivo Žídek.

Many others had various roles or functions relating to modern Czech theatre (pedagogues, playwrights, dramaturgs, critics, theorists, editors, administrators, stage technicians), but all provided me with the benefit of their experience and knowledge: Milan Calábek, Antonín Dvořák, Anna Freimanová, Aleš Fuchs, Vlasta Gallerová, Arnošt Goldflam, Václav Havel, Martin Hoffmeister, Milena Honzíková, Ondřej Hrab, Jan Kopecký, Miroslav Kouřil, Karel Kraus, Milan Lukeš, Petr Oslzlý, Miroslav Pflug, Karel Steigerwald, and Ivan Vyskočil.

For apt and expert questions, suggestions, and corrections in matters both general and specific during the evolution of the manuscript in its several stages I am grateful to Daniel Gerould, Howard Miller, Diane Mann, Evelyn Duncan, Michael Heim, Thomas Postlewait, and Kathy Lewis. I have named them in chronological order, according to when they entered the several-year process. The complex digital preparation of the manuscript prior to its submission to the University of Iowa Press was significantly enabled by the University at Albany's Department of Theatre (Langdon Brown, chair) and several of its staff: Kathryn Callan, Patrick Ferlo, Andi Lyons, and Patricia Van Alstyne.

My wife, Grayce Susan Burian, has been closely involved not only with all stages in the evolution of this work, but with all my prior research and resultant publications. Her unflagging assistance has ranged from sustained personal support during the travels and residencies underlying this study, to proofreading and secretarial activities, to valuable critical responses as this work evolved from initial notes to final manuscript. My gratitude to her lies beyond words.

Modern Czech Theatre

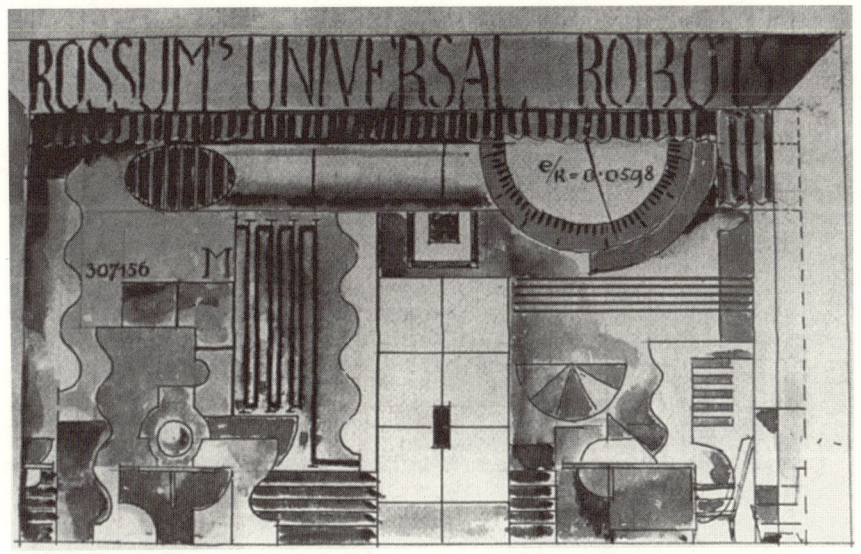

INTRODUCTION

The evolution of twentieth-century Czech theatre is a historical achievement warranting critical observation and documentation primarily because of the artistic accomplishments of that theatre. Equally important, however, Czech theatre also provides distinctive examples of the complex relations between art and society, stage and audience, which are a vital but often submerged part of an understanding of the special reality of living theatre anywhere.

When the internationally respected critic Kenneth Tynan declared in 1967 that "Prague has a strong claim to be regarded as the theatre capital of Europe,"[1] he was referring not only to a theatre of dynamic ensembles and outstanding directors, designers, and young playwrights, but also to a theatre that was responding to the social and cultural effects of some twenty years of the Czech Communist regime. It was not the first time, however, that Czech theatre confronted similar challenges. For a century preceding the opening of their National Theatre in the 1880s the Czechs experienced complex, often frustrating encounters of theatre and politics as they fought for a theatre of their own in a society dominated by German culture and language, even while Czech intellectuals, artists, and political leaders strove to raise the political consciousness of Czech citizens during the long campaign to gain Czech autonomy within — if not independence from — the Habsburg Empire.

In our own century, once Czech independence had been achieved in 1918, a repeated interplay of theatre with political realities almost became the norm, sometimes stifling or deforming the creative urge, but at other times focusing and spurring Czech theatre to greater artistry and relevance. The vital engagement of stage and society — sometimes subtle, even cryptic, sometimes harshly overt — has been a repeated condition of Czech theatre for the past two hundred years. When playwright Václav Havel became president of Czechoslovakia in 1990, it was but the latest and most celebrated example of that engagement.

Sheer geography has played a key role in the history of the Czechs, including their culture and arts. Their precarious position at the political and military crossroads of Europe has led to their destiny repeatedly being influenced and often determined by the ambitions and hostilities of their more powerful neighbors. Examples in the twentieth century alone include the founding of the Czechoslovak state in 1918 as a by-product of World War I, its sacrifice at Munich in 1938, the ensuing years of German occupation and World War II before liberation in 1945, and subsequent subordination to Russian communism from 1948 into the 1980s (including the crushing of the Prague Spring of 1968).

Not surprisingly, such momentous events (and much earlier ones as well) sensitized the Czechs to the shifting currents of European stratagems and priorities, and the Czechs' heightened political concern was inevitably echoed in the world of theatre, which in any case was traditionally responsive to the Czechs' own sociopolitical affairs. Not that the Czechs have existed in a state of chronic crisis, but the periods when their theatre has been able to cultivate its art without attention to foreign or internal pressures have been relatively rare, though not without interest. At the same time, however, the geopolitical reality of being at the heart of Europe had the long-range advantage of facilitating the Czech theatre's contacts with the traditions and practices of the French, German, and Russian theatres, to which Czech theatre has paid close attention since the mid-nineteenth-century.

Underlying all questions of the Czech theatre's relevance to its audiences is the historically and culturally shaped relationship of the two. The bond between the Czechs and their theatre had its roots in the consciously educational, moral, nation-building roles theatre played in the Czechs' nineteenth-century National Revival movement. Beginning in the 1780s, theatre joined in the broader efforts of the Czechs to reassert their language, culture, and autonomy after centuries of suppression within the Habsburg Empire. These efforts took a giant step forward with the opening of the Czech National Theatre in Prague, even though nearly forty years passed between its formal conception as a project and its opening night in the 1880s. Most of its funding came from voluntary contributions by the people, a fact memorialized in its motto above the proscenium arch: "Národ Sobě" (The Nation to Itself).

The National Theatre was intended to be not only a representative showcase for Czech theatre artists and for Czech and world dramatic literature but also an inspirational symbol of national identity and spirit. A fund appeal from the mid-1860s epitomized a recurrent theme: "If we are to be recognized as a cultured nation we must have a school of life and morals in which various strands of education and culture intertwine. . . . we must have an independent national theatre."[2] The sense of ethical responsibility and pedagogic duty implicit in such ideals persisted into the twentieth century and continued to be identified with Czech theatre, sometimes with problematic effects, as we shall see.

Several other considerations are germane to a study of Czech theatre before briefly glancing at an introductory sketch of its twentieth-century course. One is the size of the country. Here it is important to separate the Czech lands (Bohemia and Moravia) from what was Czechoslovakia between 1918 and 1993 (which included Slovakia). The Czech lands have a current population of some ten and a half million (close to that of Ohio) and occupy an area of some 30,500 square miles (close to the size of South Carolina). The sheer compactness of the country and its underlying ethnic unity have always facilitated the relationship of theatre and audience. That compactness has also contributed to the relative unity and coherence of its theatre world; playwrights, directors, designers, and actors tend to know each other and each other's work, partly because most of them are graduates of one of two theatre academies, in Prague and Brno, and partly because it is easy to travel to any given theatre.

One result of this compactness and unity has been a homogenous theatre culture that is more conducive to similar conventions and styles within the various genres of performance than to a centrifugal development of sharply variant forms and production policies. Although many theatres have had distinctive profiles, wide variations in quality and style of performance are rare. Czech theatre culture also favors certain "lines of descent" — the carrying on of certain traditions or methods from one generation to another, obviously with variations and innovations marking the work of each younger generation. Among the most notable examples were the careers of Alfred Radok and Otomar Krejča, the two most important directors of the post–World War II era. Both had significant associations with leaders of the prewar theatre, such as E. F. Burian and Jiří Frejka, respectively, who in turn had drawn from their own predecessors (e.g., Frejka from Karel Hugo Hilar). Even Josef Svoboda's scenographic mastery did not arise in a vacuum but was stimulated by the work of earlier Czech designers, such as František Tröster.

Another important ingredient of Czech theatre (indeed, of many continental European theatres) is the repertory system, a complete contrast to commercial Broadway or West End theatre, where all efforts and monies are concentrated on a one-shot production with artists individually chosen for the event, the aim of which is maximum audience impact and box office appeal, with little regard for any broader considerations. In a traditional repertory system, on the other hand, personnel are engaged on a long-term basis with relatively little turnover, and theatres are usually subsidized for at least half their budgets by local, regional, or national government. Such companies are organized to produce a body of plays to be performed in alternating sequence — a different play performed each day from an ever-freshened stock of five to fifteen plays available at any given time.

(An often forgotten and always unsung but crucial function is that of the *souffleur* or prompter, whose skillful offstage vocalizing of the script a beat ahead of the actors is a safety net for those who regularly perform some roles only once a month — with no interim rehearsal.)

Relieved of total dependence on the box office, repertory companies are in a position to foster a sustained development of actors, directors, designers, and even playwrights. The first three experience the advantage of a *variety* of ongoing assignments and challenges, and playwrights benefit from knowing the actors who will be playing their characters. Equally important, government support implies a sense of responsibility in both giver and receiver. Government commits itself to a sustained support of the arts; theatre implicitly pledges to serve the interests of its society. In its ideal form, such an arrangement can be enormously beneficial to all parties concerned, but — as history has vividly demonstrated — the arrangement can also become counterproductive and even corrupt.

The repertory system also implies the presence of a dramaturg, a crucial figure only vaguely understood in most nonrepertory theatre cultures. The usual English translation is "literary advisor," which conveys only part of a dramaturg's traditional function. The dramaturg is a virtually indispensable collaborator of repertory directors, under the overall supervision of a theatre's administrative and artistic heads. A dramaturg not only supplies in-depth information about plays and their authors, but may also function as a translator, reviser, or adaptor of plays or other text sources, usually in collaboration with a director. Some directors function as their own dramaturgs, but most directors rely heavily on the dramaturg's abilities in preparing a script for production.

Equally important, a dramaturg may strongly influence or even determine the profile of a theatre by his or her long-range planning of a repertoire with plays related to a company's abilities and goals and to the climate of the times. Often such planning develops into a conscious "program" — a philosophy and rationale defining the theatre's identity and purpose. Some theatres become primarily playwrights' theatres or theatres associated with a certain style or conceptual bias, while others concentrate their resources on actors or are dominated by one or two strong directors.

With the context of Czech theatre as well as some of its operational features in mind, we may preview some of its most distinctive "moments" and personalities in the twentieth century, as a preliminary orientation.

In 1900 Czech theatre was a youthful and earnest emulator of its older, grander counterparts on the continent. By 1920 it was in the mainstream of modern European theatre, and within the next twenty years it was arguably at the forefront of its contemporaries before being traumatized by political crises of the late 1930s culminating in World War II. Achievements of people like the Čapek brothers, Karel Hugo Hilar, E. F. Burian, and the team of Voskovec and Werich gained the praise of theatre observers whose frame of reference included all of Europe.

Soon after the stresses of World War II came the political realignment of Czechoslovakia from independent republic to Communist satellite in 1948 and years of rigidly imposed constraints. After a period of thawing, a high tide of Czech theatre returned in the 1960s, when its artists and ensembles drew international attention to their theatres in Prague as well as their performances abroad. The work of individuals like Václav Havel, Josef Svoboda, Otomar Krejča, Alfred Radok, and Jan Grossman became familiar to European and even American audiences, as did productions by ensembles of the National Theatre and new studio theatres such as the Balustrade (Divadlo Na zábradlí), the Drama Club (Činoherní klub), and the Theatre beyond the Gate (Divadlo za branou). But this breakthrough of talents was abruptly aborted by the Warsaw Pact invasion of 1968.

After an ebbtide of some ten years, Czech theatre people began to rally, focus, and finally spearhead the forces that contributed to the eventual overthrow of a moribund but still domineering Communist regime. The Velvet Revolution of 1989 was a cathartic experience crowned by the installation of a dissident playwright as president. During this era, it was a second wave of studio theatres that deserved most credit for keeping alive a spirit of resistance in their public: at the forefront were Studio Ypsilon, Theatre on a String (Divadlo na provázku), and Hana Theatre (HaDivadlo).

Czech theatre in the 1990s, like Czech society itself, is still in the process of reacting to the economic, political, and social changes following the abrupt freedoms gained at the end of 1989. It is difficult to make many secure generalizations about the present identity of Czech theatre other than to say it is trying to survive within new, more austere economic realities while sustaining its tradition of artistic quality and social awareness. New freedoms have not had a radical impact on the network of repertory theatres except to reduce subventions and place a premium on building audiences, seeking supplementary financing from sponsors, and cutting expenses. No longer subject to the political and social abuses that focused most theatre work during the Communist era, a new generation of imaginative, often unconventional directors is making its mark with productions of creative fantasy but limited engagement with issues of consequence to their audiences. The future is open.

To recapitulate, the story of Czech theatre in the twentieth century involves generations of talented artists and memorable productions. Beyond their artistic characteristics, however, lies a larger point: a theatre that has resonated with the intense concerns of its audiences is likely to acquire a significance and force beyond that which is created by random stage hits or striking individual talents. Amid the variety of Czech theatre during the past one hundred years, that basic, provocative reality has been repeatedly demonstrated, as the following studies reveal.

The chapters that follow are based primarily on my research-centered residencies in Prague since 1965 and some of the publications resulting from them. My intention has been to produce neither an anthology of random pieces nor a comphrensive survey giving equal and detached attention to all eras and all figures. Rather, I have aimed at a chronologically organized series of perspectives and observations on the most important people and critical "moments" in the evolution of this theatre in its sociopolitical context during the past one hundred years, following a brief historical background leading up to this century.

In addition to new material written specifically for this book, I have substantially edited those parts previously published and supplemented them with introductions, transitional passages, and other amplifications. Rather than cast the resulting manuscript in one consistent style or compositional point of view, I have tried to retain the original flavor of some of the writing — for example, by retaining the original present-tense point of view of some sections — in order to accent the immediacy of my personal involvement with the subject or events in question.

A few final notes and caveats concerning the scope of this book.

First, I am dealing primarily with live professional theatre for adults, not children's theatre, amateur theatre, or puppet theatre, although they have had importance for the Czechs. Moreover, I have focused on theatre that produces plays, not operas, ballets, mime, or other forms of public entertainment. The Czech language has the advantage of having one word, *činohra*, to designate this form of theatre, whereas English makes do with "dramatic theatre" or "legitimate stage." The exception to this focus on *činohra* occurs in a few passages dealing with the opera work of some Czech designers, Josef Svoboda in particular.

Second, although I comment on the work of many Czech playwrights, I do not give them sustained attention or analysis, mainly because my primary concern is with the all-encompassing phenomenon of theatre, a complex activity that absorbs the work of playwrights along with the talents and skills of directors, actors, designers, dramaturgs, technicians, and administrators to create *productions* meant to entertain, move, and enlighten an audience. It is the shifting, evolving nature of Czech theatre productions in the twentieth century in relation to their similarly evolving social and political contexts that is the subject of this study. Playwrights' texts are one component, sometimes central, sometimes peripheral, of the total theatre experience. When the contents of plays seem of particular relevance to their times or to tendencies in theatre, or when plays possess a distinctive style or form, I of course try to describe such characteristics.

Third, attention is given primarily to theatre in Prague, even though important work has long been done in other strong theatre cities, such as Brno, Pilsen (Plzeň), Olomouc, Ostrava, and Hradec Králové, to name only the first that come to mind among many others. Prague was and still is the New York City and London of Czech theatre centers.

Finally, my usage of "Czech" theatre rather than "Czechoslovakian" theatre means that my concern is with Czech theatre in Bohemia and Moravia, not with Czech theatre in Slovakia or with Slovak theatre anywhere, even though I do refer to some artists primarily associated with Slovak theatre — when they have done significant work in Czech theatre. A few words of explanation may be useful here.

Suppressed and denied adequate education by the Magyars for centuries, the Slovaks did not begin to create their own professional theatre until the establishment of the Czechoslovak state in 1918. From the beginning, Czech directors, actors, designers, and other theatre personnel began the process of training and developing a core of Slovak theatre artists in the Slovak capital of Bratislava and some other Slovak cities. In particular, the Slovak National Theatre (no connection to the Czech National Theatre) began operations in Bratislava in 1920, with a Czech ensemble and a Czech director, in a theatre building that until 1920 had performed in only two languages: German or Hungarian. Although performances of Slovak plays in Slovak intermittently occurred in the Slovak National Theatre in the 1920s, it was not until the 1930s that a Slovak ensemble began performing in Slovak, alongside the ongoing Czech ensemble. This practice lasted until the end of 1938, when all Czech involvement in the Slovak theatre ended with the establishment of the puppet Slovak state after the Munich dismemberment of what had been Czechoslovakia. In the meantime, a theatre school in Bratislava — largely staffed by Czechs — had also been training aspiring theatre artists since the early 1920s. From 1938 on, Slovak theatre became a distinct entity, even after the reunification of the two countries as Czechoslovakia in 1945 and their mutual adherence to imposed guidelines during the Communist era from 1948 to 1989. Shortly after World War II, for example, the Slovaks had their own network of state-supported repertory theatres.

In effect, despite occasional guest appearances of ensembles or individual actors, directors, and designers from the one theatre world to the other, Czech and Slovak theatres have maintained a separate existence for most of the twentieth century. One might speak of a Czech-dominated Slovak theatre until 1938, but in no case did a comparable influence work the other way. Slovak theatre warrants a full study of its own.

1

1780–1900
Some Exposition before the Main Action

A century of heightening religious tensions and subordination to Habsburg rulers culminated with the defeat of rebellious Czech Protestant forces by Habsburg Catholic forces at the Battle of White Mountain, near Prague, in 1620. It was the first significant military encounter of the Thirty Years War. Largely because of the subsequent decimation of the Czech Protestant nobility and the persecution and emigration of other educated Czech Protestants, the Czech language, banned in public use, survived for a century and a half only among peasants, servants, and small tradespeople, chiefly in rural areas. Czech literature virtually ceased to exist except for religious writings, and theatre in the Czech language vanished except for amateur performances of religiously centered folk plays in villages and marionette performances by traveling companies.[1]

A counterflow became evident toward the end of the eighteenth century. In retrospect named the National Revival movement, it began in the 1780s, following reforms during the reign of Habsburg emperor Joseph II, and it did not really end until the birth of a new independent nation, Czechoslovakia, in 1918. The movement had several interrelated goals: regeneration of the Czech language, reawakening of Czech cultural and national identity, and progress toward political autonomy. Czech theatre became intimately associated with all these aims and capped decades of organized effort with the opening of the National Theatre in 1881–1883.[2]

Although the story of Czech theatre's development during the hundred years preceding the opening of the National Theatre in the 1880s is replete with significant events and individuals, one point is central: while an infrastructure of Czech cultural institutions, political organizations, and publications was slowly evolving, theatre provided a popular and powerful instrument foregrounding the legitimacy of the Czech language, often by means of idealized dramatizations of Czech history and legend. Theatre thereby reinforced the Czechs' sense of their culture and national identity and helped to justify their increasing desire for autonomy.

For decades the effort had only intermittent and partial achievements as the Czechs, with no theatre of their own, tried to find room within the dominant German theatre system, which was centered in the Count Nostitz Theatre. It had opened in 1783, and it was on its stage that Wolfgang Amadeus Mozart conducted the world premiere of his *Don Giovanni*. Renamed the Estates (Stavovské) Theatre in 1797, it went on to play a significant though often interrupted role in the evolution of Czech theatre. Only after many decades did the Czechs have a theatre exclusively for the production of plays in their own language, the Provisional Theatre (Prozatimní divadlo), built in 1862. Until then, bilingual Czech actors were limited to one or two performances (usually matinees) in Czech in German theatres that gave them permission or, at best, in other bilingual theatres that the Czechs themselves started.

One of the key figures in the early period was Václav Thám (1765–1816), a poet, playwright, translator, and actor-director whose *Břetislav and Jitka* became the first Czech play to be performed in Czech by professional actors, in the German Nostitz Theatre in 1786. Thám later became the central artistic force in a bilingual company called the Patriotic Theatre (Vlastenecké divadlo), which performed in a temporary theatre structure (the Bouda) from 1786 to 1789 in what is now Wenceslaus Square and in other quarters into the 1790s. In a request for permission to establish the theatre, its founders referred to their desire "to contribute something to the improvement and spread of the Czech language."[3]

The Patriotic Theatre was the first to stage regular performances in Czech (along with an almost equal number in German). A visit by Emperor Joseph II to one of its performances led to the theatre receiving an official royal certificate fully legitimizing its existence; this became a significant precedent for the official request (some six decades later) for permission to make plans for the National Theatre. It is estimated that Thám wrote, translated, or adapted over 150 plays to be presented in Czech, which suggests that he was responsible for about half of the works presented by the Patriotic Theatre before the turn of the century. Although in those days it was rare for a given work to be reprised more than once or twice, the sheer numbers indicate that a constantly changing repertoire was attraction enough as long as it was in Czech. Among the foreign plays presented in Czech by the Patriotic Theatre were *Hamlet* and *King Lear*, in the early 1790s. The first Czech plays of contemporary life were two farces by Prokop Šedivý (1764–

Josef Kajetán Tyl, multitalented theatre person and activist for a Czech National Theatre.

ca. 1810), another of the playwright-translators for the Patriotic Theatre: *Prague Brewers* (Pražští sládci) and *The Meat Shops* (Masné krámy) in the mid-1790s.

Thám's successor as a multitalented, enterprising producer of Czech productions was Jan Nepomuk Štěpánek (1783–1844), a playwright, actor, and director who was the leading Czech theatre person during the first third of the nineteenth century. Štěpánek's primary affiliation was with the Estates Theatre, where he headed the Czech branch of theatre operations for almost three decades.

The first Czech playwright with a distinctive voice and undeniable talent was Václav Kliment Klicpera (1792–1859), whose forte was lively, often satiric comedy that captured something essential in Czech speech and character, whereas most earlier Czech plays were essentially imitative of German and Austrian models. Several of Klicpera's plays are still revived today, such as *Hadrian* (1821) and *Comedy on the Bridge* (1829).

Countless other actors, theatre managers, and even playwrights sustained the vitality of the emerging Czech theatre culture in the first half of the nineteenth century, but Josef Kajetán Tyl (1808–1856) was the most memorable. Like many other Czech theatre people, he was a person of multiple talents and activities: writer, editor, publisher of journals championing the revival movement, and even representative to the Diet; above all, he was an actor, dramaturg, director, and prolific playwright. Working within the German cultural and political system, he

BEFORE THE MAIN ACTION [11]

was steadfastly at the forefront of the Czech cause and laid the foundations for the further evolution of Czech theatre, particularly in heading Czech theatre activity in the German establishment's Estates Theatre between 1846 and 1851.

Tyl's own historical and socially oriented plays (many of which are still revived) reflect the Romantic movement but also foreshadow later developments of Realism. At his best, he balanced his tendencies toward sentiment and idealization with his sharp perception of the weaknesses as well as the strengths of Czech character in works like *The Bagpiper from Strakonice* (Strakonický dudák, 1847), *The Arsonist's Daughter* (Paličova dcera, 1847), and *The Hard-Headed Woman* (Tvrdohlavá žena, 1849). An early play with music, *Folk Festival* (Fidlovačka), produced in 1834 at the Estates Theatre, was a colorful depiction of contemporary Prague life, but is primarily remembered for one of its songs, "Where Is My Home?" (Kde domov můj?), which eventually became the Czech national anthem. Tyl established a model for inspirational depictions of Czech history in *Jan Hus* (1848) and *A Bloody Judgment* (Krvavý soud, 1848), dealing with an uprising of Czech miners against foreign exploitation.

More than any other theatre person, Tyl not only consciously and untiringly supported the principles of the revival movement, but proposed a concept for a national theatre as early as the 1840s. Others may have spoken of a separate theatre for the Czechs, but it was Tyl who envisioned it as something far more impressive: a force of enlightenment and morality and an expression of the national spirit that would be a school for the nation. As he put it, "Elsewhere, people may wish theatre to show them as they already are, but we must want a theatre to show us as we ought to be."[4]

Tyl's concept was taken up by a number of Czechs who were active in the complex political maneuvering for increased concessions within the Habsburg Empire. One was František Rieger, who became one of the few figures centrally involved in the campaign for a National Theatre who lived to see its completion. Rieger himself had obtained a license to launch a new Czech theatre in 1845, but the project became one of several that never got off the ground in the 1840s. In July 1850, however, Alois Trojan, a lawyer and activist who had once acted under Tyl, submitted a formal request to Habsburg authorities in Prague to form a committee to collect donated funds for the building of a National Theatre, a home for drama, opera, and ballet. The request was approved one month later. The committee, chaired by Trojan, with famed Czech historian František Palacký as president and Rieger as executive secretary, also included Tyl and Klicpera, as well as other intellectuals, artists, and political leaders.

The subsequent three decades were years of fits and starts and delays, played out in the context of confrontations and negotiations on the larger stage of Czech-

Habsburg politics. Most of the 1850s were marked by repressive Habsburg measures following the revolutions of 1848; the committee had to keep a relatively low profile to avoid arousing suspicions of subversive activity. Moreover, the committee itself was divided between those who favored obtaining funds from a relatively few powerful and wealthy sources and others who urged the broadest possible appeal to all Czechs. The choice of architects and the plans for the structure were other key issues provoking clashes. Increasingly politicized, the project became tied to pressures for Czech autonomy or even full independence. The basic plan to fund the enterprise with monies collected from the people seemed inadequate, and repeated campaigns for additional funds were necessary, including penny collections and lotteries. Nevertheless, despite a host of difficulties, the project moved ahead. A full spectrum of Czech society responded, from the nobility to agricultural and industrial laborers, who were generous not only with money but with personal items of value and building materials.

Land for the eventual site, on the right bank of the Moldau (Vltava), was purchased by the committee in 1852 from the proprietress of a salt storage building on the site. Ten years later, as an offshoot of the main drive, which had stalled in the late 1850s, the Provisional Theatre was built on the previously purchased land, with the understanding that the theatre would be converted to an ancillary, non-performance space abutting the National Theatre once the latter was built. The Provisional Theatre was the first independent, fully Czech professional theatre with a regular repertory schedule. Concurrently, bilingual operations ceased in the Estates Theatre, which became exclusively German. Two men dominated production work in the Provisional Theatre: playwright, translator, actor, and director Josef Jiří Kolár (1812–1896), an exemplar of the late Romantic era, and the great composer Bedřich Smetana (1824–1884), who was in charge of musical production.

A change of leadership in the committee in the mid-1860s placed an activist politician and editor, Karel Sladkovský, in the position of vice-president. Another inspirational milestone on the long journey toward the National Theatre was the laying of the foundation stone in May 1868, which prompted a huge three-day national and international Slav festival of pageantry and eloquence, regattas and fireworks, drawing tens of thousands to Prague. It was "the greatest national celebration of the Czechs until after World War I."[5] The stone itself was quarried from Mount Říp, a Czech site of mythic overtones from primeval times, but many other Czech cities and regions also sent symbolic stones, which are still on display in the basement of the building. Further progress, however, was stalled in the early 1870s by political tensions between the Czechs and Habsburgs, who were having major international problems and conflicts with the Hungarians, Prussians, and Italians. A more immediate crisis within the committee reflected the conflict between the Old Czech and the Young Czech political movements. The former were conservatives like Palacký and Rieger, patiently working toward Czech autonomy within a Habsburg Federation, whereas the latter, more radical group (led by Karel Sladkovský) urged complete independence.

The National Theatre project in Prague was not the only one seeking a theatre solely for Czech productions. Other cities, whose theatre activities were also subject to the German establishment and its theatres, had a similar objective, though not on as grand a scale or with such lofty intentions. Pilsen, indeed, achieved its goal shortly after the opening of Prague's Provisional Theatre when negotiations with German authorities led to the turning over of the Municipal Theatre for strictly Czech productions during the regular season, beginning in late 1865. Actually, some fifty productions had been done there each year since 1861, along with a greater number of German productions. An extraordinarily enterprising actor and director who had formed his first company in the early 1850s, Pavel Švanda (1825–1891), headed the new operation, also serving as actor, dramaturg, and director.[6] He had the good fortune of having a young associate who was perhaps even more talented than he was as an actor and director — Josef Šmaha (1848–1915). Between 1863 and 1889 Švanda produced dozens of plays, not only in Pilsen but also in temporary summer theatres in Prague. In the fall of 1881 he built a theatre in the Smíchov district, the second permanent Czech theatre in Prague after the Provisional Theatre. What is particularly impressive is that among the many routine crowd-pleasers and moderately good Czech plays in the repertoire in the 1880s were classics by William Shakespeare, Friedrich Schiller, Johann Wolfgang von Goethe, and Nikolay Gogol and some strikingly "advanced" works of critical realism and even naturalism by Emile Zola and Henrik Ibsen. Many of these challenging productions were directed by Šmaha before his departure to the National Theatre in 1883. Švanda continued operations, however, not only during the summers in Prague but also during the longer winter seasons in Brno, where in 1886 he became head of drama of the Czech theatre that had begun producing in 1884 in its own Provisional Theatre. Earlier efforts toward establishing a home for professional Czech theatre in Brno had run into much harsher resistance from the German authorities than in Prague or Pilsen. One of Švanda's coups in Brno was the first Czech production of Ibsen's *Doll's House*, in 1887, and the first Czech production of any Anton Chekhov play, *The Bear*, in 1892. For some four years in the 1880s Švanda benefited from having Eduard Vojan (1853–1920) and Hana Kvapilová (1860–1907) in his company,[7] two actors who were later to reach the pinnacle of their profession in the National Theatre.

Meanwhile, in Prague, the grand opening of the National Theatre on June 11, 1881, attended by Habsburg crown prince Rudolf and his new bride, provided the climax of more than thirty years of organized, disputatious, and interrupted effort. Smetana's opera *Libuše* had the honor of being the opening production. The costs of constructing the National Theatre had exceeded estimates by 400 percent; three more major fund drives had to be undertaken; Tyl, Klicpera, Palacký, and Sladkovský had died; but the dream of a National Theatre in a full symbolic spirit and with official status became a reality, as did Tyl's concept of a theatre of and for the people. Although major contributions came from the wealthy bourgeoisie and even nobility, as well as organizations, substantial portions of the funding came from the individual contributions of ordinary Czechs. The inscription emblazoned above the proscenium was fact, not hyperbole: Národ Sobě (The Nation['s Gift] to Itself).

Two months and several productions later, on August 12, the joyful afterglow of the June opening was agonizingly dispelled when, due to a workman's carelessness on the roof, the building burned to the ground, leaving only the walls and a few interior elements intact. The nation's grief was overwhelming, but almost immediately it became channeled into a great campaign to rebuild the theatre. In less than six months most of the funds were raised, more than two-thirds from individuals and more than two-thirds from communities outside Prague; international support once again was very strong, including donations from Czechs in America.[8] The second opening, on November 18, 1883, is the one now cited as *the* opening. Once again, Smetana's opera *Libuše* had the honor of being the first production, as it had been for the opening two years earlier. *Libuše* celebrates the title character, a mythic queen of Bohemia, and her vision of the Czechs' glorious future, including an image of the Hradčany Castle, which has dominated Prague since the late 1300s.

. The Czechs' pride of personal involvement in an idealistic enterprise centering in theatre as a symbol of national identity fused with the concept of theatre as a moral and educational force. It became a cultural legacy. Sometimes obscured or faded, sometimes distorted and abused, that legacy has remained an intangible component of Czech theatre and society. It surfaced most recently and forcefully a century later, in the hectic days of the Velvet Revolution of 1989.

Subject as it was to strict censorship, Czech playwriting in the nineteenth century after Tyl was not in a position to confront the issues of nationalistic aspirations as directly or forcefully as did the practical activities of the Committee for the National Theatre or other Czech political endeavors. Nevertheless, by drawing on inspirational historical material such as the Hussite era (e.g., Tyl's *Jan Hus*)

The Czech National Theatre, in its 1883 form, on the banks of the Vltava in Prague. Photo by Vladimír Hyhlík.

or even earlier royal eras such as those of Bohemian kings Václav I and Charles IV, Tyl and subsequent Czech playwrights fed the Czechs' need to associate themselves with glories in their past in order to strengthen their sense of the rightness of their present thrust toward autonomy. Direct handling of controversial contemporary material and explicit calls for independence or throwing off of oppression were out of the question. Moreover, the broad flow of events as the century progressed gave hope for increased Czech self-direction, not only in theatre but also in education and other institutions.

What of other drama in the new National Theatre in the remaining years of the nineteenth century? Heading its three divisions of opera, drama, and ballet until 1900 was František Adolf Šubert (1849–1915), whose unenviable task it was to satisfy many conflicting artistic and political demands, the chief of which was sustaining a representative cultural showcase equal to models in French and German capitals. The initial seasons were marked by late Romantic, poetic, and historical drama with emphasis on elaborate scenic displays in the manner of Vienna's Burgtheater or the Meiningen players (who had already visited Prague several times before the National Theatre opened) and by superficially realistic conversation pieces in the French boulevard mode. Indeed, many Czechs were disappointed that the drive for a meaningful national theatre seemed to be embodied in a place of ostentatious bourgeois entertainment. The fight to stage foreign and native plays that would depict contemporary life realistically and critically was led by dramaturg and playwright Ladislav Stroupežnický (1850–1892) and actor-director Josef Šmaha. Indeed, most of the strongest work in the National Theatre before the turn of the century was the result of Šmaha's artistry. Beyond productions of Shakespeare, Molière, Schiller, Gogol, Alexander Ostrovsky, Ibsen, Gerhart Hauptmann, and earlier Czech playwrights, he also successfully staged the premieres of what became milestone Czech realistic dramas of contemporary social criticism centering in village life.

The 1887 production of Stroupežnický's village comedy *Our Swaggerers* (Naší furianti), as directed by Šmaha, became a landmark of Czech drama and theatre in its lively yet critical portrayal of Czech character types and behavior. The play deals with a ludicrous quarrel between two posturing elders of a contemporary south Bohemian village. At issue is the position of night watchman of the village, with each elder backing his favorite candidate. Before the dispute is settled, the whole village becomes involved. A good-natured but tartly satiric view of traditionally sentimentalized types, the play pioneered a movement toward a maturer vision of the realities of Czech life.

Darker views of village relationships and passions were evident in Šmaha's productions of *Household Woman* (Gazdina roba, 1889) and *Her Stepdaughter* (Její pastorkyně, 1890) by Gabriela Preissová (1862–1946), a playwright far ahead of her time in powerfully depicting the plight of unempowered rural women in a tradition-bound, male-dominated society. Each play subsequently became a libretto, for Josef Bohuslav Foerster's opera *Eva* (1899) and Leoš Janáček's *Jenufa* (1904), respectively. Two other plays, *Vojnarka* (1890) by Alois Jirásek (1851–1930) and *Maryša* (1894) by Vilém Mrštík (1863–1912), continued the unsparing critique of the previously idealized role of women in bucolic life. *Maryša* in particular achieved classic status in portraying a frustrated woman's murderous response to the callous social practice of loveless marriage against one's will.

The recurrent use of a village setting reflected the historical reality of Czech culture being centered in rural life for over two hundred and fifty years. Despite the great strides in reviving Czech culture and political presence in urban centers during the nineteenth century, most Czechs remained more familiar with village life than with life in the city. Moreover, village life seemed to provide richer material for the dramatic embodiment of elemental passions and states of mind within a social framework of inflexible traditional values and practices. Finally, it is likely that these Czech writers were inspired by the treatment of similar themes in the work of the Russian masters Alexander Ostrovsky and Lev Tolstoy.

A key actor in most of these plays and others demanding detailed character drawing with psychological insight was Jindřich Mošna (1837–1911), whose talents were such as to inspire playwrights (Stroupežnický and Jirásek, for example) to write roles for him. His match in many respects was Marie Hübnerová (1865–1931), who joined the National Theatre in the mid-1890s and was one of its mainstays until her death.

Czech drama in the last two decades of the nineteenth century was not limited to folk-centered realistic plays or Czech variations of Eugène Scribe and Victorien Sardou. Poetic treatments of Czech history, myths, and fairy tales were also staples of literature and the stage. Perhaps the best-known Czech representative of this more consciously artistic playwriting was Jaroslav Vrchlický (1853–1912), a prolific lyric poet, translator, and critic whose learning and taste were cosmopolitan. His trilogy based on Greek tragic myth, *Hippodamia*, with music by Zdeněk Fibich, is a self-conscious late Romantic verse drama, which had its premiere at the National Theatre in 1893. A much livelier and entertaining work was his earlier *A Night at Karlstein* (Noc na Karlštejně) presented at the National Theatre in 1884. A lyrical comedic romance dealing with Czech emperor Charles IV and his court, it has been successfully revived countless times down to the present.

Similar to Vrchlický, yet perhaps more uncompromising as a poet, Julius Zeyer (1841–1891) also wrote numerous works that ignored the realist movement. His best-known and most successful play was *Radúz and Mahulena*, a poetic and dramatically effective tale of young love drawn from Slovak legend, with a musical accompaniment by Josef Suk. One of the first Czech plays to reflect the increasingly important symbolist movement, it was performed in the National Theatre in 1898 and, like Vrchlický's *Night at Karlstein*, has held the stage to the present.

The influence of Ibsen was clear in the plays of Jaroslav Hilbert (1871–1936), especially in his first work, *Guilt* (Vina, 1896), a highly concentrated, psychologically centered study of moral values in a bourgeois urban setting.

The National Theatre's only serious rival remained the Švanda Theatre, which had been operating across the river since 1881, before the rebuilding of the National Theatre. This alternative major theatre had several distinctive features. It was from its beginning a private enterprise with no state support. Moreover, although its complete dependence on the box office prompted its staging of many flimsy farces, operettas, and star vehicles, it also included serious new dramas that surpassed in quality much of the work at the National Theatre. The theatre remained in the Švanda family even after founder Pavel Švanda's death in 1891. In the late 1890s, his son Karel consciously formulated a repertory program comprising both popular classics (Shakespeare and Czech comedies) and a series of contemporary chamber plays by foreign and Czech writers, perhaps in emulation of André Antoine's Théâtre-Libre in Paris and Otto Brahm's Freie Bühne in Berlin. Švanda's program included works by Arthur Schnitzler, Henri-François Becque, and Ibsen as well as some provocative recent Czech works, such as Preissová's *Household Woman*.

As the century drew to a close, Czech drama was approaching the level of its more established, long-practiced European models. In language, form, creative imagination, and theatrical effectiveness, it had developed significantly from its tentative, imitative roots earlier in the century, although it was still looking to foreign dramatic models and theatrical patterns. Similarly, although the Czechs now had two major Prague theatres producing entirely in Czech, a body of strong actors, and some skilled, creative directors, Czech theatre had yet to demonstrate a sustained record of distinctive achievement comparable to the best of European theatre. That goal was to be reached in the new century.

2

1900–1938
From the Turn of the Century to Munich

Despite interesting and varied theatrical activity by others, the work of two men dominated Czech theatre in the early years of the twentieth century. Then, soon after the birth of the Czechoslovak Republic at the end of World War I, other, more youthful, talents emerged, and by the mid-1930s Czech stages were at the forefront of innovative, imaginative European theatre. But this promising evolution was aborted by the disastrous international events at Munich in the early fall of 1938, when Czechoslovakia's independence was radically curtailed.

FROM 1900 THROUGH 1920

In the first two decades of the new century, Jaroslav Kvapil and Karel Hugo Hilar led the efforts to create modern Czech theatre, even as the Czech people were continuing a century-long campaign to achieve autonomy. Were it not for World War I, most Czechs would probably have remained content with gradually increasing reforms by the Habsburgs while retaining a degree of security as one of the constituent members of the empire. Autonomy within a federation seemed a realizable goal to the majority of Czechs, including history professor Thomas G. Masaryk (1850–1937), future president of what would become Czechoslovakia. But the war sparked hopes of complete independence in both the Czechs and the Slovaks. While Masaryk led the intensive efforts of Czechs and Slovaks to gain Allied support abroad, other Czechs worked within the establishment at home to gain added concessions from Vienna. This total effort culminated in 1918 with the creation of the Republic of Czechoslovakia, which joined the Czechs and their ethnic cousins, the Slovaks, in a single new state sponsored by the victorious Allies.

In the meantime, Kvapil and Hilar had begun their theatre careers in the two largest Czech theatres in Prague, Kvapil at the National and Hilar at the Vinohrady (which was built in 1907). Like many before them in Czech theatre, both had a literary background as writers, editors, translators, and critics, and their first duties at these theatres did not involve directing. For Kvapil, the end of the war marked a high point in his theatre career; for Hilar, it became simply one of several milestones.

Before tracing the careers of these two major figures, it may be worth noting the evolution of the Švanda Theatre, which represented the best of a number of smaller-scale, privately operated, popular theatrical companies running parallel to companies at the more prestigious state- or municipal-supported National and Vinohrady theatres. The Švanda Theatre continued its productions into the new era under the leadership of Karel Švanda and then, from 1903 to 1906, his sister Marie. Her noteworthy achievement as a producer and artistic director of a major theatre was then carried on by another important woman, Ema Jelinková-Švandová, an actress married to Karel Švanda. In 1906, after Marie's death, Ema took over as actress-manager of the Švanda Theatre. For the next several decades, the Švanda Theatre was primarily a theatre of boulevard entertainment providing a showcase for Ema Švandová's histrionic talents. Nevertheless, realizing that her impact would be heightened by occasionally undertaking some challenging roles, she included works by authors such as Maurice Maeterlinck, Henrik Ibsen, Maxim Gorky, and George Bernard Shaw. As noteworthy as the Švanda Theatre's efforts at a serious repertoire may have been, however, it was the sustained creativity of Kvapil and Hilar in Prague's two high-profile theatres that lifted Czech theatre to international stature in the early decades of the century.

Jaroslav Kvapil (1868–1950) significantly advanced the move of Czech theatre into the flow of twentieth-century Western theatre, both in his choice of plays and in his methods of staging at the National Theatre, where he directed an astonishing number of productions — over one hundred and fifty in less than twenty years. He began directing at the National Theatre in 1900 while employed as a dramaturg there, became chief director in 1906, and functioned as head of drama from 1911 to 1918, which meant that he supervised all nonmusical productions there, not only the plays he himself directed. Until his era, as we have seen, the National Theatre was primarily an actors' theatre, with productions in the familiar genres of historical dramas and folk plays, romantic realism, early naturalism and critical realism with a social focus, and boulevard comedy and melodrama, echoing French, German, and Russian models. Notable work in these genres had

Jaroslav Kvapil in his sixties.

already been done by earlier Czechs in the previous decade or two, especially by Josef Šmaha, whom Kvapil later called the first "modern" Czech director. Šmaha was limited, however, by his dual activity as actor and director.

In his efforts to upgrade the repertoire of the National Theatre, Kvapil, the first major Czech director who had not been an actor, drew on his sophisticated literary background. Central to his interests were the classics, above all Shakespeare, but also the Greeks and Molière. These were supplemented by his strong attraction to contemporary international drama: works by B. M. Bjørnson, Ibsen, Chekhov, and Gorky, but also new Czech plays by Alois Jirásek, Fráňa Šrámek, Viktor Dyk, and many other contemporary Czech playwrights.

Equally important, in his efforts to set Czech theatre on a new course, Kvapil willingly learned from his study of foreign exemplars: Otto Brahm, Max Reinhardt, Konstantin Stanislavsky, and the Munich Artists' Theatre, all at the cutting edge of innovative theatre in Europe in the early years of the century. Kvapil was able to observe their productions on tour in Prague (Brahm and Reinhardt in the Neues Deutsches Theater, built in 1888 partly in response to the Czechs' new National Theatre, and Stanislavsky in the Estates Theatre) or in their own theatres, just as earlier Czech directors had observed the duke of Saxe-Meiningen's players on their visits to Prague. Moreover, through reading, Kvapil was also familiar with the radical (for the time) theories and methods of Adolph Appia and Gordon Craig, including their advocacy of the director as the prime creator of the production as a whole.

Eduard Vojan as Hamlet, 1905.

Kvapil's work represents a synthesis of the approaches of the major artists just noted. Essentially conservative, and highly respectful of playwrights (he himself was an author of plays and a librettist), as a director Kvapil was inclined toward a subtle psychological realism in acting and a lightly stylized, atmospheric staging perhaps closest to that of the evolving symbolist movement. It is not surprising that he felt a special affinity for Chekhov, Paul Claudel, and the later plays of Ibsen. His crucial contribution to Czech theatre lay in fully establishing the director as the unifying shaper of all production elements, although he had a partial precedent in Šmaha's best work. Eclectic in his tastes, never imposing a strongly personal interpretation, Kvapil blended all elements into a harmonious whole, which almost always included a strong musical accompaniment.

In his efforts to bring Czech theatre up to current European standards, Kvapil was fortunate in being able to draw on a core of experienced, highly gifted actors, above all Eduard Vojan (even today considered the greatest of Czech actors, whose last name became a generic term for "actor") and Hana Kvapilová for protagonist roles and Marie Hübnerová and Jindřich Mošna for character parts. In addition he had youthful Leopolda Dostalová (1879–1972), whose career in the National Theatre was to last sixty-eight years. Kvapil adopted a supportive approach with them, relying more on their creativity than on his own subjective slant on a play. His work with designers was essentially conventional, reflecting the transition from painted, representational scenery to more selective, simplified realism with symbolist overtones.

Although Kvapil inclined toward a *l'art pour l'art* approach to theatre and his work focused on aspects of individual character and on human relationships rather than on overtly social or political issues, he was nevertheless sensitive to theatre's responsibility to issues involving the national cause of the Czechs. In the midst of the world war, with the Czechs still a province of the Austro-Hungarian Empire, Kvapil was very active in the Czech "Mafie," a covert resistance effort by influential Czechs working within the law to promulgate the Czech cause. One of his achievements was the staging of a cycle of sixteen Shakespeare plays in the spring of 1916 (most of which he had previously directed), as if to align the Czechs with England. (It says much of Habsburg toleration that no move to stop the cycle occurred.) During this cycle Vojan performed the astonishing feat of acting the leading roles in eight of the plays, including the four great tragedies. In May 1917 Kvapil composed a Writers' Manifesto addressed to Czech members of the imperial council protesting against a previous declaration of loyalty to the monarchy by some of the Czech members themselves. One year later, in April 1918, he organized an even more stirring action: a National Oath of allegiance to the Czech cause by leading representatives of Czech cultural and political life in Prague's Municipal House. And the following month, to honor the 50th anniversary of the laying of the National Theatre's foundation stone, he arranged the performance of several dozen works by Czech authors to underline the Czechs' yearning for autonomy. Characteristically, when autonomy and independence were achieved in October 1918, Kvapil took leave of theatre to assume an important function for several years in the new nation's Ministry of Education, thus becoming one more example of a Czech theatre person whose commitment to the national cause was equal to his love of theatre.

In the meantime, K. H. Hilar (1885–1935) was making his mark as an even stronger directorial presence at Prague's Vinohrady Theatre from 1910 to 1920. Seventeen years younger than Kvapil, Hilar responded more fully to the vigorous dynamics of the new century than to the relatively more genteel practices of Kvapil's generation. Coming of age at the turn of the century, Hilar was part of the far-flung movement that rejected realism outright as a meaningful artistic mode. Obviously influenced by the symbolists, yet inherently eclectic and too vigorous a man of the tangible world to reside in a passive aestheticism, Hilar was drawn to the expressionist movement that was gathering full force as he began his work in theatre.

A published poet and novelist, editor, and critic, Hilar joined the Vinohrady Theatre as a secretary and reader in 1910, as Kvapil was about to become official head of drama at the National Theatre. Hilar began directing almost immediately and two years later took on the post of dramaturg. In 1914 he capped his swift rise

A drawing of K. H. Hilar in the 1920s, by H. Boettinger.

by becoming head of drama at Prague's second most prestigious theatre. In the next six years he staged a series of productions that took Prague by storm and brought Czech theatre abreast of the front ranks of contemporary European theatre. His achievements at the Vinohrady made him the obvious choice to succeed Kvapil as head of drama at the National Theatre after Kvapil left to work for the new state. Indeed, Kvapil was one of the important people to recommend Hilar for the post. Between late 1918, when Kvapil left, and 1921, when Hilar took over, drama activity at the National Theatre was ineffectively supervised by a number of stopgap personnel.

Eduard Kohout, a major actor under both Kvapil and Hilar, described the difference between them: "Kvapil created harmony, Hilar drama. To go from Hilar to Kvapil meant going from expressionism to impressionism. As if you walked out of the studio of Van Gogh or Munch into the time of Monet or early Pissarro."[1] Hilar's own appreciation of Kvapil's contributions and limitations is perceptive, even if a bit biased:

> Kvapil's work seemed to have valuable decorative refinement but without true dramatic rhythm and tension, because the improvisation of the actors' ensemble and the license of individual acting mannerisms scattered the rich and cultivated taste of the director. Kvapil's direction seemed to me a cluster of lucky accidents, not the work of a powerfully cast, unifying artistic program.... He created moods rather than drama.... [On the other hand,] in an era of dilettantism, Kvapil's work was ... the first Czech stage direction to be a conscious synthesis of stage crafts according to creative and poetic aesthetic principles.[2]

Hilar went farther than Kvapil in embodying the Craig ideal of autonomous, absolute directors like Reinhardt or Vsevolod Meyerhold, who use all production elements, including the script, as raw material for a unifying creative vision embodied in a production marked by theatrically striking, imaginative exploitation of stage space, lighting, and dynamically expressive acting, all closely controlled and sensitively orchestrated by the director. Unlike Kvapil in temperament and instinct, Hilar had little interest in a theatre of psychological complexity or nuance, witty or philosophic conversation, nor (despite an early flirtation with the decadents) in a theatre of symbolistic atmosphere. Instead, Hilar saw theatre as a Dionysian or Baroque rite, a full-blooded, provocative, vibrant celebration. His instinctive histrionic, hyperexpressive sense evolved and manifested itself in various forms, often in grotesque distortions, sometimes in more moderate forms.

Several of Hilar's recurrent characteristics as a director appeared in his earliest work: restricting actors' habitual mannerisms to the immediate demands of the play at hand, tightly controlling their intonation, expression, and rate of speech, drawing on the theatrical stylization of *commedia dell'arte* even for modern works, and introducing elements of the grotesque in characterization, movement, and delivery, especially in such works as Molière's *Georges Dandin* (1913) and Carl Sternheim's *Merchant Schippel* (1914). It was a sharper, more concentrated, heightened form of theatre than Kvapil's, more aggressive and hard-edged, with a distinct inclination toward irony and satire.

Many of these very tendencies were encouraged by the example of several guest-directed productions in Prague during the spring of 1914 by František Zavřel (1879–1915), a Czech who had learned his craft under Reinhardt in Berlin and then pursued a successful career of his own in the leading theatres of Berlin and Munich. After directing a production of *King Václav IV* by Viktor Dyk (1873–1931) at the National Theatre in January, Zavřel directed a production of Frank Wedekind's *The Earth Spirit* in April at the Švanda Theatre, starring Ema Švandová in the role of Lulu, an example of her undertaking more demanding roles than her repertoire usually allowed. Hilar himself invited Zavřel to the Vinohrady later that spring to stage a Czech play based on *Don Quixote*, Dyk's *The Coming to Wisdom of Don Quixote* (Zmoudření Dona Quixota). Zavřel represented a concentrated dose of contemporary world theatre with a vivid, personally distinctive style that reacted against the harmonious, sensuous theatre of Reinhardt or Kvapil and pointed toward the nervous excitement of expressionism. Hilar described what Zavřel's example meant to him: "His directorial efforts toward a simplification of means, concentration, and intensity of effect were for me a confirmation of my own directorial inspiration."[3] Hilar added that Zavřel opened his eyes to something perhaps even more important: the cutting, transposing, and general editing of the text to make it stageworthy and dramatically more effective, as well as the drastic modifying of stage directions concerning scenery and properties to make the staging more expressive. "Zavřel dared to support the poet against the inexperienced playwright, and the dramatic work against the inexperienced poet. . . . he dared to give a helping hand to an untried play against the experienced spectator. This co-creative work of the director-dramaturg became for me a model."[4] Hilar clearly admired a "daring" that would have been totally alien to Kvapil.

From *Penthesilea* (1914) onward, Hilar was evolving his own brand of expressionism, which for him was far less a matter of theory or quasi-mystical ideology than of performance style and spirit as a reflection of the age: "Intensity of expression, condensation of form, concentration of feeling and meaning, that is what — aesthetically and not merely sociologically — conveys the spirit of our age."[5] The specific manifestations of Hilar's expressionism were a constant stylization, if not distortion, of voice and body to produce a highly dynamic, rhythmicized total performance with a stress on sheer theatricality. Characterization was often sacrificed to artificial configurations of essential forces and ideas; physical staging and lighting were deliberately and drastically manipulated to achieve striking contrasts and confrontations; the grotesque was a constant though variable element; and a middle range of emotional display was rejected in favor of extreme pathos or ecstasy.

His penchant for satire with grotesque, *commedia* overtones found expression in productions like Sternheim's *The Snob* (1915), Richard Brinsley Sheridan's *The School for Scandal* (1916), and Molière's *Don Juan* (1917), while darker, more spastic variations of this tendency were evident in his staging of *The Dance of Death* (1917) by August Strindberg, a playwright who never appealed to Kvapil. Hilar did not abandon the grotesque but heightened and expanded it in other works that strove for a certain heroic, monumental pathos: for example, Shakespeare's *Antony and Cleopatra* (1917) and Pierre Corneille's *The Cid* (1919). Psychological realism was subordinated if not suppressed in favor of markedly stylized, rhythmically orchestrated voices, sculpturesque blocking, and artificially imposed movement as if Hilar, master shaper of the total stage work, were releasing his will toward expressive form.

Although expressionistic characteristics were widespread in European theatre at the time, Hilar's form of expressionism was distinguished by a balance and resultant enrichment rooted in his inherent common sense and wit, freedom from didacticism, respect for literary values, and affinity for the sensual and physiological rather than the mystical or allegorical. Moreover, his penchant for the grotesque seems less a matter of arbitrary "effect" or self-indulgence than an appropriate reflection of wartime stress and horror.

As the war drew to a close and was followed by revolutionary movements and the birth of new states throughout Europe, Hilar and other European theatre artists were attracted to plays dealing with the masses, their turbulence and aspiration, their ecstasy and pathos. For Hilar, perhaps the most apolitical of all major Czech theatre people, the war and the turbulence of peace were equal inspirations for what concerned him most — his creative work in theatre. In productions like Z. Krasiński's *The Undivine Comedy* (1918), C. Van Lerberghe's *Pan* (1919), Arnošt Dvořák's *The Hussites* (1919), and Emile Verhaeren's *The Dawns* (1920) Hilar reflected the postwar spirit of feverish social turmoil and class conflict not literally but metaphorically. As one Czech critic pointed out, these were not "Reinhardt spectacles of mass movements, but dramatic battles of individuals and collectives for truth and justice."[6] The same critic went on to say: "No one else on the Czech stage showed a collective hero, presented by a collective, with a comparable sense for its powerful moving drama and suggestive force."[7]

By 1920, thanks to the special talents and total dedication of Kvapil and Hilar, as well as their associates, Czech theatre did indeed belong among the front ranks of European theatre. In the next two decades, until stifled in 1938 by events preceding World War II, Czech theatre established itself even more firmly as a powerful voice in contemporary theatre and in the life of its young nation, thanks to the ongoing work of Hilar and a cluster of new talents from a younger generation.

THE SEIZURE OF A THEATRE AND SOME RELATED ETHNIC MATTERS

In November 1920, as if to crown their independence and reclaim a part of their heritage, Czech demonstrators (some of them actors) seized the Estates Theatre in a spontaneous, problematical show of patriotism triggered by clashes between the Czech army and Germans in Cheb and Teplice, two Czech cities near the German border. The clashes were symptomatic of other political, social, and even military problems in the new republic during the early years of its independence, such as the integrity of its borders. The Estates Theatre, which had been German in origin and exclusively so since 1862, became a second stage of the Czech National Theatre. The Czech national comic opera, Smetana's *The Bartered Bride* (Prodaná nevěsta), was performed there the very night of the takeover, and the first new production on its stage was Tyl's *Arsonist's Daughter* the following month.

Although the seizure of the Estates Theatre was criticized by President Masaryk himself, it was a fait accompli — and a striking exception to most potentially controversial Czech-German issues in the early years of the new republic. As a testimonial to the toleration of minorities in Czechoslovakia, German theatres established in Bohemia and Moravia during the nineteenth century (one in almost every large city) remained German after 1918 until the end of World War II. In Prague, where Germans constituted between 5 percent and 10 percent of the population, the Neues Deutsches Theater remained in full operation after 1918 as one of the most recent and well-equipped large theatres of the capital.

The broader context of Czech and German relations in the Czech lands suggests that the society remained largely bilingual and that the coexistence of the two cultures was complex but essentially peaceful, particularly in cosmopolitan Prague, until 1938 and the Sudetenland-Munich disaster. Each culture had its own educational institutions, press, and other organizations, both social and political, and each had a vote in the shifting governments extending back to the late nineteenth century. The distinction between the Czechs' perceptions of the Germans and Austrians, however, warrants a few more words. Though the two groups are often lumped together as German because of their common language, there is no doubt that the Czechs related Germans to militaristic Prussians, a force to be feared despite their cultural achievements. Austrians, on the other hand, although the principal authority figures for Czechs for centuries, were viewed as less threatening, less severe, more approachable, essentially more familiar than the Germans. For theatre people, in any case, the German-Austrian distinction was essentially irrelevant. The issue was a matter of creativity, artistry, freshness, and relevance to the times. Until ideology became decisive (e.g., nazism, communism) foreign artists like Stanislavsky, Reinhardt, Jacques Copeau, Craig, Leopold Jessner, Alexander Tairov, or Meyerhold were judged not by nationality but by their talent and professionalism.

To return to the broader question of Czech and German theatre in the Czech lands, the separation of Czech from German, which began in 1862 with the building of the Provisional Theatre for strictly Czech productions, had one theatrical exception: the world of cabarets, an often neglected variant of traditional theatre that attained great European popularity in the first quarter of the new century, with Prague as one of its chief sites of performance. Two Prague cabarets, the Lucerna (1910) and the Montmartre (1913), provided entertainment that featured alternating Czech and German numbers on the same program; but certain other cabarets had individual numbers actually blending the two languages, much as Czechs (and probably some Germans) did in everyday idiomatic speech, sometimes making a consciously ironic point: "Ano, já jsem správný pražák, *durch* a *durch*," meaning "Yes, I'm a real Praguer, through and through" — with the italicized words in German, and the rest in Czech.

Related to the Czech-German issue and the cabaret phenomenon is the question of Jewish involvement in Czech theatre, for it was in Czech cabarets that one was most likely to find Jewish material in the form of musical numbers or skits in Yiddish. There is no evidence of a Jewish theatre company other than one or two touring groups from abroad (Austria or Hungary) that appeared sporadically, performing in Yiddish with some success in Slovak towns, but less frequently and with much less success in the Czech lands. Various factors were involved, including apparently unseasoned performers, but the principal reason for lack of a more sustained presence is that Jews were rather thoroughly assimilated into the Czech or German cultures. One rarely comes across reference to a "Jewish" actor, director, or designer in sources dealing with Czech theatre of the nineteenth century and onward, although such artists existed. On the other hand, especially in Prague, where the German, Czech, and Jewish cultures were most thoroughly mingled, Yiddish performers or Yiddish numbers did appear in some cabarets. Evidence is scanty, but it seems that Franz Kafka, for example, witnessed performances by "a troupe of Yiddish actors . . . installed in a Prague coffeehouse" in 1910 and 1911,[8] although another source declares that "prior to 1918 the Yiddish theatre was unknown in the territory which later formed the Czechoslovak Republic."[9] This latter source then describes some Yiddish theatre in Slovakia, chiefly a troupe from Vienna (HaOr) in 1920. Subsequent Yiddish touring groups from abroad appeared intermittently and with little acclaim between 1921 and 1928, principally in smaller cities and towns, mostly in Slovakia and in the most eastern province of Czechoslovakia, Subcarpathian Ruthenia. In the 1930s a few local amateur and semiprofessional Czech Jewish groups sporadically and briefly appeared in German-language productions in Brno and Prague (e.g., the Jungjüdische Bühne of Brno and the Jüdische Kammerspiele of Prague).

In terms of mainline cabaret activity, the early Czech cabarets evolved from nineteenth-century song-centered entertainments in taverns or pubs called *šantány* or song-locales (from the French *chanson*). Influenced by German cabarets in Munich and Berlin (dominated by Wedekind and Reinhardt, respectively), Czech cabarets became more literarily centered, evolving away from strictly vocal numbers to include monologues, skits, and even short plays, especially parodies of literary classics.

The most important of these new cabarets was the Red Seven (Červená sedma, named after its founder, Jiří Červený, 1887–1962). Many other Prague cabarets were popular, but the Red Seven combined originality, longevity, and a variety of thematically relevant material more successfully than its contemporaries. Opening in Prague in 1909 on an amateur basis, it became professional in 1914 and performed until 1922; its principal home was a converted ballroom in a hotel. At one time or another virtually all the major cabaret performers appeared in its shows: Vlasta Burian (1891–1962) and Ference Futurista (1891–1947), both great comedians at the beginning of their careers; writer, director, and actor Artur Longen (1885–1936), "the most bohemian of bohemians"; Eduard Basse (1888–1946), writer, actor, and master of ceremonies. Among standard playwrights and other writers whose works were written for or adapted to the cabaret setting were G. B. Shaw and Czechs Jiří Mahen, Arnošt Dvořák, František Langer, Jaroslav Hašek, and Karel Čapek. The Red Seven's popularity peaked in 1918–1920, when its satiric, witty parodies and skits were freer than established theatres to attack both the dying Hapsburg monarchy and the Czech bourgeoisie. The Red Seven and its less celebrated contemporaries represented a lively strand of Czech popular theatre, the off-off Broadway of their day. Most of their work was ephemeral, but they established a mode of performance that evolved into new forms of significant studio theatre in the interwar era and even bore fruit in the subsequent studio theatres in the 1960s and beyond.[10]

1920–1938

Considered as a whole, theatre in the First Republic (1918–1938) had great vitality and variety. The vitality was due largely to the enormous release of spirit accompanying the creation of an independent republic after several centuries of alien citizenship within the Habsburg Empire, and the variety to Czechoslovakia's critical location between East and West, which facilitated its access to the theatrical avant-garde of France, Germany, and the Soviet Union, exemplified by directors such as Jacques Copeau, Erwin Piscator, Bertolt Brecht, Vsevolod Meyerhold, Alexander Tairov, and Eugene Vakhtangov. Equally important stimuli were American jazz and film (Buster Keaton, Lillian Gish, Charlie Chaplin, Douglas Fairbanks), which were sweeping the continent.[11]

The Czechs' efforts to sustain their new independent cultural identity went hand in hand with a desire to become worthy of world citizenship by keeping abreast of significant culture abroad. In Czech theatre this tendency toward self-improvement by learning from others produced an exceptional potential for creativity. Probably no other country in postwar Europe possessed the combination of a firmly rooted repertory theatre system and theatre artists who were not only talented but as a whole free of feelings of national or cultural superiority or of commitment to native theatre traditions or conventions. The Czechs were eager and receptive. Moreover, they had been spared most of the ghastly wounds suffered by their grander neighbors in the great war, and they were exhilarated by the prospects of a brave new world of national independence and unfettered participation in the artistic turbulence revivifying European culture. For the Czechs, it was one of the rare times when the external pressures of economics or politics were minimal. They were free to create at will.

Not all Czech theatre during this era was provocative, original, or exciting. As in all theatre eras, there existed a body of competent professional work in many theatres, the chief appeal of which was the charisma of the actors, a provocative but shallow new script, or well-packaged kitsch. But the *significant* contribution of Czech theatre to the great flowering of adventurous European theatre of the 1920s took the form of several pairs of contrasting tendencies. Its notable achievements included the work of both large institutionalized theatres and small experimental studios operating on minimal or nonexistent budgets. The plays ranged from standard classics to original plays to works that were less plays than innovative scenarios drawn from fiction, poetry, and journalistic data. Moreover, the plays and the methods of producing them also embodied virtually all current artistic modes, with the most significant productions having one tendency in common: the flight from the dead center of illusionistic realism. Instead, expressionism, constructivism, dada, surrealism, theatricalism, and the special Czech variation of these isms — poetism, which accentuated playful fantasy — marked much of the outstanding work of this era, as did the esprit of such paratheatrical forms as the circus and the cabaret.

Two other general observations may be made about the theatre of the 1920s and 1930s before proceeding to specifics. First, although the name of Karel Čapek towers above all others if we consider the period with regard to playwriting, the theatre, as theatre, was dominated by its directors, first, and its scenographers and actors, second. Czech playwrights, with the striking exception of Čapek and perhaps František Langer,[12] did not measure up to their fellow theatre artists.

Second, to speak of an overall evolutionary tendency or direction in theatre during the twenty years of the First Republic, one must turn for guidance to events dominating life outside the theatre during that period, namely the sometimes meandering, sometimes rushing stream leading from the first heady days of Czech independence to increasing stability and prosperity, only to be followed by economic crisis and the growing threat of fascism and militarism, culminating in the ignominious capitulation of England and France to Adolf Hitler's demands in the autumn of 1938 at Munich.

Profoundly influenced by these events, the theatre at first passed through an exuberant, richly inventive phase that lasted until approximately 1930. It was a phase marked by aesthetic considerations, whereas the following years increasingly revealed moral or ethical preoccupations which at times became flatly ideological or political, all in response to pressures from the evolving domestic and international crises preceding the devastation of World War II.

In addition to the National and Vinohrady theatres, several other prewar and wartime theatres and artists previously mentioned continued into the new era. For example, the privately run, commercial Švanda Theatre on the left bank of the Vltava had been producing since 1881. Ema Švandová, its head since 1906, continued her policy of selecting plays on the basis of the roles they offered her, but even such plays were occasionally several cuts above the routine boulevard entertainment of the day. Moreover, when she ran into prolonged slack attendance, she would temporarily lease the theatre to others. Among those who made the Švanda Theatre their temporary home during the interwar era were several of the cabaret stars we met in the previous chapter. Nevertheless, even the best work at the Švanda Theatre did not prove memorable on a more than domestic scale. For impact that reached beyond Prague and sometimes even beyond Czech borders, one must trace the careers of others, some of whom had already achieved renown, and some of whom were just beginning their careers in theatre.

A convenient way to perceive the highlights of the period is to focus on several specific seasons with primary attention to the work of a half-dozen notable individuals who dominated the theatre of the time, while also mentioning the work of a few others in passing. Before tracing the careers of the artists in the top echelon in some detail, a brief introduction to each may be helpful.

Playwright Karel Čapek (1890–1938) was probably the best-known Czech theatre person in the world until another Czech playwright, Václav Havel, gained international attention for his plays and his political stance from the late 1960s onward. To put things in proportion, however, it is best to start by acknowledging that most critics regard some of Čapek's novels and even short stories as more profound and significant than his plays,[13] several of which can — with some justice — be regarded as melodramatic and awkwardly constructed. Nevertheless, it was his plays that drew the widest audience.

Čapek's complex personality was that of a skeptical humanist and ironic, satiric humorist. A journalist and literary person for most of his life, Čapek also sat close to the seats of power as a member of an informal inner circle around Czechoslovakia's first president, Thomas Garrigue Masaryk.[14] Keenly aware of the enormous potentials and pitfalls of contemporary industrialization and technology, Čapek had deep faith in life, in human reason and even goodness, but he was also subject to profound despair at human folly, greed, and lust for power. He rejected all attempts to apply easy solutions to the mystery of human identity and relation-

Josef and Karel Čapek in the 1920s.

ships or to provide formulas or ideologies for the improvement or salvation of societies.

Čapek's plays, which range from light, lyrical comedies to satiric fantasies to tense dramas, are primarily plays of ideas, of conflicting principles, rather than studies of character; they prompt audiences to think rather than feel. Similarly, the form of his plays is less distinctive than their provocative ideas. Nevertheless, he is far from a closet dramatist; he had a sharp sense of theatrical playfulness and dynamics, and an ear for effective dialogue and dramatic confrontations. For several years, in fact, he was a highly regarded dramaturg and also a stage director of about a dozen productions. As a playwright in the interwar period, he evolved from a position of philosophical critical detachment to engaged partisanship. A final point not to be ignored is that he intermittently teamed with his brother Josef (1887–1945), a painter and stage designer who collaborated on several of his productions and co-authored several of his plays.

Karel Hugo Hilar, who worked exclusively in large institutionalized theatres and was probably the single strongest director in the history of Czech theatre, already had a significant career underway as the war ended and the First Republic was established. His innate flair for dynamic, highly expressive spectacle was reinforced by his most frequent designer-collaborator, Vlastislav Hofman (1884–1964). Surpassing the considerable achievements of his older contemporary Jaroslav Kvapil, Hilar's blend of Dionysian force and expressionistic intensity in the National Theatre thrust the Czech stage onto the international theatre map by the mid-1920s. His remaining career was severely curtailed by a stroke, although he maintained his leadership in the National Theatre and directed a number of major successes before his death in the mid-1930s. Kvapil himself, after several years of important service in the new Ministry of Education, returned to steady theatre directing for six more years in 1921.

Jiří Voskovec (1905–1981) and Jan Werich (1905–1980) in their Liberated Theatre (Osvobozené divadlo) of the late 1920s and 1930s created an entirely different sort of theatre. Law students untutored in the crafts of theatre when they launched their first jerry-built production, they captured the imagination and love of their audiences with a series of semi-improvised revues with music which always had cathartic laughter as their central dynamic but which increasingly matured to important sociopolitical satire as conditions deteriorated in the 1930s. Their unsubsidized theatre, in which they were authors, librettists, star actors, and occasionally even directors and designers, known simply as v + w, became by far the most popular and commercially successful one in Czechoslovakia and a bulwark against the realities of encroaching fascism.

Emil František Burian (1904–1959) was for years a composer and actor before turning to direction. Ultimately he established his own theatre in the 1930s, a frankly partisan, Communist-oriented tribune of social criticism where Burian presented works ranging from semidocumentary agitprop to productions of high poetic and lyrical imagination in which his musical orientation was always evident. Working almost entirely in limited studio conditions with relatively small budgets, Burian nevertheless was also responsible for the development of forms of staging which foreshadowed many of the more sophisticated evolutions of such techniques in the Czech theatre of the late 1950s and 1960s. His achievements in these areas gained international recognition.

During the interwar period, the careers of Jindřich Honzl and Jiří Frejka often converged with each other and with those of others already mentioned. Although neither possessed the unique theatrical powers of the artists already discussed, each was responsible for important work in varied forms. Honzl (1894–1953), especially, had a checkered, at times seemingly inconsistent career. A secondary-school science teacher and a committed Communist intellectual with a strong interest in Soviet theatrical practice, he devoted himself at first to theatre by and for the proletariat. Concurrently, however, he became actively involved in the early 1920s with the Devětsil organization, a loosely structured leftist group of artists, poets, and intellectuals whose work echoed many radical departures from realism, essentially (and ironically) more elitist than proletarian in their appeal. This apparent contradiction (somewhat analogous to inconsistencies in Burian's own work) surfaced more than once in Honzl's subsequent career, which included extensive work as the director of most of v + w's productions, as an important critic and theorist of theatre and film, and as an independent director of national and foreign classics in state theatres as well as cryptic surrealist works in improvised studios.[15]

In contrast, Jiří Frejka (1904–1952) was in the apolitical Hilar tradition. A pioneer and leading figure in the consciously avant-garde, semiprofessional studio theatres of the 1920s, he had a sensibility especially attuned to lyrical, poetic theatre with improvisatory qualities and conventions reminiscent of the *commedia dell'arte*. By the 1930s, however, Hilar had taken Frejka into the National Theatre as his protégé, and in this center of tradition and large-scale production Frejka matured into a more socially and politically responsible artist, but without losing his lightness of touch and poetic sensitivity. Moreover, Frejka, who consistently sought creative work with talented young designers like Antonín Heythum (1901–1954) in the 1920s, also evolved into a major director of theatrically impressive *mises en scène*, particularly in his collaborations in the 1930s with František Tröster (1904–1968), the most significant designer in the generation following that of Vlastislav Hofman.

A look at the work of these key figures in four different years or theatrical seasons provides a cross-sectional perspective on certain key milestones of Czech theatre in the 1920s and 1930s.

In 1921, when much of Europe still feared the specter of Bolshevism, the official establishment of the Communist Party in Czechoslovakia testified to the essentially liberal and tolerant government of the First Republic under the leadership of President Masaryk. Ema Švandová was again appearing as Lulu in a revival of Wedekind's *The Earth Spirit* and *Pandora's Box* at the Švanda Theatre, while Artur Longen opened his short-lived Cabaret Bum in rivalry with the Red Seven, taking the hugely talented, dadaistic clown Vlasta Burian with him. In the fall Longen started his more successful Revolutionary Stage by directing Vlasta Burian in Longen's adaptation of *Don Quixote*; later, Longen staged his dramatization of Hašek's *The Good Soldier Schweik*.

It was the premiere of Karel Čapek's *RUR* (Rossum's Universal Robots) at the National Theatre in January 1921, however, that brought world attention to Czech theatre for the first time. It was directed by Vojta Novák (1886–1966), a prewar and wartime director in small avant-garde theatres as well as at the Švanda Theatre, and designed by a young architect who would do important work in the 1920s and 1930s, Bedřich Feuerstein (1892–1936). In the fall of that year Čapek also assumed the duties of dramaturg and director in the Vinohrady Theatre at the invitation of Kvapil, who had left government work to replace Hilar as head of drama at the

Bedřich Feuerstein's rendering for Čapek's RUR, *National Theatre, 1921.*

Vinohrady. Earlier, Čapek had written two other plays: an unproduced witty, lyrical one-act comedy in the *commedia dell'arte* vein, The Fateful Play of Love (Lásky hra osudná) in 1910, on which his brother Josef collaborated, and The Brigand (Loupežník), over which he labored for almost ten years before its National Theatre premiere in 1920. *The Brigand*, a comedy of conflicting generational values, demonstrated Čapek's gift for provoking laughter while also touching on painful human relationships. It is probably his most realistic play with regard to characters, situation, and form.

   RUR presents a prototypical Čapek situation: a fantasylike plot device is introduced into a contemporary realistic frame of action. In this case it is a formula for the creation of lifelike robots, who will eliminate human toil and give promise of a paradise on earth. In essence it is a science-fiction melodrama, symptomatic of Čapek's concern for the survival of human values in an increasingly mechanized, technocratic world. The robots rebel and almost wipe out the entire human race except for one survivor — the man who invented the formula. He is saved from complete despair when he realizes that two of the robots, a male and female, show signs of affection for one another. He sees Adam and Eve in them — the beginning of a new, still human race. This arbitrary, sentimental resolution is symptomatic of other flaws in the play: contrived situations and stilted characters and dialogue. Nevertheless, the play created a sensation and was performed all over the globe. Underlying the melodrama is a recurrent Čapek action: a wonderful, miraculous discovery becomes destructive or unbearable. Utopian dreams may turn nightmarish. It is a dramatic action that reveals Čapek's sense of dark irony as well as his skepticism toward all technological marvels or salvationist ideologies — in short, all absolutes.

An event of equal and perhaps longer-lasting significance for Czech theatre in 1921 was Karel Hugo Hilar's assumption of leadership of drama production at the National Theatre as a successor to Jaroslav Kvapil, who, as noted, subsequently took over Hilar's abandoned position at the Vinohrady Theatre, where he served until 1928. For the next decade and a half Hilar dominated all drama work on the National Theatre stages, maintaining his stature as one of Europe's major theatre artists. His expressionistically slanted approach was seen to full effect that year in productions of *Coriolanus*, *Medea*, and *The Doctor in Spite of Himself*. The following year Czech theatre and Hilar achieved even greater renown for his direction of the Čapek brothers' *The Insect Comedy* (Ze života hmyzu), designed by Josef Čapek. Although the play has three acts, the action throughout is presented in a series of lively short scenes or "numbers," and for that reason it was often dubbed a "revue." The basic conceit is an expressionistic depiction of humanity's follies and horrors in the guise of insect life, as observed (or dreamed) by a likeable, thoughtful, but aimless tramp who falls asleep outdoors. Each act focuses on a certain segment or aspect of insect-human life: butterflies depict the frivolousness and waste inherent in faddish high society; dung beetles, grubs, parasites, crickets, and killer flies embody a materialistic, acquisitive, Darwinian world of survival by any means, including murder to feed one's own; rival colonies of red and yellow ants present the horrors of militarism and totalitarianism as they strive to exterminate each other for the possession of perhaps a square foot of soil and grass; and delicate, expiring moths convey the ephemerality of life. The tramp finally has an epiphany about the sheer value of life and how it ought to be lived, but he experiences it in the midst of a fatal heart attack. The Čapeks' original version ends very pessimistically, or at best ambivalently — so much so that they wrote several alternate endings which offer a not entirely persuasive view that ordinary, simple life will endure and find value in honest work.

Overall, *Insect Comedy* is a much more interesting dramatic work than *RUR*, offsetting its grimmer insights with genuinely comedic, even farcical byplay and a gallery of entertaining, often grotesque types. The first play by a Czech author to have more than one hundred performances in the National Theatre, it also became an international hit and has had many successful revivals. Hilar's original production involved colorful, eccentric costuming to emphasize the blend of insect and human in the characters. For the butterfly sequence, a gauzy appliquéd material backed a curved, raked platform on which lay a carpet with bold floral patterns and large pillows equally embellished. Frequent projections were used

Josef Čapek's setting for act I of the original production of the Čapeks' Insect Comedy, *National Theatre, 1922, directed by K. H. Hilar.*

on the cyclorama (e.g., black smokestacks against a red horizon in the ant sequence), and a glass floor facilitated special lighting effects for the choreographed play of the moths.

In the meantime, from November 1921 until March 1924, Karel Čapek directed some dozen productions at the Vinohrady, including works by Molière, Percy Bysshe Shelley (*The Cenci*), Aristophanes, and several Czech playwrights, plus his fourth full-length play, *The Makropulos Affair* (Věc Makropulos), in 1922. The work is more similar to *RUR* than to *Insect Comedy* in that it presents another science-fiction, utopian miracle in a realistic contemporary setting: a formula for eternal life has proved successful in a woman who is three hundred years old but appears to be a glamorous singer approaching middle age (played by Dostalová). The point of this essentially serious melodrama is that she has come to hate her condition and that life with its mortal limits is much preferable to the folly of eternal youth. It is a happy moment when the formula is destroyed and she is able to die. (The play was adapted to form the libretto of Leoš Janáček's 1926 opera with the same title.)

Jindřich Honzl was already active in theatre in 1921, directing the proletarian Workers' Dramatic Chorus (Dědrasbor, an acronym for Dělnický Dramatický Sbor), which mounted mass choral recitations of leftist proletarian poetry. The following year, in addition to participating in the previously mentioned Devětsil, he would be instrumental in the work of another Communist cultural organization, Proletkult. Meanwhile, E. F. Burian was studying composition in the Prague Conservatory, while Jiří Frejka, Jiří Voskovec, and Jan Werich were students of liberal arts in secondary schools.

By the 1926–1927 season modern Czech theatre had taken its place in the mainstream of significant world theatre. Hilar's work had reached a peak of success with his production of *Romeo and Juliet* in 1924, but within a few weeks of its premiere he suffered a crippling stroke that incapacitated him for the better part of two years. Nevertheless, during the season on which we are focusing he had recuperated enough to stage one of his most notable productions, *Hamlet*, with starkly expressive scenography by Hofman and with the services of two of the major actors of the interwar period, Eduard Kohout (1889–1976) as Hamlet and Václav Vydra (1876–1953) as Claudius; Leopolda Dostalová played Gertrude. By this time Hilar had toned down his expressionistic extremes in order to concentrate more fully on internal, humanistic values. Hamlet was a delicate youth trying to cope with the harsh, often grotesque world of the Danish court, a world depicted by the black void encompassing Hofman's sharply illuminated, hard-edged scenic pieces. That same season Hilar also directed his second play by the Čapek brothers, *Adam the Creator* (Adam stvořitel), which did not measure up to the success of the earlier Čapek works. Once again the basic plot device is a utopianlike miracle, the ability to create the world anew, from scratch, but this time the play as a whole is a fantasy, with Adam destroying creation and God giving him the chance to recreate it. The results of Adam's efforts prove at least as bad as the world that was destroyed, and Adam is content to leave the world as it is. The action resembles *Insect Comedy*'s series of short, primarily comic sequences, but the underlying motifs are often strained and inconsistent. Čapek did not write another play for ten years.[16]

Of the four major Čapek plays of the 1920s, *RUR* and *Makropulos Affair* share characteristics of traditional realistic form, science-fiction motifs, and an absence of humor and textured characterization, while *Insect Comedy* and *Adam the Creator* are more nearly expressionistic in style and revuelike in structure, with capricious, grotesque characters, abundant humor, and themes that are closer to medieval moralities than to science fiction. The divisions, rough as they are, strongly suggest the influence of Josef as a direct collaborator in *Insect Comedy* and *Adam* and the absence of his influence in the former two plays, which Karel Čapek wrote by himself.

Hilar's Hamlet *in Vlastislav Hofman's setting, National Theatre, 1926.*

The most important event of the 1926–1927 season was the start of the careers of Voskovec and Werich with their amateur, minimalist production of *Vest pocket revue* (the title was in English) in a tiny makeshift theatre in the Malá Strana section of Prague in April 1927. By now law students, they were an overnight sensation in this zany, lighthearted spoof of contemporary mores. What had been planned as a one-night fund raiser for Voskovec's preparatory school's alumni club eventually ran for over two hundred performances. What was the essence of its appeal? The performance consisted of some eight to ten short satiric scenarios in a revue format with music. The topics were local as well as international, and the wit and great good humor resonated completely with the essentially optimistic mood of the time. A paid professional orchestra played contemporary American swing music with lyrics by Voskovec. Beyond these elements was the semi-improvisational nature of it all, which climaxed in the inadvertent collapse of a stage flat. To cover the pause until it was set up again, v + w improvised totally on the stage apron and did it so well that this segment became the peak of the whole production. Their literate, spontaneous wit, fresh and seemingly naive, was the key. In virtually all of their subsequent productions, this 90 percent improvised

TURN OF THE CENTURY TO MUNICH [41]

Frejka's adaptation of Cirkus Dandin, *based on Molière's* Georges Dandin, *with setting by Antonín Heythum, 1925.*

forestage sequence — shared directly with the audience, drawing on contemporary events, never the same from performance to performance — became the jewel in their crown.

In many respects, *Vest pocket revue* can be viewed as a product of natural evolution from the cabarets of the earlier years of the century. Indeed, the two major figures from the cabaret era that I have been tracing, Artur Longen and Vlasta Burian, had by now also abandoned the cabaret format for more conventionally patterned plays, however bizarre their plots or actions might be. In the 1926–1927 season they collaborated on productions in the Adria Hotel on Wenceslaus Square (Václavské náměstí), putting on vehicles exploiting Burian's great comic talents, with Longen as author or adaptor as well as director.

The response of the first-night audience to *Vest pocket revue* led to additional performances sponsored by the recently established Liberated Theatre (Osvobozené divadlo), which had been casually launched by Frejka somewhat more than a year earlier. Prior to that, Frejka had several other studio productions dating back to 1923, such as his own adaptation of Molière's *Georges Dandin*, which he staged in 1925, with Heythum, in a combined constructivistic–*commedia dell'arte* manner and retitled *Cirkus Dandin*. As a formal organization, however, this new Liberated Theatre was sponsored by Devětsil and had Honzl as its official co-director. Honzl himself, like Frejka, had been directing relatively short avant-garde French

[42] MODERN CZECH THEATRE

and Czech plays during the previous season for this theatre — dadaistic, surrealistic works such as Guillaume Apollinaire's *The Breasts of Tiresias* and Georges Ribemont-Dessaignes' *The Mute Canary*. But in the spring of 1927 irreconcilable clashes of temperament and policy between Honzl and Frejka forced Frejka's departure from the Liberated Theatre, leaving Honzl in charge.

Frejka went on very quickly to form his own Theatre Dada, in which he continued to perform the light, eccentric work that attracted him, such as Jean Cocteau's *Wedding on the Eiffel Tower*. Honzl similarly pursued his own brand of avant-garde repertoire, such as Alfred Jarry's *Ubu Roi*, Cocteau's *Orphée*, and evenings of poetry by the Italian Futurist Filippo Marinetti and the Czech Vítězslav Nezval (1900–1958), who exemplified the avant-garde spirit of the time in poetry.

Although Voskovec and Werich became formally affiliated with what was now Honzl's Liberated Theatre (and played roles in *Ubu* and *Orphée*), their continued popularity in *Vest pocket revue* was so great that within two years they took over the company from Devětsil and Honzl and moved to larger, commercial theatre spaces in the center of Prague. Thereafter, the theatre came to be known as the Liberated Theatre of Voskovec and Werich, with Honzl assuming an important but secondary role as their director, supervising the work of the other performers (under v + w's ultimate authority), while Voskovec and Werich wrote the scripts and were in complete control of their own central roles in each production. Their eventual, fully established professional theatre was unusual for two more reasons: it was not subsidized and it presented productions one at a time in series, rather than maintain a number of plays in repertoire. Nevertheless, v + w still maintained a stable ensemble (including musicians and dancers) instead of casting each production afresh.

Not the least important event in this milestone season of 1926–1927 was the emergence of E. F. Burian as a director. A Communist Party member since 1923, he divided his time and work between choral music for leftist poetry recitals and background music for several National Theatre drama productions. Indeed, one of his own operas, *Before Sunrise* (Před slunce východem), was performed there in 1925.[17] He had also begun to act in the avant-garde productions of Honzl and Frejka. But in the same month that witnessed the opening of their *Vest pocket revue*, Burian first presented his own initial production of what he called Voiceband, under the aegis of Frejka's Theatre Dada. It was a striking performance form that blended complex choral recitation, chant, and other nonverbal human sounds with strongly rhythmic, syncopated music of his own composing. For the next season or two Burian continued to act for Frejka and present further recitals of his Voiceband, which attracted enough favorable attention to be invited abroad to an international music festival in Siena, Italy, in 1928.

The 1926–1927 season was also the high point of the brief career of the multi-talented Vladimír Gamza (1902–1929), who grew up in Russia, where he was influenced by Stanislavsky and Eugene Vakhtangov. After a brief engagement under Hilar at the Vinohrady Theatre (1920–1921) Gamza succeeded in launching two avant-garde studios, in Brno (the Czech Studio) and Prague (the Art Studio), the latter in the fall of 1926. In both he consciously emphasized art above political relevance. His experimental approach sought to fuse the internalized realism of the Moscow Art Theatre (MAT) (e.g., Charles Dickens' *The Cricket on the Hearth*, 1927) with Vakhtangov's near expressionism (Gogol's *Marriage*, 1927), but he never found sufficient audiences for his productions, which he not only directed but also designed. Chronically ill, he was nevertheless engaged as a director and actor in the National Theatre in 1928, where he directed a few productions (e.g., Ivan Turgenev's *A Month in the Country*) before his untimely death.

In short, the modern Czech theatre was in the full vigor of its early maturity in 1926–1927. Thanks to economic prosperity and political stability, Czech theatre artists were able to devote themselves to the most varied creativity, from full-blooded mountings of classics like Shakespeare to frequently self-centered experiments and even fads. Theatre activity as pure entertainment — with only incidental social relevance — almost became an end in itself. This would not happen again for more than sixty years.

Conditions had altered radically by the season of 1933–1934. The international economic crisis had resulted in massive unemployment in Czechoslovakia. In January 1933 Hitler became chancellor in Germany and shortly thereafter secured even greater powers as a result of the Reichstag fire. So began twelve years of state-sponsored atrocity and mayhem that would affect all of Europe and much of the rest of the world as well — including Czech theatre. In October of the same year a new German political party was formed by Konrad Henlein in the Czech borderlands with Germany, the Sudetenland. Henlein, with Nazi German support, stressed irredentist issues in these borderlands, where Germans were in a majority.

During the next five years hundreds of German (and even some Czech) writers, artists, and intellectuals previously residing in Germany were to stream into these borderlands as well as into Prague, Brno, and other large cities. They had become personae non gratae in the new Nazi Reich and sought refuge in democratic Czechoslovakia. The German theatres in the Czech borderlands (Liberec, Teplice, Ostrava) as well as in Prague itself were able to provide such refugees with at least some relief, even if only temporary. Those passing through Prague included Max Reinhardt, Bertolt Brecht, and Thomas Mann, on their way elsewhere. Others, specifically theatre people, found employment in Prague's Neues Deutsches Theater: Alexander Moissi, Ernst Deutsche, Albert and Else Basserman, Max Pallenberg. Other refugees from Nazi Germany organized small groups to perform as guests in some Prague theatres. The cooperation of Czech and German theatre people was made more formal by the Club of Czech and German Theatre Workers, formed in 1935 in Prague.

The world outside the theatre was becoming impossible to ignore, but the implications of what was to come were not yet obvious in the fall of 1933, when the single most important theatrical event of 1933–1934 occurred — E. F. Burian's establishment of his own theatre in Prague, D34, the D representing the Czech word for theatre (*divadlo*), and the numbers changing annually to represent the forthcoming year. Burian had spent three years in Brno and Olomouc (1929–1932) gradually developing his skills as a director in plays by authors from Niccolò Machiavelli and Molière to Brecht and Eugene O'Neill, while trying to reconcile his aesthetic inclinations toward a Tairov-like artistry with his commitment to proletarian-slanted social criticism. Finally, he experienced enough frustrations in working for others to open a theatre of his own, focused more consistently on Communist goals.

The embodiment of this objective, D34, opened on September 1, 1933, in a small converted concert hall, the Mozarteum, in the center of Prague. The production was *Life in Our Days*, a semidocumentary, propagandistic collage which he adapted from a German text by Erich Kästner. During the next several years, in addition to foreign travel that included Moscow in 1934, he ripened his inherently strong theatrical talents by continuing to stage at least a half-dozen original works or adaptations each season. These productions alternated between Brechtian or Piscatorian sociopolitical commentary (e.g., *Threepenny Opera*, 1934), his own unwavering concern for poetic, musical values, and his keen interest in folk motifs. The most successful fusion of these two tendencies was his memorable achievement in *War* (Vojna) in early 1935, his own lyrical, deeply moving antiwar choral drama rooted in the ceremonials of village life. Also interesting were Burian's free adaptations in 1934 of Molière's *The Miser* and Shakespeare's *The Merchant of Venice*, both of which were slanted toward attacks on capitalism and class oppression, as were his productions of Soviet plays, such as Gorky's *Yegor Bulychov* (1934), the first production of that play outside the USSR.

Like the v + w theatre, Burian's was unsubsidized through most of its 1930s existence, but it played in much more restricted quarters and hewed to the repertory system of alternating productions. The legacy of both theatres was to become very influential in subsequent decades, but Burian's work, while attracting a loyal, enthusiastic following, never experienced the broad popularity of v + w's.

Voskovec and Werich, after a shaky season or two when they diverged from the revue form, settled into a successful format of "Jazz Revues" combining their distinctive brand of partially (at times wholly) improvised humor and light satire with essentially escapist entertainment loosely tied to a farfetched action in exotic settings. *Fata Morgána* (1929) was the first of these new revues that revived their popularity. *The Golem* (1931), the last of this series, was the most finished in its imaginative re-creation of the sixteenth-century Prague court of Emperor Rudolph and his astrologers and alchemists. One reason for *Golem*'s superiority may have been its direction by Honzl, who returned to v + w after an absence of two seasons. In these revues v + w usually played characters who inadvertently become embroiled in the main action and periodically step outside it to comment on it and on related issues.

Not the least factor in their ongoing success was the contribution made by Jaroslav Ježek (1906–1941), a classically trained composer with a flair for improvisation, who became their permanent composer in residence in 1929. Also important were fairly elaborate song-and-dance routines presented by professional choreographers and dancing girls. The designer for most of the Jazz Revues was František Zelenka (1904–1944), whose fresh, capricious style was appropriate for them and the rest of their professional company.

During the 1933–1934 season a transition was becoming increasingly evident in v + w's work. In 1932, when Burian was finishing his work in Brno, they had already staged *Caesar*, a more tightly shaped revue that sharply extended their satire to flaws in the contemporary Czech political scene (early signs of Fascist elements) and the grotesque phenomenon of dictators like Benito Mussolini and Hitler. Aristophanic laughter was still present in abundance, but v + w's basic orientation had shifted.

The move from high-spirited entertainment to a concern for sociopolitical relevance and the need to take a stand on public issues was probably due in part to the return of the ideologically inclined Honzl as their director. The next two plays focused on economics and unemployment problems; v + w then returned to the offensive against totalitarianism in their production of *Ass and Shadow* (Osel a stín) in October 1933, one month after Burian launched his D34 theatre. Set, like *Caesar*, in Roman times, *Ass and Shadow* was more nearly a play with musical numbers than a revue and also more aggressive in its attack. It presented a thinly disguised, stinging caricature of Hitler and the Fascist menace that drew complaints from the German Embassy in Prague. The apolitical phase of their career was over; with only incidental exceptions, Voskovec and Werich then continued to evolve their response to the forces threatening the very existence of the First Republic.

The finale of v + w's Caesar, 1932, brought the action into the present. Voskovec and Werich are at lower right. Photo by Alexandr Paul.

Among the most sensational of the productions was a spinoff from *Ass and Shadow* to start the following 1934 season: *Executioner and Fool* (Kat a blázen), an even harsher depiction of menacing dictators set in a contemporary but mythical Mexico. Actual riots took place in the theatre between Fascist sympathizers and the greater part of the audience, which was beginning to contain more members of the working class. Despite the more fully engaged, partisan slant of the productions, laughter was still at the core and happy endings resolved matters.

Meanwhile, Honzl, like Burian, had also spent several seasons as a director at the State Theatre in Brno after temporarily breaking with v + w in 1929, but he experienced only mixed success and returned to Prague in 1931 to resume direction of the remaining v + w productions. On the side, however, he visited both

An informal photo of the creators of the Liberated Theatre of v + w. From left to right, Voskovec, Werich, Ježek, and Honzl, during the run of their Caesar, 1932. Photo by Alexandr Paul.

Moscow and Paris and occasionally accepted an assignment in larger theatres — for example, guest directing Vladislav Vančura's (1891–1942) *Alchemist* at the National Theatre in late 1932. Despite this experience, Honzl was unsuccessful in his efforts to become a permanently appointed director at the National Theatre in the 1935–1936 season. Frejka was one of a four-member committee of the permanent staff who decided against recommending him, an action probably not forgotten by Honzl in later years. Although Honzl directed in the National Theatre once more as a guest (1938), he obviously felt frustrated. It is impossible to gauge the various factors involved in the decision against Honzl, but the question of Honzl's abilities was probably secondary to his explicit affiliation with the Communist Party. The National Theatre was ultimately an organ of the government, and in those increasingly politicized times Czechoslovakia was trying to steer a centrist course between the right and left.

By the 1933–1934 season Frejka had become a permanent director at the National Theatre, after having been invited by Hilar to become an assistant director in 1929. During his first few apprentice seasons there he managed to organize an informal Studio project in which he could concentrate on the relatively small-scale lyrical and fanciful works that had been his trademark earlier. One of them, indeed, was the official premiere of the Čapeks' very first play, the highly theatrical *Fateful Play of Love*, on a bill of one-acts in the spring of 1930. By 1933–1934, however, he had begun to take on works of more substance and larger scale, such as J. K. Tyl's Czech classic *Jan Hus* and Aristophanes' *The Birds*, a production in which he, too, began to take a more direct stance vis-à-vis the external sociopolitical events in Europe by equating the central manipulators in the classic comedy with contemporary dictators. Like Honzl and Burian he also took an extended trip to the Soviet Union in 1934 to observe its theatre, but in his case political feelings were not an additional motivation.

In 1933–1934 Karel Hugo Hilar was approaching the end of his career. Although he never regained his full strength and drive after the stroke of 1924, he succeeded in mounting a series of impressive productions at the National Theatre that revealed a profounder sense of life's complexities while retaining his genius for total staging. Perhaps the most powerful of these productions was his 1932 *Oedipus*, with Kohout in the title role and a monumental and superbly functional set by Hofman. This was nearly matched by Hilar's penultimate production in 1934, *Mourning Becomes Electra*, with the same designer, and with Dostalová playing Christine Mannon. Both works still retained expressionistic elements, but these were subordinated to a deeper perception of the mystery of human destiny. It is fascinating to speculate on how Hilar's work would have evolved in the following years of growing European crisis had his health and spirit held firm, but in

A model of Vlastislav Hofman's setting for Hilar's production of Oedipus, *National Theatre, 1932.*

March 1935 he suffered a second and fatal stroke, thus ending one of the great eras of the National Theatre.

In the meantime, the paths of Ema Švandová and Vlasta Burian had briefly crossed in 1928 when he leased the Švanda Theatre. He performed there with Longen until 1930, when he moved into a theatre bearing his own name in the heart of Prague, where he would remain for the next fifteen years. In the 1933–1934 season he began work with a new director, Julius Lébl, who brought a more systematic approach to the staging of Burian's serial productions, which began to have runs of over a hundred performances. Like v + w, Burian also began to appear in films. After Burian left the Švanda Theatre in 1930, Ema Švandová leased it for a year to another comic, Jára Kohout (1904–1994), but in 1932 she once again formed a company and performed in her theatre until 1935, at which time she retired and sold her theatre concession to Jára Kohout.

Not only the National Theatre, but every theatre in Czechoslovakia was entering a period of maximum challenge as events relentlessly drove toward the crises of 1938. The surviving artists with whom I am dealing, however, were by now in their peak creative years, and it is interesting to note their stance and their activities in what would be the final full season of independent theatre, in 1937–1938. In September of 1937, almost as an ill omen, former President Masaryk died; he had abdicated in 1935 and was succeeded by his longtime associate, Eduard Beneš (1884–1948).

It was the career of Voskovec and Werich that most nearly coincided with the timing and import of events in 1937–1938. Henlein's Nazi-affiliated Sudeten Party had been presenting increasing demands for Sudeten autonomy during the previous year or two. In 1938, not long after Hitler occupied Austria in March (the Anschluss), a series of inept interventions by the British and French brought increasing pressure on the Czechs to accede to Henlein's demands. It was in such perilous times, when Czech mobilization was imminent and war or peace in the balance, that the last two v + w productions were staged. The final productions, *Heavy Barbara* (Těžká Barbora, the Czech equivalent of World War I's huge cannon Big Bertha) in November 1937 and *A Fist in the Eye* (Pěst na oko) in April 1938 (one month after the Anschluss), exhibited their ripened artistry. *Heavy Barbara* contained their fully evolved satire within a sustained plot that presented a thinly veiled parallel to the territorial ambitions of Germany and the Sudeten Germans in Czechoslovakia in the form of rival lands in the medieval era. *A Fist in the Eye*, by comparison, was a masterful culmination of their revue form directly relevant to the problematics and absurdities of the Sudeten crisis. With deliberate echoes of their previous work, but now in a theatre-in-theatre frame, it presented a series of sketches from myth and history showing the common people as the real protagonists behind the heroic facades of history. These two final productions, performed in unaccustomed (for them) rotating repertory during the late spring and summer of 1938, reinforced the morale of their packed audiences with their dynamic optimism and faith in the strength of ordinary but united people. Each performance became a manifestation of the public's solidarity and will to resist the threat to their short-lived independence as a nation. With the fall of the First Republic at Munich in late September 1938, however, the official license of their Liberated Theatre was denied, and less than three months later v + w emigrated to the United States. The most popular theatre in prewar Czechoslovakia was only a memory, but it helped sustain the Czechs in the dark years to come. Before their departure, in an effort to shelter members of their company, Voskovec and Werich worked out a deal with Jára Kohout to have him take over their theatre and employ their personnel. He agreed and kept performing in their theatre for the next eight years with serial productions of depoliticized musical farces or outright operettas.

Karel Čapek also responded directly to the pressures of the times. He had devoted himself to essays and novels for ten years after *Adam the Creator*. But the rising political and military crises affecting not only Czechoslovakia but all of Europe drew him back to the public tribunal of theatre. His very last play, *The Mother* (Matka), was produced in the last free (1937–1938) season at the National Theatre. During the previous season, his *The White Disease* (Bílá Nemoc) — a more powerful, imaginative work — had also been produced at the National Theatre.[18] Both plays foreshadowed the horrors imminent in Europe, *The White Disease* metaphorically, *The Mother* more literally. The former, set in a nameless contemporary country, presented a military dictator on the brink of war but threatened by a mysterious, deadly plaguelike disease ravaging the globe. A modest, pacifist doctor discovers a cure but refuses to reveal it — even to innocent sufferers — unless the dictator abandons his militaristic goals and establishes peace. When the dictator, who has himself contracted the disease, finally caves in to the doctor's demand, the doctor rushes to provide the wonder-drug, only to be accidentally killed on the way by a hysterical, war-intoxicated mob. The basic situation of a seemingly marvelous discovery with complex, humanistic implications was similar to both *RUR* and *The Makropulos Affair* but now had direct topicality. Čapek clearly favors the doctor over the dictator, but complicates the issue by the doctor's seemingly unhumanistic refusal to save others unless his will prevails. The tightly constructed play, full of highly charged confrontations between firmly drawn types, is ultimately pessimistic and despairing. No compensating factor is present, no redeeming element, unlike the denouements in *RUR* or *The Makropulos Affair*.

The Mother, by contrast, culminates with a positive act. The play takes a new tack for Čapek in focusing on a crisis in a single family in a nameless country and their response to a war in progress. The surface realism extends to every aspect of the play except one plot premise: the father, husband, and four sons of the mother — a cross section of personalities and sociopolitical points of view — are already dead and now, in a very normal-seeming way, reappear and converse with each other and the live mother, who deals with them as if they were still alive. The running debate is whether the sensitive youngest, living son should join the battle. Will the mother allow him to do so? She resists the varied arguments of the dead, who say the living son should go. But when she hears the latest radio news bulletins about the senseless killing of innocent women and children by the enemy, the mother finally thrusts a rifle into his hands and sends him off to probable death. War is seen as irrational and destructive, but the killing of innocent victims, including children, by the aggressors has to be resisted.

As a play, *The Mother* is a simplistic, schematic, routinely developed melodrama, but nevertheless generates a degree of tension in its dialogue and confrontations. Produced in early 1938, as Czechoslovakia was edging toward a decision to mobilize its forces against the German threats, the play had immediate resonance. Its run ended early in September as the repeated summit meetings of European powers on the Czech-German crisis were intensifying toward their climax in Munich at the end of the month. For Čapek, the enlightened, philosophic patriot, a confidant of Masaryk and Beneš, the Munich decision to sacrifice Czechoslovakia to appease Hitler was devastating; he died three months later of natural causes, undoubtedly exacerbated by the stresses of that international betrayal.

Honzl, of course, directed both of the final v + w productions. He also directed Bohuslav Martinů's surrealistic opera, *Juliette*, at the National Theatre in March 1938, a work with no apparent connection to the tense realities beyond the theatre's walls. Like a bill of one-acts by Nezval, Louis Aragon, and André Breton which he had directed in a small studio setting in 1935, the Martinů work seemed to reveal Honzl's need to balance his sociopolitical concerns with more purely aesthetic activity.

Two of Frejka's most striking productions at the National Theatre during the years of growing crisis had been Lope de Vega's *Fuente Ovejuna* in 1935 and Shakespeare's *Julius Caesar* in 1936, both of which clearly responded to the increasing dangers of fascism and showed Frejka's growing mastery of large-scale staging in collaboration with František Tröster. Tröster's scenography for *Caesar* was especially powerful. Its grotesquely angled platforms and statues grossly disproportionate in scale to the characters conveyed some of the angst of the world outside the theatre as well as the world on the stage. Frejka continued directing a series of major productions at the National Theatre during the final free year of 1938, the most notable being *Romeo and Juliet* in June 1938 and Jaroslav Hilbert's *Falkenštejn* (celebrating a late thirteenth century Czech patriot) in October 1938.

Burian's D theatre had continued a mix of productions reflecting his multiple talents: productions of poetry and music alternating with semidocumentaries attacking the bourgeois capitalist system and its acquisitive morality. His innate gift for effective staging that exploited the values of complex lighting was reinforced by the design and technical skills of Miroslav Kouřil (1911–1984), who was Burian's associate from 1934 to 1941 and again in 1945. Their projects extended beyond staging to include plans in 1938 for a state of the art Theatre of Work (Divadlo

A model shows Tröster's starkly expressive scenography for Frejka's Julius Caesar *at the National Theatre, 1936.*

práce) in which Burian's productions would be supplemented by other cultural and social activities. The project was never realized, but it indicates Burian's goal of a complex, multicultural, socially relevant institution, not merely a place for producing plays.

Producing in the Mozarteum, a small, rudimentary facility, Burian developed his theatre of synthesis: a conscious fusion of media, a contemporary, politicized version of Richard Wagner's *Gesamtkunstwerk* in miniature, in which, it was generally conceded, Burian demanded skill and discipline from his actors rather than individual creativity. A special embodiment of Burian's theatre of synthesis was the innovative *Theatergraph*, a complex mixture of mood-evoking projections and other lighting effects integrated with the play of live actors in productions such as Wedekind's *Spring's Awakening* (1936) and Alexander Pushkin's *Eugene Onegin* (1937), the first of which especially succeeded in being strong social criticism as well as lyrically expressive stagecraft drawing on sophisticated use of the technology of his day. It was work that inspired many young theatre aspirants, who flocked to his provocative theatre.

Although these and other works were leftist in their orientation, they did not seem to confront the Fascist menace as directly as did the work of many other artists at the time. One exception to this was Burian's adaptation of Pierre Augustin de Beaumarchais' *Barber of Seville* in 1936, which Burian turned into an eloquent statement against fascism in the Spanish Civil War. One partial explanation for Burian's only intermittent engagement in the leftist anti-Fascist campaign, beyond his innately complex temperament, may be that he was undergoing an internal crisis related to the conflicting claims of his Communist ideology and his consistently intense feelings as an independent artist. Having been severely shaken by news of the persecution of his idol Meyerhold in the Soviet Union in 1935 and 1936, he went so far as to challenge openly the Communist line that championed Socialist Realism against so-called formalism. In 1937 and 1938 two of his productions in particular, *Hamlet III* (his adaptation of Shakespeare and Jules Laforgue) and Goethe's *Werther*, may be seen as metaphoric personal statements defending his stature as a free artist rather than as reflections of the immediate threats to the nation's existence.

The Munich extortion meant the loss of about one-third of the land and population of Czechoslovakia, mainly in Bohemia. The loss of the Sudetenland, a heavily industrialized area with many mineral resources as well as the Czechs' Maginot Line of defenses, effectively castrated the Czechs. Aggravating the trauma in the following weeks were increased Slovak demands for autonomy, in part incited by a German-engineered plan to isolate the Czechs completely. Denuded and abandoned, they lost their independence entirely less than six months later when unopposed German troops streamed across the borders and established a "protectorate" of Bohemia and Moravia. March 15 was a dark, chill day; rain mixed with snow as German troops occupied Prague and its Hradčany Castle, seat of Bohemian kings centuries earlier. Hitler himself arrived at the castle the following day. Concurrently, Hitler's negotiations with Fascist and chauvinist elements in Slovakia succeeded in creating a Slovak state, in effect a German satellite. Less than a year after Munich, Hitler invaded Poland on September 1, 1939, and thereby ignited World War II.

To recapitulate, the Czech theatre of the interwar period, led by cosmopolitan artists, exhibited world-class standards and was in the vanguard of significant staging. A full spectrum of innovative production modes could be seen on its stages in perhaps greater profusion than elsewhere in Europe, especially in the 1930s as increasing conformity and even censorship restricted full creativity in other theatre centers. Equally important, especially in the 1930s, the Czech theatre was able to respond vitally to forces affecting the life of the young state and the fate of its people. In doing so, it recaptured some of the nineteenth-century Czech theatre's sense of mission and focus in the Revival Movement. At its best this theatre combined high artistry with genuine relevance, whether on the stage of the National Theatre, at the commercially successful Liberated Theatre, or in the cramped quarters of Burian's Mozarteum. Not the least of its achievements, finally, was its legacy of general inspiration for future generations, who would be experiencing crises and challenges of their own. In the meanwhile, however, in the spring of 1939 all Czechs were experiencing the anxieties of life in a homeland occupied and ruled by alien forces, with no light gleaming in the distance.[19]

3

Theatre during the Occupation and War Years

The period from the full occupation of Czechoslovakia by German forces on March 15, 1939, until the liberation of Czechoslovakia by the Soviet and American forces on May 9, 1945, is often ignored or given scant attention in commentaries on Czech theatre. Yet a number of events and activities relating to the main flow of theatre during those years are worth noting.

All plays by Jewish authors and others unacceptable to the Nazi regime, such as political emigrants and most authors from countries at war with Germany, were banned. (Shakespeare and Molière were rare exceptions, occasionally permitted.) Conversely, pressure was applied on all theatres to stage works by acceptable German authors, both classic and contemporary (but *not* people like Brecht). All Jewish theatre artists, German or Czech, were forbidden to work in theatre. Few or none had publicly identified themselves as Jewish, assimilated as they were in Czech or German theatre activity, but such subordination of their Jewishness was irrelevant in the new Nazi order. Needless to say, a great many Jewish artists, writers, and ordinary citizens fled the country if they could, even before March 15.

The Germans took over the second stage of the National Theatre in Prague, the Estates Theatre, in July 1939, an action that could not have surprised the Czechs too much because the theatre had been under German control since it was built in 1783 until it was commandeered by the Czechs after World War I, in 1920. An alternate venue for this branch of the National Theatre was found in a *variété* theatre in the Karlín section of Prague, less than a mile from the Estates Theatre. The new theatre was renamed the Provisional Theatre, a deliberate echo of the Czech theatre that preceded the National Theatre. The final Czech production in the Estates Theatre was Jirásek's folk classic *The Lantern* on July 1, and the first production in the new Provisional Theatre was Smetana's *Bartered Bride* in September.

The basic routine of theatre performances continued with minimal change, except that all theatre activity was forbidden for a month or two in the fall of 1941 when Hitler's deputy, Reinhard Heydrich, took over as "Protector" of the Czech lands. A second extended suspension of all theatre occurred between September 1944 and May 1945 because of Germany's desperate need to conscript labor and conserve resources. Otherwise, few theatres were closed or restricted in the number of performances they could give. In fact, attendance was at an all-time high during the whole period. As more than one observer noted, each performance in each theatre, especially the National Theatre, became an implicit *sub rosa* tribunal on the German occupation. That Czechs were able to assemble legally in theatres was in itself an attraction, particularly in theatres that had special Czech significance, such as the National Theatre. Moreover, audiences could almost always perceive morale-reinforcing verbal or visual signals in the productions' incidents, themes, or dialogue.

Productions involving any form of tyranny or oppression were always relevant, but with the unspoken understanding that nothing blatant would be permitted, including overt reactions from audiences. Prime examples included even German works: Schiller's *Maid of Orleans*, Goethe's *Torquato Tasso*, or Ludwig van Beethoven's *Fidelio* (which was banned after its 1944 premiere). But Shakespeare's *Macbeth, Richard III*, or even *Hamlet*, Molière's *Tartuffe*, and Plautus' *Pseudolos* also provided a variety of "messages" confirming the injustice and sense of evil felt by Czechs or offering ways of coping with the daily realities of life outside the theatre (for example, ingenious cunning, as in the Plautus play). At the other extreme were productions like Burian's *Manon Lescaut* by the contemporary Czech poet Vítězslav Nezval, which drew Czechs to the theatre for the sheer beauty of Nezval's use of their language. Other plays by Czech authors offered implicitly patriotic elements or other forms of comfort for the audiences. Director Jan Bor's original play *Zuzana Vojířová* focused on a strong Czech protagonist of the Renaissance era and his love of the Czech lands. It opened at the National Theatre in February 1942 and became the single most performed play of the entire wartime era, reaching over one hundred reprises.

Other theatrical activity directly involving the major theatre figures of the prewar era can be recapitulated briefly. During their exile in the USA, Voskovec and Werich occasionally performed before Czech audiences and made many broadcasts beamed back to Europe. Their brightest moment came in a Broadway appearance as Shakespeare's clowns Trinculo and Stephano, respectively, in Margaret Webster's well-received production of *The Tempest* in the spring of

1945, which I saw as a college freshman. They were very effective, even with their Czech-accented English.

In Prague Burian, Frejka, and Honzl all presented a variety of morale-strengthening productions for as long as possible. For reasons unrelated to the German takeover of the Czech lands in March 1939, Burian's D39 theatre was finally able to move out of its inadequate, deteriorating quarters at the end of the 1938–1939 season and begin producing as D40 in the fall of 1939 in the larger space of a subterranean concert hall a mile from its former home in the Mozarteum. Until March 1941, when Burian was arrested, his theatre was closed, and he was sent to a concentration camp, he created a repertoire of new and revived works, straight plays as well as programs of poetry, music, and dance. Virtually all his twenty-five productions in the new quarters were Czech in source, such as the *Manon Lescaut* mentioned above (1940). Others included Burian's own opera version of the Czech classic *Maryša* (1940), Zeyer's *An Old Story* (Stará historie, 1940), and Nezval's *Loretka* (1941), a nostalgic Prague-centered period piece with music and dance. Unlike Honzl and Frejka, however, Burian spent most of the war in concentration camps.

Frejka stayed at the National Theatre throughout the war, producing works with covert and sometimes not so covert significance for Czech audiences, such as the Plautus comedy (1942) mentioned above, Klicpera's *Evil Stag* (Zlý jelen, 1942), and Tyl's classic *Bagpiper from Strakonice* (1943). During these years Frejka also published several thoughtful theatre studies.[1] Honzl remained in Czechoslovakia throughout the war years, keeping a low profile and directing a few staged readings of Czech centered literary works with his Theatre for 99 (Divadlo pro 99) in a tiny hall in 1940 and 1941 before going underground for the duration of the war because of his explicit Communist affiliation.

Of equal significance, all three directors began to pass their respective skills and insights on to the next generation. Burian had begun an acting school as an adjunct to his theatre as early as 1939; Honzl did something similar though more informally with his actors in his *sub rosa* Theatre for 99; and Frejka, along with his leading actor, Ladislav Pešek (1906–1986), became a faculty member of the Theatre Conservatory in 1941, where he especially focused on techniques of *commedia dell'arte* and circus clownery.

The fruits of these efforts began to appear even during the wartime occupation with the creation in June 1941 of a young ensemble called the Windmill (Větrník) after the close of Burian's D41. Former students of Burian's acting school, led by Josef Šmída (1919–1969), formed the core of the group, but they were joined by several of Frejka's students from the Theatre Conservatory. The Windmill pleased wartime audiences by producing several original works notable for synthesizing

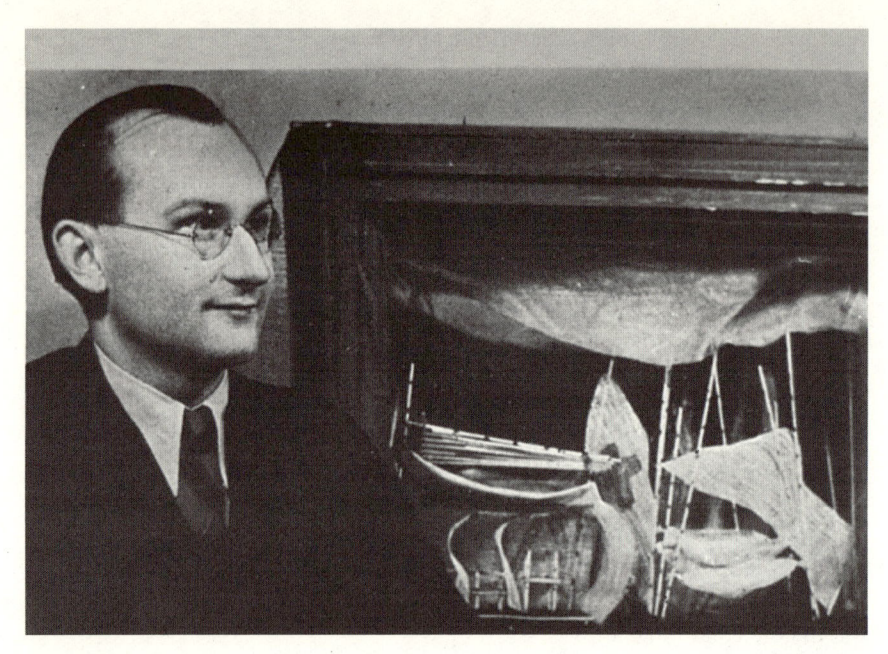

Jiří Frejka in the 1940s.

and carrying on the prewar avant-garde work of its mentors. In doing so the theatre gained a strong following that sustained its existence beyond the liberation in 1945. Somewhat similar though more limited activity was evident in the remnants of Honzl's Theatre for 99 ensemble, who put on a few undergound performances, culminating in one performance of *Ubu Roi* in 1944.

In the meantime, representative examples of theatres stressing sheer entertainment included the remarkably popular Theatre of Vlasta Burian, which continued to operate serially throughout these years, as did the Theatre of Jára Kohout. Although both theatres chiefly appealed through broad farce with musical elements, Burian's was unquestionably of higher quality, centering on his remarkable talents as a character farceur with a genius for mimicry, vocal and physical agility, and sheer madcap improvisatory riffs, for which all scripts had to allow room. His final production ran for the entire 1943–1944 season, totaling 350 performances.

A different sort of theatre actually began in the fall of 1939, the Theatre of Anna Sedláčková (1887–1969). She had been an extremely popular, sophisticated romantic comedienne at the National and other theatres since the early years of the century. Now she organized a small company, which included her daughter, and operated in repertory fashion in the theatre space vacated by E. F. Burian at the end of the 1938–1939 season, the Mozarteum. For the first few seasons, in an effort to establish a serious reputation, she appeared in a number of challenging roles in plays by Ibsen, Čapek, and even Shakespeare, but the talents of the rest of her company were not equal to hers. For the final season or two before all theatres closed in the fall of 1944, her repertoire leaned strongly toward standard boulevard comedies and detective thrillers.

Another wartime group that would continue its activity after the liberation was the ensemble of young amateurs from Pelhřimov, a town outside Prague. Known at first as the Dramatic Studio for Youth, they mounted several revues from assemblages of material from various sources, much in the vein of E. F. Burian. Their staging, too, echoed in minimalist fashion his use of scrims and projections. After September 1944, when all theatre activity was forbidden, they covertly prepared and rehearsed a satiric three-part script, *The Broken Trilogy* (Rozbitá trilogie), focusing on aspects of Czech life of first earlier eras, then the occupation era, and finally the immediate present. These montages of various materials were clearly influenced not only by the work of Burian but also by v + w. The group staged an illegal, very secret performance for a selected local audience in February 1945 and then a completely public performance on May 18, shortly after the liberation, perhaps the very first postwar production of a new work on Czech soil.[2]

The wartime era also witnessed the early theatrical work of three men who would become the leading figures in the great creative surge of Czech theatre in the postwar decades. Alfred Radok (1914–1976), after work as assistant director at Burian's D41, performed similar work and also directed in Pilsen and at the Vinohrady Theatre in Prague, but in 1944 he was sent to a labor camp until the liberation because of his part-Jewish background. Josef Svoboda (b. 1920) worked with an amateur group in his home in Čáslav before continuing his studies in Prague, where he did his first semiprofessional stage design work with a young group, the New Ensemble, in 1943–1944. Otomar Krejča (b. 1921) began his career during the war as an actor in the provincial theatres of Jíhlava and Kladno.

Darker realities of the wartime era were the deaths of numerous important theatre people. Some, like National Theatre director Jan Bor, died of natural causes. Others (Jewish or not) died in concentration camps, like directors Viktor Šulc (formerly of the National Theatre), Oldřich Stibor (Olomouc), and Josef Skřivan (Brno), designers František Zelenka and Josef Čapek, and cabaret star Karel Hašler (1879–1941). Some, like playwright Vladislav Vančura, were executed with hundreds of other citizens following the assassination in May 1942 in Prague of Reinhard Heydrich, who had earned his reputation as "the Hangman." The Nazis also retaliated for the death of Heydrich by arbitrarily razing the village of Lidice and killing all its male adults and, in a more bureaucratic way, by summoning representatives of all Czech theatres to the National Theatre that June to pledge fidelity to the Third Reich.

All the more striking in the face of such events and the greater atrocities that came to be known as the Holocaust, and yet symptomatic of theatre's inherent life force, was the organizing of theatre performances in concentration camps by their Czech inmates. Of course, such activity was not restricted to the Czechs. Theatre, music, art, and related cultural entertainment were no doubt produced by many nationalities in virtually every camp. E. F. Burian, for example, during his imprisonment in Dachau, participated in several cabarets for the Czech inmates, but also in multilingual entertainments; later, in the camp at Neuengamm (near Hamburg), he composed a Voiceband cantata for Christmas 1943: "Our Daily Bread" (Unsere tägliche Brot) with and for his fellow German inmates. Similarly, Josef Čapek worked alongside Germans and other nationals on selections from *Hamlet*, Goethe's *Faust*, and Hauptmann's *The Beaver Coat* in Sachsenhausen; and Nina Jirsíková (1910–1978), former choreographer for both v + w and E. F. Burian, organized dance and poetry performances in Ravensbruck. Indeed, even in Auschwitz, Czechs participated in Polish performances; and, in Auschwitz-Birkenau, some Czech families carried on cultural activities they knew from the Czech internment camp at Terezín (the Czech name for the German Theresienstadt), where they had been temporarily placed.

Terezín is perhaps the most remarkable of the camps in terms of the quantity and quality of Czech theatre and other arts produced there. Formerly a military garrison town in northern Bohemia, Terezín was chosen as the place to hold all Jews from Bohemia and Moravia, but by the end of the war it had also received Jews from virtually all of occupied Europe; the total number of prisoners who experienced Terezín was some 140,000, with as many as 58,000 being present at a given time. The camp received its first transports of Czech Jews in November 1941 (shortly after Heydrich took command in Prague), although individual prisoners, not always necessarily Jews, had temporarily been held in its small fortress earlier. Burian himself was briefly a prisoner in the small fortress in March and April 1941, shortly after his arrest. On the eve of May 1 that year he recited Karel Hynek Mácha's great romantic poem *Máj* from memory to a handful of his fellow prisoners.

From the end of 1941 to April 1945, with one major interruption, Terezín became a hotbed of cultural activity despite its terribly overcrowded, diseased, stress-filled conditions. For the first few months the cultural programs were spontaneously improvised recitals and cabaret-type entertainments in attics or other restricted spaces in the special barracks that housed the incoming Jews. Terezín's inmates were largely self-administered by a council of elders, who in the spring of 1942 generated a subsidiary recreation committee (Freizeitgestaltung) to super-

František Zelenka's sketch of the attic of a barracks in Terezín, one of the performance spaces used by the concentration camp inmates.

vise a growing number of inmate-initiated cultural events: musical recitals, poetry readings, cabaret evenings, lectures, marionette plays for children, and eventually plays for adults, which were presented in either German or Czech, depending on the performers involved. In any case most of the cultural programs in Terezín were done by and for Czech Jews in Czech and involved Czech texts or scores.

The cultural programs expanded following the formation of the Freizeit committee, which became officially legalized by the Nazi camp command in the fall of 1942. Another event that expanded these activities was the evacuation of all Aryan citizens from the town of Terezín in June 1942, which meant that the entire town became a concentration camp in anticipation of the increased entry of Czech Jews as well as a smaller number of Jews and others from other countries. More space for the cultural programs became available, as well as more encouragement with less tight controls by the Nazi wardens.

One reason for this uncharacteristic beneficent policy on the part of the Nazi German authorities would apply to all the concentration camps: cultural entertainments and other recreational activity, obviously monitored as to content and extent, helped distract people and mollify tensions that might lead to disturbances that would complicate the efficient, controlled maintenance of the camp and its flow of human traffic. In Terezín a grimly ironic second factor was present. In the context of their "final solution of the Jewish question," Nazi leaders had decided that Terezín would become a model camp, a showcase for international inspection teams, such as those of the Red Cross. Terezín was to send the message that the concentration camps were more like retirement communities, where culture flourished. Terezín became a Potemkin Village, a huge stage set, within which theatre and other cultural activities could be displayed, especially when foreign visitations were to occur. In advance of such known visits, beautification (Stadtverschönerung) projects occurred to display the camp at its best, including the repair and rehabilitation of living quarters, planting of flowerbeds, and artistic performances of various types. Once the visits were over, camp life quickly returned to bare survival levels, but, even then, reduced cultural activities initiated by the inmates went on. The prisoners realized they were being used, but took advantage of the greater opportunities for creativity. What the inmates, like the rest of the world, did not know until late in the process was that facilities and procedures for their extermination in other camps were already being put in place.

It was in this context that a remarkable number and variety of stage performances took place, especially between the summer of 1942 and the fall of 1944, when cultural programs were sharply cut back because of greatly increased numbers of transports conveying the still unknowing inmates to the gas chambers of Auschwitz and other camps. Needless to say, there was an ongoing turnover of inmates throughout the camp's existence, which severely affected the already difficult production conditions. Even with the Nazis' pseudo-liberal support of the cultural activities, the inmates had to make do with improvised spaces, equipment, and materials and had to prepare their performances in the very limited available time after they had fulfilled their daily workloads.

There are no definitive records of all the cultural activity, but certain specific production data have become available, even though information concerning dates and personnel is often conflicting or ambiguous. Nevertheless, the following selection of names, titles, and dates relating to productions in Czech provides a representative impression. Ironically, plays or abridgments in 1942 included some that would not have been permitted on Czech stages outside the camps: Cocteau's *The Human Voice* and several sets of one-acts by Chekhov or the Czech poet Jiří Wolker; in 1943, Langer's *Camel through the Needle's Eye*, the Čapeks' *Fateful Play of Love*, a Czech play by Václav Štech, *The Third Ringing* (Třetí zvonění), Molière's *Georges Dandin*, Olga Scheinpflugová's *The Killed* (Zabitý), and Peter Kien's *Puppets*; in 1944, Rostand's *The Romantics*, an evening of Gogol works, Gogol's *Marriage*, and Tyl's *Bagpiper from Strakonice*.

Operas or plays with music included a concert version of *The Bartered Bride* (1942); Jan Karafiat's *The Bugs* (Broučci, in 1943), for children, which was performed thirty times; *The Magic Flute* and Smetana's *The Kiss* (Hubička), both in 1943; and Vilém Blodek's *In the Well* (V studni) and Norbert Fryd's *Esther*, an adaptation of folk materials with themes echoing the oppression of the Jews, which had been prepared for Burian's D theatre before its closing, both in 1944. The single most successful theatre work in Terezín was probably *Brundibár*, a children's opera previously written by Adolf Hoffmeister and Hans Kras, to be performed by children. It was produced in Terezín in 1943 and repeated for a Red Cross visitation in July 1944. It achieved fifty performances, and in August and September 1944 was filmed for propaganda purposes, as part of a German propaganda film entitled *The Führer Gives the Jews a Town as a Gift* (Der Führer schenkt den Juden eine Stadt).

Revues and cabarets with music, many deliberately in the vein of V + W productions, were ongoing presentations from the first six months of the camp, as were readings of poetry, musical recitals and concerts, and lectures. The very last production efforts were again initiated by the Nazi command in anticipation of another Red Cross visitation: a revival of the children's musical play *The Bugs* and scenes from Jacques Offenbach's *Tales of Hoffmann* were being rehearsed in March and April 1945, a scant month or two before the end of the war. Then the chaos of retreating German armies and transports of Jews now from the east and other parts of Europe wiped out all activities other than those for survival.

Hundreds of people were involved in these varied programs, only a few of whom had had professional experience, but perhaps a half-dozen Czech Jews stand out as the leading organizers, directors, and performers at Terezín. František Zelenka, previously mentioned as the designer of many productions for the National Theatre and for V + W, continued to function in a design-technical capacity for most of the major presentations at Terezín until his transport to Auschwitz. Gustav Schorsch (1918–1945), a student of Karel Dostal of the National Theatre, was responsible for a number of plays produced, in particular Gogol's *Wedding*. Vlasta Schonová (b. 1919) was probably the single most active producer, director, and performer of work staged at Terezín, from plays to recitals of poetry. Rafael Schachter (1905–1944?), a pianist, was responsible for most of the operas, including those mentioned plus some in German; Karel Reiner (1910–1979), a composer for Burian's D theatre in the mid-1930s, provided the music for *Esther* and several other plays. The person most associated with original cabarets and revues was Karel Švenk (1907–1945?), although a number of others also presented them.

Theatre at Terezín was a unique phenomenon running parallel to the theatre on Prague stages and elsewhere before Czech audiences. In its complexity of elements, its creativity in the midst of immediate and longer-range difficulties that blended into horrors, it was both grotesque and inspiring. Bořivoj Srba, one of the chroniclers of theatre in the camps (not only Terezín), made an observation that seems especially apt for the activities at Terezín: "The elementary power of theatre to elevate a person to a truly human level demonstrated itself in no other surroundings in the years 1939–1945 as convincingly as it indeed did here — behind bars and barbed wire."[3]

4

The Postwar Years and the 1950s

By the middle of the 1960s theatre in Czechoslovakia had drawn the attention of the rest of Europe and was beginning to be mentioned in American theatre publications. Prewar Czech theatre of the 1920s and 1930s had also achieved international recognition and even acclaim for its imagination, social relevance, and expressive theatricality. But between the prewar achievements and those of the 1960s lay the shadow not only of the war, but of the 1950s, or, to be more precise, of the decade from 1948 to 1958. Writing in retrospect, Ota Ornest, head of Prague Municipal Theatres from 1950 to 1973, pinpointed the special torments of the period:

> The 1950s (and actually even the end of the 1940s) were years of fright and terror, and large-scale murder. Those years meant Stalinism at its peak, which differed very little from Nazism and in fact had many more flunkies (not merely collaborators but ideological flunkies) than Nazism. And then [there were] the people who kept silent and thereby became accomplices. I belonged to their number, as did most of those, almost without exception, who worked in the arts — Party members and non-Party members alike. Moreover, in addition to keeping silent, every now and then they had to comply with some "sacrifice to the gods" if they wanted to keep working, if they wanted to retain some values . . . if they simply wanted to stay alive.[1]

How did this grim era come about? What was it like? Some exposition is necessary to clarify the context in which postwar Czech theatre developed.[2]

PART I: 1945–1948

In terms of material damage from warfare, Prague as a city suffered little, with theatre being perhaps the most serious victim. Three months before the end of the war, in February 1945, one of the infrequent Allied bombing runs did incidental damage to a suburb of Prague but largely destroyed much of the National Theatre workshops, including several generations of stored scenery by some of Czech theatre's early designers. The war itself ended for the Czechs on May 8, 1945, after three days of intense fighting between Czech civilians and remnants of the German army in the streets of Prague, chiefly in the area of the Old Town Square (Staroměstské náměstí), where several historic buildings were severely damaged.

The next day, with the battle essentially over and the German forces gone or in flight, the Red Army entered Prague as its official liberator. The Soviet forces, aided by Czech units, had been fighting their way from eastern Slovakia to Moravia and then to Prague for over a month. Meantime, U.S. Army forces under General George Patton had entered western Czech territory on April 18 and proceeded to set up headquarters in the Pilsen area. Prague could have been liberated by the U.S. Army well before May 9, but tactical and political decisions made at top levels among the Allies at Yalta in 1944 meant that as of May 5 the U.S. forces were to stay west of the line from Budweis to Pilsen to Carlsbad while the Red Army "liberated" Prague. Thus the USSR gained an enormous political and psychological advantage in the next few years in the struggle to determine whether Czechoslovakia would be aligned with the West or the East, capitalist democracy or Communist totalitarianism.

A few critical demographic facts should be noted as a background for postwar theatrical activity. The war itself, the Holocaust, and the postwar expulsion of Germans from the Czech lands led to significant changes in the cultural topography in which postwar Czech theatre operated. The figures for the Jewish population are better expressed in real numbers than in percentages. Of some 120,000 prewar Jews in the Czech lands, less than 20,000 survived the war and still resided there. Indeed, subsequent Jewish emigration in 1948 and 1968 left fewer than 4,000 Jews residing in the Czech lands by 1993. The German population before the war was approximately 30 percent of the total population of the Czech lands; after the war and the mass expulsion of the Germans from the borderlands, their number had fallen to less than 2 percent of the total population. For the first time, the Czechs were on their own in their own lands. Many may have celebrated this, but the resulting cultural loss must surely have been drastic, although it may not have been immediately or dramatically apparent amid the pervasive euphoria of liberation and intensive planning and negotiating for the future. I am not aware of anyone having made a study of this sociocultural phenomenon.

Those theatre people who survived the years of occupation and war (1939–1945) were eager to build on the achievements of the past but faced a new age and a new audience marked by experiences, memories, and attitudes with roots in prewar confrontations with fascism, which culminated in the Munich capitulation of 1938. The immediate postwar period witnessed the reunification of the Czechs and Slovaks and the restoration of the pre-Munich government, but with a substantial new Communist component as a result of wartime negotiations among government leaders and others in exile. If the prewar government was moderately conservative in its social and political profile, the postwar government was from the beginning already tilted to the left, largely because the prewar regime was associated with the political disaster of Munich and the protectorate under the Nazis. With a new coalition government committed to a degree of moderate socialism, a jockeying for power developed between the more hardline conservative and leftist political forces. The momentum of the latter, led by the Communists, resulted in their taking 40 percent of the votes in the spring 1946 elections. Combined with the leftist Social Democrats (16 percent), they now held a clear majority. The path was open to the full seizure of power by the Communists less than two years later, in February 1948.

One of the basic and generally accepted socialistic measures was the nationalization of traditionally profit-making, capitalistic enterprises, including theatre. All theatres previously operated for private profit were placed with others under state or collective control, and an official advisory council was established to determine who would be put in charge of each theatre; it was headed by Miroslav Kouřil (E. F. Burian's former associate). A separate decree called for the establishment of an extended theatre network, which by 1949 consisted of forty-six state-supported theatres in the Czech lands. It was a lively, stimulating, but unsettled time as new theatre companies competed with established ones, and a new generation of actors, directors, designers, and playwrights began to work with veterans of the prewar era. Another symptom of new beginnings was the establishment of a university-level Academy of Performing Arts (AMU [Akademie múzických umění]; its theatre section was designated DAMU [Divadelni akademie múzických umění]) in Prague in 1945 and in Brno in 1947. For theatre students it meant a five-year curriculum for actors, directors, and designers. The number of students admitted each year was in direct proportion to the anticipated future needs of the network of theatres throughout the nation.

The National Theatre revived production less than a week after hostilities ended, with an informal performance of *The Bartered Bride* on May 13, followed by the official reopening on May 27 with Smetana's *Libuše*. Meantime, the Estates Theatre reverted to the Czechs as the second stage of the National Theatre. What had been the major German theatre since 1887, the Neues Deutsches Theater, which had been largely dormant during the war years except for guest musical performances by German or Italian companies, was appropriated by the Czechs and turned over to a talented and aggressive group of young people.

The initial postwar positioning of the major prewar figures is worth noting. Especially significant was a switch involving Frejka and Honzl, most likely due to the latter's advantages as a Communist vis-à-vis Frejka's political neutrality. Honzl, long frustrated in his wish to direct in the National Theatre, now became part of its leadership as one member of a troika named to head drama activity there, even as Frejka moved from the National Theatre to become artistic head of the Vinohrady Theatre, where the prewar work of Kvapil, Hilar, and even Čapek had made its mark. Their first postwar ventures were promising, as described below.

The status of E. F. Burian was complicated by his delayed return to Prague from a north German concentration camp almost a month after the resumption of normal life after the war; he very nearly lost his life during an inadvertent bombing by the British of several ships carrying prisoners in the Baltic in the war's closing days. Because no other steps were taken to place him more favorably, he had to settle for his old, essentially limited subterranean quarters of 1941, which he later called a "rat's hole" (*krysí díra*). His resentment at having to settle for a much less impressive platform than those given to Frejka and Honzl, or even to the young people who took over the former large German theatre, was evident in his reference at the time to his own theatre as a "theatre that was left over" (*divadlo který zbylo*).

That a simple renewal of prewar theatre activity would not be possible in postwar Czechoslovakia was also clearly evident in the career of Vlasta Burian, the "King of Comics." His enormously popular theatre never reopened after its 1943–1944 season. In Marxist terms, he was a wealthy capitalist entrepreneur. It was this as well as his apolitical, individualistic persona that lay behind false accusations of his collaborating with the Nazis during World War II when he continued to operate his theatre. His profit-making theatre was liquidated by Communist functionaries immediately after the war, and he himself was arrested for over three months, underwent three trials, and was not allowed to perform again until 1950. Other privately owned theatres such as Anna Sedláčková's theatre in the Mozarteum were also closed. Her theatre was taken over by a young Communist-centered ensemble, and her career was over. Jára Kohout's privately owned theatre of lightweight musical farces was taken from him by the state, but he continued to run it for a season before the return of Voskovec and Werich, whose theatre it had been and who were allowed to use it but not own it.

Compared to their professional peer Vlasta Burian, Jiří Voskovec and Jan Werich had less drastic but nevertheless disenchanting experiences following the victorious liberation. They returned separately to Prague from the USA: Werich in 1945, Voskovec in 1946. The duo that had entertained and inspired audiences in the turbulent 1930s with a string of unique productions combining the best of strong political cabaret and musical revue managed but one production as an onstage team in their revived Theatre of v + w: a modified reprise of their last prewar production, *A Fist in the Eye* (April 1947). Although they did a few other, more conventional, productions separately, or with Voskovec directing Werich, they realized that their work no longer resonated with the new sociopolitical context, and they dissolved their theatre and their partnership at the end of the 1947–1948 season, following the Communist takeover. Their last production was an adaptation of *Finian's Rainbow* (March 1948), directed by Voskovec and starring Werich. It was still running when Voskovec departed for France, and later the United States, never to return to Czechoslovakia. Werich stayed on in Prague as an unfailingly popular actor-entertainer.

Two much newer theatres entered the postwar era on a wave of enthusiasm, but also ran into difficult times. The Windmill ensemble, which successfully produced a number of works in the Burian-Frejka manner during the war years, did well during the first year of liberation but in the fall of 1946 was forced to close because of a weakening box office and the departure of a core of actors for greener fields. Another theatre's experience a year or two later made it clear that the new Communist era was not very tolerant of public, though indirect, criticism. The Theatre of Satire became the new name of the fresh, youthful theatre established during the war by amateurs in Pelhřimov. It met with great popularity in Prague for some three years after its initial performances there in the summer of 1945 with *Broken Trilogy*. This was followed by an even more successful cabaret revue, *Cirkus Plechový*, which achieved more than 300 performances. Although lacking the personal genius of Voskovec and Werich, the Theatre of Satire was fully in the vein of the prewar v + w revues: clever, cheeky, imaginatively staged critiques of the contemporary scene. Several of its later successes were guest directed by Alfred Radok and designed by Josef Svoboda, who were principally employed at another theatre. Nevertheless, the Theatre of Satire became one of the early victims of the new ideological tone after the February 1948 Communist putsch by running afoul of guidelines insisting on the presence of "positive" elements even in satire, as a reflection of the official optimism decreed by the Communist Party central committee. Because it no longer received the bureaucratic support all theatres had to have, the theatre was obliged to terminate its activities by the end of the 1948–1949 season.

Another postwar variation of a new theatre bringing an infusion of fresh talent before encountering non-negotiable decisions by the new Communist cultural hierarchy was the Theatre of the Fifth of May (Divadlo 5. května), named after the date of the Prague uprising against the German occupants. A more ambitious, larger-scale enterprise, in normal circumstances it might have become a major new arts showcase in Prague. During its relatively short existence, it was already drawing favorable international attention and outshining the postwar work of the National Theatre, and that in itself created problems for the post-February Communist regime. Its core personnel, several of whom were inspired by the prewar avant-garde, especially by E. F. Burian, were loosely organized as early as 1944, so the theatre was ready to function right after liberation. The talented and enthusiastic company consisting of an opera ensemble and a drama ensemble took over the large, well-equipped former Neues Deutsches Theater in Prague in the first days after the liberation. Alfred Radok, Josef Svoboda, and the opera director Václav Kašlík (1917–1989) were among its major artists. Kašlík, like Radok, had worked with Burian in his last prewar season.

The original aim of the drama ensemble was to be a frankly political theatre supporting the socialist cause, with an emphasis on Slavic plays, but these aims were modified by the inclusion of Western plays in the second season to bolster attendance. The opera company was more successful in realizing its intention of employing nontraditional, avant-garde theatrical methods to stage an international repertoire. Like the Theatre of Satire, it had only a three-year life. By the spring of 1948 the new, post-February regime had decided that the drama ensemble had served its purpose as a politically relevant force and that the opera company would serve better if amalgamated with the National Theatre's opera wing, thus providing the National Theatre with a third major stage, which was renamed the Smetana Theatre. The company felt betrayed by conservative forces within the new ruling establishment who preferred to have one major company, the traditional National Theatre, rather than the National Theatre *and* an unorthodox, successful alternative.

Not all new or revived theatres had such short lives. A small group from Ostrava under the leadership of Jan Škoda (1896–1981) had moved to Prague during the war years and performed a few times in a recently formed theatre on the left bank, the Intimate Theatre. Almost immediately after the war this theatre was reconstituted as the Realistic Theatre and moved into what had been the Švanda Theatre. Škoda himself had also directed previously in Slovakia and in Brno in the 1930s. He and the company were devoted to a realistic treatment of socially centered plays. This and the group's Communist orientation assured them of favored treatment in the new scheme of things.

PART II: THE DARK ERA OF MODERN CZECH THEATRE, 1948–1958

The political watershed of February 1948 (known to this day simply as *únor* [February]) that preceded the last days of the Theatre of Satire and the Theatre of the Fifth of May occurred less than three years after the end of the war. Czechoslovakia experienced a governmental crisis in which the essentially democratic but weak regime under ailing President Eduard Beneš was thoroughly outmaneuvered and outfaced by a highly organized, militant Communist Party with crucial behind-the-scenes support from Moscow. The bloodless putsch was welcomed by many in the arts who had leftist sympathies dating back to the 1930s or at least were willing to let the Communists demonstrate the alleged advantages of their system. But the "years of fright and terror" soon began, most shockingly in 1950–1952, with massive show trials and executions designed to eliminate opposition to the new regime and to intimidate the general public. How Czech theatre might have evolved had it been spared the overwhelming changes in all aspects of life following the Communist seizure of power in February 1948 will never be known.

Within a year after the February putsch, all cultural activity began to be regimented and codified as an instrument of the Communist Party program to create a new society presumably dedicated to the working-class masses. A hierarchy was established, with each theatre being answerable to the Ministry of Education and Information. This in turn took orders from the Central Committee of the Communist Party, which was programmed to echo the current line of the Communist Party in the USSR. The result was that the Party had total power over the arts, power often in the hands of shadowy figures behind the facade of a self-styled "people's democracy."

Symptomatic of the new order was the redesignation of the Estates Theatre; in the fall of 1948 it became the Tyl Theatre in honor of that nineteenth-century Czech theatre pioneer. More immediate and painful were elaborate personnel screenings of all cultural workers to establish the degree of their political correctness and reliability. In all schools, including the Theatre Academy (DAMU), Marxism-Leninism became a required course each year under the title of Political Education. Other symptoms included the renewed promulgation of the Socialist Realist aesthetic articulated by a Soviet politburo chief, A. A. Zhdanov, in the 1930s: art was to be based on nineteenth-century realism in form and Marxism-

Leninism in content. In theatre, this led to a distorted oversimplification and uncritical application of what was thought to be Stanislavsky's system; what had been dismissed by the prewar avant-garde — literal reproduction of external reality — was now prescribed as theatre's salvation.[3] The former Švanda Theatre under Jan Škoda and Karel Palouš (1913–1999), now designated the Realistic Theatre of Zdeněk Nejedlý (the cultural czar), was identified with a supra-Stanislavsky approach and soon became the butt of jokes, despite the total sincerity and commitment of its staff to the goal of playing truthfully. The problem lay in the unqualified and simplistic acceptance of *some* of Stanislavsky's practices. Such excesses affected most theatres for a season or more in the early 1950s.

Also symptomatic were the arbitrary establishment and liquidation of theatres and ensembles and the appointment, removal, or never explained work suspensions of actors and directors. Innumerable meetings of theatre administrators and directors became routine, mostly to approve previously decided plans. One notable meeting occurred in Bratislava in January 1949, establishing what came to be wryly known as the "Bratislava Ladder," essentially a formula for choosing repertoires for each theatre each season: the staples were to be, in order of priority, politically correct Czech, Russo-Soviet, and classic works, with a perhaps 10 percent allowance for works from the West, if they were acceptable, which is to say anticapitalist. Offshoots of such programmatically imposed formulas were periodic waves of new plays celebrating Communist-inspired resistance to fascism, Communist work ethics in factories, farms, and villages, and Communist resistance to capitalist exploitation and aggression.

Why the strong move toward socialism and communism on the part of theatre people, especially by people like Frejka, who had not committed to those causes earlier? Several explanations may apply, some of which I have already touched on. Prewar experience made a persuasive case for the position that the only consistent opposition to fascism was communism. By the same token, the Munich capitulation became identified with betrayal by the West and by the prewar, bourgeois First Republic of President Beneš. Moreover, the Soviet army's liberation of most of the country, including Prague, in the closing phase of the war intensified already existing pan-Slavic attraction to things Russian. The Communist Party, much more organized and focused than any other political group, consistently propagated the idea that its program provided a well-planned, logical solution to social problems in the wake of six years of wartime suffering and deprivation. In the eyes of many people communism became a universal formula for social justice and well-being, a higher ideal to fight for.

A special sense of mission also came into play. The challenge of creating a new citizenry for a new society, a new order, undoubtedly appealed to many intellectuals and artists, especially the seductive idea that theatre had the power to play a major educational and inspirational role in the process, thus promising a special importance to every theatre worker. In this sense the deeply rooted nineteenth-century concept of the moral and educational role of theatre experienced an ironic, perhaps even perverse, rebirth. Originally tied to the ideals of national identity and autonomy for the Czechs, the concept was now co-opted by an ideology designed to frustrate both ideals in the name of universal social engineering designed and controlled by Moscow. More immediately, the Communist promise that theatres would no longer be run by profit-minded entrepreneurs but by theatre people themselves fulfilled the ideal of "theatre belonging to those who create it," as E. F. Burian had put it back in the 1930s. Finally, these powerful appeals were enhanced by the Soviet assurance that the Czechs would be able to formulate their own version of communism, and not simply be stamped in the Soviet mold. Illusory as most of these assurances and ideals proved to be, they help explain the initial decisive move to the left in Czech theatre.

It is tempting to regard the years following 1948 monolithically, as an unrelieved dark era during which normal critical judgment and independence of expression were frighteningly purged or paralyzed, an era of great waste and damage with little of value to warrant closer study, especially when contrasted with the startlingly creative era of Czech theatre in the 1930s or associated with the Prague Spring in the 1960s. But in 1967, when Kenneth Tynan called Prague the theatre center of Europe,[4] he was not referring to the work of theatres and individuals suddenly appearing in the 1960s but of those that developed in that previous dark era itself, 1948 to the late 1950s, cited so pointedly by Ota Ornest, above. According to others, it was an era marked by "sheer, inexcusable stupidity that lasted relatively long."[5] How can one reconcile the demoralizing and destructive abuses in the world of Czech theatre during those years with the concurrent development of talents that led to the achievements of the Czech theatre in the 1960s? As I shall try to explain, part of any answer would be that although distressful and frustrating in most respects, it was *not* a monolithic, universally dark and sterile era.

What was it like in individual and existential terms to be in Czech theatre during this dark era, and how did Czech theatre emerge from it? A consideration of the role of some of its leading players may help explain the twists and turns, the paradoxes and ironies, and the ambiguities of the postwar decades leading to the celebrated 1960s.

At the heart of the drama of the postwar era were the three leading prewar avant-garde directors, Jindřich Honzl, Jiří Frejka, and Emil František Burian, whose careers entered their final phases, and two directors whose careers were just starting to mature, Alfred Radok and Otomar Krejča.

The three veterans set about reviving their careers in a familiar but profoundly changed environment. In the three years between liberation and the Communist putsch, they all had a number of successes that gave promise of developing a productive synthesis of their prewar avant-garde work with a greater sense of social and political responsibility in support of the reconstituted state. Even in the years following the February 1948 takeover by the Communists, each would have the satisfaction of producing at least some work of quality, but only Frejka did so consistently, thereby managing to sustain and even build on the quality of the work he had previously achieved. Each one also produced inferior work whose main virtue was a simplistic propagating of the current Communist line. (Frejka was least guilty of this.) Tracing their postwar careers is a fascinating and disturbing experience. The specific pressures and conflicts they faced, especially after the full takeover by the Communists in 1948, produced crises in their careers and even their lives as they tried to maintain their artistic integrity while serving the cause of the new society, to which each one was committed. Even Frejka, although not yet a Communist Party member, clearly aligned himself with the move toward a socialist order.

Of the three artists, Honzl was the most intellectually committed and orthodox in his Marxist-Leninist ideology. In the interwar era, despite his commitment to theatre in support of the class struggle and the masses, he had devoted himself to surrealist and other markedly apolitical, elitist stage pieces. In his postwar career, such deviations — which would have been labeled degenerate formalism — disappeared. In fact, he renounced most of his earlier artistic experimentation, calling the artistic reality of illusions "an escape from the world" and otherwise condemning apolitical art as playing into the hands of the enemy.[6] His interest in experimental work after 1945 seemed satisfied by creating within the National Theatre an ancillary Studio in which he could work with young actors on special smaller, noncontroversial projects under less pressure than in his regular work in the main theatre.

All in all, Honzl probably experienced fewer radical stresses in the postwar era than did Burian or Frejka. Essentially more detached and analytical than they were, he accepted the increasingly restrictive, indeed oppressive, measures that followed February 1948. But there were problems even earlier. The gratification he doubtless experienced in being one of the three heads of the National Theatre drama company lasted less than one season,[7] for as a result of elections in the spring of 1946 the new minister of culture, a strong anti-Communist, removed him from that position, although he continued to serve as a director. But two years later, immediately after the Communist takeover, Honzl was put in sole charge of the drama company. The satisfaction of holding this powerful position was offset by his having to terminate his Studio because he could no longer handle the demands of both tasks. Moreover, working with the entrenched, experienced actors in the National Theatre had not been easy from the beginning. They were irritated by Honzl's cold, sometimes caustic manner; moreover, as established, socially privileged artists, they were uncomfortable with his proletarian, intellectual orientation.

Nevertheless, Honzl succeeded in mounting a total of sixteen productions (mainly in his Studio) for the National Theatre after the war. A number of them were carefully prepared, primarily realistic Czech and Russian dramas with relevance to the changing social forces of the day, such as the Czech historical drama *Jan Hus* (1945), the nineteenth-century Czech naturalistic social drama *Maryša* (1948), and Gogol's *Revizor* (1948). Observers of both Frejka's 1936 *Revizor* and Honzl's 1948 *Revizor* noted a characteristic difference of tone: Frejka's prewar production had an almost eerie, dreamlike quality, whereas Honzl's was in the spirit of an Honoré Daumier caricature. This quality was effectively captured by the youthful Josef Svoboda's set, which was based on the contrast between attractive though philistine facades and ramshackle, often squalid behind-the-scenes realities. These classics were balanced by less orthodox choices, such as Čapek's *The Insect Comedy* (1946, with Svoboda) or Federico García Lorca's *Blood Wedding* (1946, in the Studio), although both lent themselves to Honzl's strong social slant. (My recollection of the *Insect Comedy* production is of a colorful, dynamic spectacle with a very strong performance by Jaroslav Průcha in the role of the tramp.) More indicative of the times and of Honzl's acceding to their pressures were his final two productions, in 1949: *The Great Smelting* and *Moscow Character*. Schematic, propagandistic Soviet works, they revealed more about Honzl's Communist orthodoxy than about his stature as an artist.

Seriously ill after years of chronic intestinal disorders, Honzl withdrew from his work at the National Theatre at the end of 1949 and focused on his writing, editorial work, and teaching at DAMU until his death in 1953. In retrospect, his postwar years were a less than satisfying conclusion to a long career, but probably not as frustrating and agonizing as the experiences of Frejka and Burian.

If Honzl seemed able to reconcile the tensions between art and politics, his will and that of the Party, Frejka succumbed to them. More intuitive and poetic than Honzl, though less disciplined, he was more subtle and literary than Burian, though less strikingly theatrical. He proved to be more vulnerable than both. All three were masters at synthesizing the elements of text, acting, and scenography, but whereas Honzl tended to focus on the text, and Burian on the musical expressiveness of performance, Frejka was primarily attuned to bringing out the utmost from his actors. More than Honzl and Burian, he gravitated toward large-scale, classic works requiring imaginative vision, complexity of characterization, and a unifying, suggestive atmosphere, but he never lost his special sense for playful, lyrical theatre. In his five postwar seasons at the Vinohrady Municipal Theatre he progressed in his artistic evolution from the previous two decades, avoiding in his art the frustrating compromises found in Honzl's and Burian's postwar work while adding emotive force and sharpened social awareness to his already formidable talents.

Although instinctively averse to any party affiliation or even the overt inclusion of politics in theatre,[8] Frejka nevertheless seemed to accept and support the positive aspects of the new order — its presumed concern for social justice and true democracy and its "scientifically" based program for creating a new world order. Rather than lower his standards regarding choice of plays or methods of staging, he constantly strove to slant his very best efforts toward *indirectly* reinforcing the spirit of postwar liberation and the feeling of new beginnings and later the ideals, values, and goals of the Communist Party. In the best sense, he was a fellow traveler, but this ultimately proved insufficient. Among the most outstanding of his seventeen productions at Vinohrady were Romain Rolland's *The Fourteenth of July* (1945), Georges Neveux's *Theseus, the Seafarer* (1946), Alexander Griboyedov's *Woe from Wisdom* (1947), Shaw's *Saint Joan* (1948),[9] Gorky's *Dostigayev and the Others* (1948), Shakespeare's *Merry Wives of Windsor* (1949), and V. V. Ivanov's *The Armored Train* (1950), which many critics considered one of the best postwar productions of a Soviet play.

It is true that Frejka was subjected to varying degrees of criticism for the stylization of some productions, the shortage of Socialist Realism in his repertoire, and the insufficient degree of "Stanislavskian" naturalism in his work with actors, but the high quality of his work had to be acknowledged, and he kept fulfilling all administrative duties and directives from above. Despite many inner uncertainties, he even applied for Communist Party membership in 1948.[10] There is also evidence to suggest that he attempted to join the Communist Party as early as the spring of 1946 but was dissuaded by top Party people in the arts because, tactically speaking, he would thereby be less subject to pressures from the anti-Communists then in power. At the time, not belonging to any party seemed to be in his favor. But other problems developed.

Frejka's story was tragic in the classic sense: his own tactics and temperament were as responsible for his defeat as were the oppressive measures of those in power. His associates and contemporaries agreed on several aspects of his character: he was inherently retiring if not shy, perhaps even timid; he unnecessarily complicated his personal and professional relationships; and his aversion to direct confrontations led to his preference for strategic maneuvering, which often backfired.

An example of Frejka's tactics occurred almost immediately after the liberation in May 1945, when he may already have had premonitions about some of the problematic politics to come. Having learned that Honzl, with whom he had differences reaching back to the 1920s, would become not only his colleague at the National Theatre but also one of his superiors, Frejka arranged to be reassigned to the Vinohrady Theatre. Concurrently he also began negotiating to have that theatre be sponsored by the Czechoslovak army as a form of extra security. He went so far as to have letterheads for the theatre include reference to its being a theatre of the army, but the reorganization failed to occur at that time.

Like Honzl, Frejka confronted an established older group of actors at the Vinohrady, with whom it would not be easy to deal. Turning to his strengths, Frejka imported some dozen young actors into his company, thereby enhancing his artistic potential but clearly alienating many of the actors already present, especially when he began to favor the new ones in casting. One significant example was his employment of Otomar Krejča, then strictly an actor, who left E. F. Burian's troupe at the end of the 1945–1946 season to join Frejka. With more than one older actor assuming he would play Macbeth for Frejka in the fall of 1946, Frejka proceeded to cast Krejča, who became a mainstay for the next four seasons, while resentments accumulated.

With the coming to power of the Communist Party in 1948, the internal political situation at the Vinohrady Theatre became more tense. Although he followed all official guidelines, Frejka's fellow members in the inner Party councils and committees of the theatre proved largely uncooperative and even hostile, partly for reasons of dogma, partly because of personal and professional resentment. Moreover, although he publicly apologized for his bourgeois family background and upbringing — and the values and habits they implanted — his failure to renounce his prewar *work*, as both Honzl and Burian had done, heightened his problems. Similarly, although never openly criticizing the doctrine and practices of Socialist Realism, Frejka obviously did not incorporate them in his work. Adding to his increasing levels of stress was his forming of a liaison (while married) with a young actress in his company.

In the season of 1949–1950, as prescribed proletarian plays were becoming fashionable and political events were building toward the notorious show trials of the early 1950s, Frejka more actively courted important politicians and army generals, again trying to get under the protective shield of the military. It was in vain. Decisions to reorganize many theatres had been made at upper levels, and — a sharp irony — although the Vinohrady Theatre was officially declared the Theatre of the Czech Army at the end of the 1949–1950 season, the two generals in charge dropped Frejka as artistic head. Had his entire theatre, especially its hardcore, careerist Communist members, supported him, he might have been able to survive, but he had alienated many by another tactic: in an effort to obtain their support, he promised the role of Hamlet to three different actors, who inevitably discovered his deception.[11] Underlying the Communist Party issue was the essential fact that Frejka was never "their man"; his hard-line Communist colleagues never felt he was really in their camp.

Badly demoralized, Frejka was temporarily "saved" by being assigned to the artistic leadership of the Music Theatre in the Karlín section of Prague, a traditional home of operettas and other popular entertainment. His successor in 1952 became Jan Škoda, from the Realistic Theatre. Swallowing his remaining pride, Frejka accepted and, remarkably, threw himself into his work, imbuing several lightweight productions with unexpected distinction. The first was a revised version of one of V + W's lesser vehicles, *Heaven on Earth* (Nebe na zemi, 1950), starring Vlasta Burian in his first stage work since 1944. But Frejka was a broken man, sleepless, constantly taking medications for his nerves, with his tendency toward a persecution complex increasing. Three events seemed to be decisive in the end. His extramarital lover left him; a final tactic misfired when it was discovered that a published letter in a Prague weekly critical of the new Vinohrady program but praising his Karlín operation was ghostwritten by Frejka himself over the signature of one of his students in the Theatre Conservatory;[12] and he witnessed a hugely successful public rehearsal of a new production at Karlín, directed by Alfred Radok. The juxtaposition of his own perceived failures with the obvious popularity of a younger contemporary was decisive. On October 17, 1952, he shot himself in his office; ten days later he died. His handwritten note addressed to the Central Committee of the Communist Party of Czechoslovakia is surely one of the most poignant theatrical documents of the era:

> I thank the Party for discovering a new life.
> I fall like a soldier at the front. I think that I fought honorably and to the advantage of the Party. I am no longer able to create anything except death, but within it is an important conclusion.

Emil František Burian in the late 1940s. Photo from the National Theatre Archive.

    Note the conclusion: Czechoslovakian theatre is being drained by the triumvirate of Kouřil — Šmeral — Feldstein. They ought to be removed. In their place perhaps Burian, Vnouček.
    In conclusion I ask the Central Committee to take care of my son.
All honor to labor!
Jiří Frejka[13]

    E. F. Burian survived Honzl and Frejka. Viewed as a whole, his career after the war revealed a series of strained, painful, even embarrassing efforts to keep proving himself as the greatest Czech director (which many thought him in the 1930s) while striving to satisfy the Party's priorities without compromising his own high standards. Immediately upon his return from internment in concentration camps, he had to swallow his disappointment at having to resume operations in his old theatre instead of being given a more prestigious venue. As if to compensate for this slight, he undertook what seemed a hubristically ambitious project of being in charge not only of his old D theatre (now designated D46) but three theatres in Brno and another in Prague, very nearly burning himself out in less than a season before cutting himself off in the spring of 1946 from all but his home theatre.

In that first season he directed *fourteen* productions and supervised several others; before he was finished in 1959 he would direct some fifty more.

Many contemporaries said in retrospect that Burian's first full production after returning was not only his best postwar work but one of his best ever. His highly subjective version of *Romeo and Juliet* (1945), which he subtitled *The Dream of a Prisoner*, directly reflected the traumas of his own wartime experience. It was vintage avant-garde Burian in its emotively charged, lyrically expressive, and musically orchestrated staging, with political-ideological implications secondary if present at all. Setting the production in a concentration camp, Burian retained the integrity of most of Shakespeare's text in playing out the vision of one of the prisoners, occasionally creating additional dialogue to establish the updated environment. The concentration camp context intensified by contrast the lyric pathos and humanity of the work, the power of love to defy even the most horrendous oppression. It was Burian's statement on behalf of the victims of the camps, with whom he had shared dreams of freedom and human happiness.

His subsequent work, whether revivals of his prewar productions, contemporary plays of a Socialist Realist stamp, or new adaptations of nondramatic pieces, hit the mark only in isolated productions; he seemed not able to find the right wavelength, not able to adjust to the new audiences and the new social realities, try as he fervently did. His disorientation may have had to do with his no longer having anything to rebel against; all that he had fought for, socially and politically, seemed to have been accomplished. Although relatively well done, his revivals of his prewar productions prompted only academic interest, and new plays, including his own, seemed undeveloped, tainted by the distortions and oversimplifications inherent in plays written according to the politically correct Socialist Realist formulas of the day. Most painful of all, he seemed unable to connect with the very audience he so sincerely sought, the proletariat. The malaise at the core of his efforts was evident at the end of his first season: fifteen of his actors left the company for the promise of better roles elsewhere, because they felt not enough attention was devoted to rehearsals, or because of backstage personal differences. The defections were not a good sign.

February 1948 brought increased pressure to do contemporary, Socialist Realist work. Burian presented one of the more successful, albeit simplistic, new plays dealing with sociopolitical aspects of the factory workplace, *Grinder Karhan's Team* (Parta brusiče Karhana) by Vašek Káňa (1905–1985), in 1949. The following year brought the beginning of the notorious show trials, modeled, like so many other aspects of Czech life, on Soviet prototypes. Burian responded by writing and staging a quasi-documentary, *The Hotbed* (Pařeniště), in 1950, which exploited the recent show trial of Milada Horáková and other political figures who had opposed the regime, were tried on false charges, and were executed. A cheap, sensational play, it revealed the lengths to which Burian seemed ready to go in demonstrating to the regime his loyalty and reliability.[14] Both works were staged in a stereotypically realistic fashion, a far cry from the imaginative theatrical staging inherent in his prewar work. In a larger sense, the *Hotbed* production also suggested the degree of mortal fear afflicting many people, even someone as seemingly secure and proven as Burian. Ironically, he was severely criticized because the play was judged insufficiently positive in portraying its central Communist protagonist.

Soon after, in the fall of 1951, partly for protection, partly for financial reasons, and partly for prestige, Burian negotiated the conversion of his theatre to an auxiliary unit of the army, to be known not as D52, but as the Army Art Theatre. In doing so, he echoed the earlier efforts of Frejka, in 1945 and again in 1950; but Burian was successful. For the next four seasons, until the fall of 1955, Burian ostentatiously wore the full uniform of an army colonel, causing more than a few colleagues to think he had lost his mind, but the temper of the times was such that his action seemed appropriate to many others.

During those four years, four notable deaths occurred within six months of each other. Jiří Frejka died in October 1952, and Honzl in April 1953. In the interim, in March 1953, and of greater public consequence, were the deaths of both Josef Stalin and Klement Gottwald, Czechoslovakia's hard-line Communist president, a virtual protégé of Stalin. No overtly dramatic events resulted, but a crucial milestone had passed; the darkest days were over. Almost as a sign of the beginning of a different atmosphere, *Bearers of Honors* (Nositelé řádů) by Miloslav Stehlík (1916–1994) had its premiere in Pilsen a few weeks after the leaders' deaths. It was the first Czech play after February 1948 to contain a degree of criticism of the new proletariat.

Despite his theatre's affiliation with the army, Burian's insecurity and wavering continued. In 1952 he had overtly renounced his avant-garde past and pledged to follow the Socialist Realist line more consistently; in 1953 he added a second recantation of his past production approaches, declaring that he had been mistaken in his admiration for Meyerhold. His poetically styled productions were few and far between for a number of seasons. In the fall of 1954 he accepted an invitation from Bertolt Brecht to direct a play in the latter's Berliner Ensemble. The play, *The Winter Battle*, was by German playwright J. R. Becher; Burian had successfully staged the premiere of this play in his own theatre two years earlier. The Berlin experience was not a happy one. After four or five weeks of rehearsal, Brecht asked Burian to relinquish his direction because of complaints from Brecht's actors about Burian's concept and his seemingly unstructured rehearsal methods.

Brecht completed the preparation of the play, which opened in January 1955. The incident was never reported or openly discussed in Prague.

Burian's next production work occurred in the spring of 1955 when he staged the first of the poetic plays by Josef Topol (b. 1935), *Midnight Wind* (Půlnoční vítr), which was not particularly well received but marked the beginning of the playwriting career of the man whom many came to regard as the most gifted Czech playwright of the century. At the beginning of the 1955–1956 season Burian had his theatre drop its army affiliation and revert to its very first name, D34, which it retained until Burian's death. As if following through on the choice of the Topol play and the renaming of his theatre, Burian decided to dedicate the next two seasons to a sustained retrospective of his earlier, primarily stylized, imaginatively staged productions, as a way of documenting a historically important form of Czech theatre. Perhaps more to the point, he was obviously concerned with asserting the innovative significance of his work in the face of recent productions by others who had, he felt, plagiarized from him.

In February 1956 the Twentieth Congress of the Communist Party of the Soviet Union, led by Nikita Khrushchev, publicly reviewed and condemned many of the worst excesses of the Stalinist era. Again, no overt changes became quickly evident, but a larger crack had appeared in the foundation of the monolithic system. Later that year, Zdeněk Nejedlý (1878–1962), the hard-line minister of education, science, and art since the change of regime in 1948, was eased out of his position.

Twelve of Burian's fourteen productions between 1956 and 1958 were essentially revivals, but the public showed only moderate interest in them. The one success among the productions was Vladimir Mayakovsky's *The Bedbug* (April 1956), one of the plays he had not staged earlier; his treatment of it contained some genuine touches of satiric verve, which had echoes of Burian at his best. The mere fact of his choice of these productions and being able to do them is another indication that a thaw was in progress, eventually to culminate some ten years later in the Prague Spring. But it was to be a long and not steady or uninterrupted process.

Burian's own inner insecurities and compulsions took one final turn, in part triggered by the comments of Soviet director Nikolay Okhlopkov, who witnessed several of the retrospective productions when the company toured to Russia in May 1958. Okhlopkov noted that, while Burian's theatre was noteworthy in its attacks on the bourgeoisie, it was mature and secure enough to address not only negative but positive themes and that it would be good to see at least half of his future productions consist of contemporary plays.[15] Burian had heard this critique often enough in Prague, and he resolved on yet one more *volte face*: his next season (1958–1959) would consist of new plays, not written according to a Socialist

Realist formula, but capturing the real life of recognizable, ordinary citizens of the day. It was a bold move in what was to prove his final season.

Three of the seven new plays he directed were his own, but the entire repertoire failed to live up to his hopes; with rare exceptions he was at his weakest in writing or staging straightforward realistic drama. By this time other Czech playwrights had been writing more honestly, critically, and successfully about contemporary social problems and personal relations,[16] and other directors had staged Czech and other works that were dramatically effective and relevant to many issues Burian had been trying unsuccessfully to address. Two directors in particular were rising stars: Alfred Radok, who had been Burian's assistant in 1940–1941, and Otomar Krejča, who had acted under both Burian and Frejka. Burian accused Radok of stealing from him and resented the resources available to Krejča at the National Theatre, where Krejča had become head of drama in 1956. Burian was particularly upset at Krejča's successful work with the new playwrights that he himself had been seeking so desperately.

By this time, too, Burian was in poor health. The stresses had taken their toll. He died on August 9, 1959. One of his critics and biographers, Adolf Scherl, who saw most of Burian's postwar productions, offered several overall assessments:

> His tragedy was that he stopped believing in his poetic, avant-garde type of theatre. His talent wasn't cut short by wartime and concentration camps, for he could still produce outstanding work; for example, his *Romeo and Juliet* and some other poetic adaptations. The worst was his erratic wavering; it was abnormal.... It was the problem of a talented artist being destroyed when forced to accept an official aesthetic. You can't simply blame it on Stalinist excesses. It was a matter of inherent coercion.... His tragedy was that of an artist being at a crossroads and unable to decide which path to take — an awful sort of schizophrenia but typical of life here at the time.[17]

With Burian's death, one of the last major links to the prewar avant-garde Czech theatre was broken, but its influence lived on. Jan Werich, in fact, revived several of the prewar v + w works between 1955 and 1958, but with a new partner, Miroslav Horníček (b. 1918). Moreover, as mentioned above, Radok and Krejča, the two leading directors of the new generation, were tied to the heritage of Honzl, Frejka, and Burian. They were subject to the same postwar artistic and political stresses, but being younger they were probably more resilient and adaptable and were in the process of developing their artistic identities rather than having to live up to previous achievements. Why focus on them rather than on any of the other hundred or more professional directors of that era? Because their work most strongly resisted the counterartistic flow of the theatre of their time. It was their vision, artistry, and will that most decisively broke the pattern of the Socialist Realist formula and, along with the later development of new, nonestablishment studio theatres, inspired the surge of creativity leading to the peak years of the 1960s.

Characteristically, Radok's contribution was relatively spontaneous, almost inadvertent, a product of his ever fresh creativity, whereas Krejča's was a more deliberately planned strategic campaign. Though sharing a number of characteristics, as individuals they were distinct in temperament as well as in their approach to staging. Their careers not only overlapped with the final years of their predecessors but involved a number of direct working relationships with them.

Radok is perhaps best remembered as the most intuitively creative Czech director of the entire postwar era, including the 1960s. Colleagues still speak of his sixth sense, his sorcery with actors and other components of production. Although he was in no sense a rebel or dissident, his temperament and creativity were absolutely at odds with the prevailing norms, which led to his virtually chronic problems in a number of theatres. With his roots in E. F. Burian's prewar theatre, and after wartime direction in Pilsen, he joined the young Theatre of the Fifth of May and dazzled, startled, and irritated audiences with radically fresh, irreverent musical productions such as *The Merry Widow?* in 1945 (the question mark reflected Radok's good-natured satiric slant on the material), *The Tales of Hoffmann* (1946), and *Rigoletto* (1947), the last two with Josef Svoboda, whose metaphoric scenography excellently complemented Radok's ironic, exuberant powers of fantasy. Their *Rigoletto* could serve as a fine example of pre-postmodernist staging. A scaled-down reproduction of a Verdi-era opera stage, including proscenium and curtain, was placed on a turntable within the regular main stage. During certain sequences, the turntable would rotate and thereby expose the wings of the Verdi stage, with singers, dancers, and backstage personnel flirting or carrying on other non-Verdi matters, while the onstage singers were impassionately singing into what was the offstage area of the main theatre. Radok also directed one other opera, *Pagliacci* (1948), and several plays with the company and, as noted previously, a few productions with the Theatre of Satire.

In 1948, the watershed year of the Communist takeover, Radok joined the National Theatre with the rest of the Fifth of May company. Between his final production with the Fifth of May theatre in March 1948 and his first with the National Theatre in January 1949, Radok shot his first of three feature films, *A Distant Journey* (Daleká cesta), a remarkable stylized version of the Terezín concentration camp experience focused on the story of one family. Characteristically, it was marked by Radok's sense of irony and the grotesque, which seized upon the inherent irony of Terezín as a showcase Nazi camp. The film, which won acco-

Alfred Radok in the 1950s with his wife, Marie Radoková, his lifetime theatre collaborator. Photo from the Theatre Institute, Prague.

lades internationally,[18] never achieved wide distribution in Czechoslovakia and was completely barred after Radok's self-exile in 1968.

Radok did three productions at the National Theatre before being forced to leave in 1949 (one year before Frejka was forced to leave the Vinohrady Theatre); his offense was an insufficiently Socialist Realist production of a minor Czech play, *The Bride from Chod* (Chodská nevěsta), by D. C. Faltis. During this first tenure with the National Theatre his most notable production was Lillian Hellman's *The Little Foxes* (1948), which opened one month before the Communist takeover and created tensions simply by being an American play, even though harshly critical of bourgeois capitalism.

After several seasons of peripheral theatre activity, which nevertheless included a significant experimental production with Svoboda in 1950 involving filmed projections, F. Šamberk's *The Eleventh Commandment* (Jedenácté přikázání), Radok was able to rejoin the National Theatre in 1954 as Krejča was coming to power there. This time he stayed until 1958, when he left to head innovative work on a multimedia form of live stage action juxtaposed with concurrent filmed images which he had developed with Josef Svoboda in the *Eleventh Commandment* production. A project that had its roots in Burian's Theatergraph of the 1930s, it became known as Laterna Magika and caught the world's attention at the Brussels Expo 58, thereby contributing to the breaking up of the ice pack that had chilled Czech theatre for ten years.

In the meantime, Radok had directed a number of controversial, theatrically striking productions at the National Theatre, including Hedda Zinner's *The Devil's Circle* in 1955 (which starred Krejča), Nezval's *Atlantida* in 1956 (which toured to Paris, probably the first major Czech theatrical export to the West in the post-1948 era), Leonid Leonov's *Golden Carriage* and Hellman's *Autumn Garden* (the entire set was in white), both in 1957, and culminating in John Osborne's *The Entertainer* (1957), all again with Svoboda. *The Entertainer* had a chacteristic Radok sequence, the burial of Billy Rice, the "entertainer"'s music hall father, which is not called for in the stage directions. A mime of lowering a casket into the ground with all due reverence and solemnity was carried out with an old upright player-piano, closely associated with Billy, instead of a casket.

Despite his success at Brussels Expo 58 and the relatively freer atmosphere back home, Radok's association with Laterna Magika was relatively short-lived once he disturbed authorities in 1960 by his totally non–Socialist Realist treatment of a scenario to accompany Bohuslav Martinů's cantata *The Opening of the Springs* (Otvírání studánek), in the new multimedia form. Radok's next work was with the Municipal Theatre before finally returning (for the third and last time) to the National Theatre in 1966.

In the meantime, in 1959 the last of the prewar avant-garde, Burian, had died, but new small theatre ensembles were beginning to take root in Prague and elsewhere, like the Theatre on the Balustrade, which was to figure prominently in the vital new wave of Czech theatre of the 1960s. Also, Krejča had been leading a renaissance at the National Theatre.

Krejča, unlike Radok, seemed able not only to operate but to grow and flourish within the post–February 1948 system; for a time, indeed, he forced his own vision on it, thereby profoundly altering the face of theatre in Czechoslovakia. Unlike Radok, Krejča was a strong-willed, dominating personality; with his innate intelligence and rhetorical skills he was also remarkably effective as a tactician and leader. He worked almost entirely with large theatre companies and for relatively long periods. After serving as an actor under Burian in the first postwar season, he was with the Vinohrady Theatre from 1946 to 1951 under Frejka, almost exclusively as an actor, and then joined the National Theatre, where he remained until 1965. During this latter engagement 1956–1961 were crucial years, for in 1956 he became head of the drama company and shifted his primary stage activity to directing. Inheriting a corps of seasoned, gifted actors, Krejča proceeded to build a team around him, consisting of Karel Kraus (b. 1920) as dramaturg and Jaromír Pleskot (b. 1922) as staff director (both had been his colleagues at the Vinohrady under Frejka). Pleskot went on to stage a memorable production of *Hamlet* in 1959, starring Radovan Lukavský (b. 1919). In 1959 Krejča imported still another strong young actor-director, Miroslav Macháček (1922–1991). Meanwhile, from within the National Theatre he had supplemented his team with scenographer Josef Svoboda. And, as noted, he could also build on some of the work of Radok's second tenure (1953–1959) in the National Theatre.

To provide the crucial fuel for his high-powered production team, Krejča and Kraus then brought in a number of promising, mostly young dramatists. Working with these dramatists and the rest of the team, he made the National Theatre the most meaningful and exciting theatre in the country by mounting a series of original plays and revivals that reflected, sometimes indirectly, contemporary life with honesty, psychological complexity, and theatrical power. The plays included works by contemporary Czechs: *A Sunday in August* (Srpnová neděle, 1958) by the poet František Hrubín (1910–1971) and *Their Day* (Jejích den, 1959) by another poet, Josef Topol; a nineteenth-century Czech: *The Bagpiper from Strakonice* (1958) and *Drahomira and Her Sons* (Drahomíra a její synové, 1960), both by Josef Kajetán Tyl; and a foreigner: (*The Sea Gull*, by Anton Chekhov, 1960). These productions formed a conscious program in their subjects, dramaturgical slant, and staging; the focus was on individuals or domestic groupings but clearly had reference to broader social problems in the new order. Krejča, speaking from authority as a major actor himself, demanded from his veteran actors fresh honesty and thought in order to embody his deep analysis of texts and his complex insights into characterization. Krejča also had the advantage of some of Svoboda's most innovative, expressive scenography.[19] It all came together and set a new standard for modern Czech theatre.

The career relationships and resultant influences among the five chief figures under consideration are worth noting. Radok had a crucial, close association with Burian in 1940–1941 when he served as his assistant until D41 was closed and Burian arrested. There is no denying that he was profoundly influenced by Burian's synthetic, metaphoric approach to staging, his musical orientation, and his penchant for adapting texts, as well as by his significant use of scenography, particularly lighting and projections. Radok had no direct association with Frejka, but he had something of Frejka's sensitivity and intuitiveness, and, indeed, his fears. Radok worked as a colleague of Honzl in the National Theatre for a year and a half in 1948 and 1949. They were totally incompatible politically and artistically, and Honzl was responsible for Radok's first dismissal from the National Theatre; in fact, Radok suffered a heart attack directly related to Honzl's vituperative attack following Radok's production of *The Bride from Chod* in 1949.[20] The larger point, according to many contemporaries, is that Radok's unique talents were a sty in the eye of those less gifted.

Krejča was directly associated with Burian in the first postwar season, when he was in the ensemble of D46. He played Prometheus in Aeschylus' tragedy under another director, but then acted Cyrano for Burian. Much as he respected Burian, he chose to leave him for Frejka's company at the Vinohrady Theatre, where he performed major roles for five years, undoubtedly learning a great deal, perhaps especially from Frejka's painstaking work with texts and actors, although their styles differed. By the time Krejča joined the National Theatre, Honzl was gone.

To summarize, both Radok and Krejča were clearly the offspring of the prewar Czech theatre, primarily its avant-garde practitioners, with Burian and Frejka, rather than Honzl, as the chief influences. Clearly, however, Krejča and Radok were far more than imitators or clones. Radok and Krejča (the latter, perhaps, to a lesser degree) were inheritors of a nonrealistic, poetic, consciously theatrical, metaphoric approach to theatre which was developed by all three major prewar directors. And with the addition of their own distinctive talents, they carried this approach forward into the 1960s, the third great era of Czech theatre in the twentieth century (viewing the 1915–1930 Hilar era as the first, and the 1925–1938 avant-garde era as the second).

A comparison of Radok and Krejča would include several additional points. Krejča was both a notable actor and a significant director, whereas Radok never had any sustained interest other than directing. Radok had been directing for some fifteen years before Krejča began directing steadily. (Krejča had directed only three productions during the fifteen years prior to his first major production at the National Theatre.) Krejča acknowledged the high quality of Radok's work and even spoke of basing his program at the National Theatre in part on the work Radok had already achieved there. Radok, in the Burian tradition, always edited and altered texts extensively to adapt them to his vision and make them maximally conducive to striking metaphoric, theatrical images. In his work at this time, Krejča, working with Karel Kraus, rarely made serious changes in texts other than occasionally transposing scenes; rather, the effort was to penetrate deeply and reveal the full complexity of the characters and thought.

Radok rarely tackled major classics (never a Shakespeare play), preferring to work with lesser-known texts that could more readily be manipulated. He almost never staged original plays, except for one play of his own, *The Village of Women* (Vesnice žen) in 1945. Krejča's repertoire, on the other hand, was heavily represented by classics and original plays. Radok did a number of impressive operas and other musical works; Krejča never staged an opera, and only rarely a play with music and song. Radok had a flair for comedy and even farce, whereas Krejča's *naturel* inclined toward serious drama, with a strong penchant for Chekhov (with his farce unemphasized) and similar works.

In the rehearsal process, Radok, much like Burian, worked primarily intuitively and improvisationally and would probably have had difficulty in rationally explicating his concepts, which in any case would have been evolving during the rehearsal process. Krejča prepared elaborate notes and charts, which could easily have been transformed into lecture notes for a seminar. Both recognized the value of spectacle, and both worked very productively with scenographers, the chief one for both being Svoboda, although Radok also did important work with Ladislav Vychodil (b. 1920), such as *The Play of Love and Death* in 1965 at the Municipal Theatre. In the best sense, Radok and Krejča complemented each other in their work; and in 1954–1959, when they were both in the National Theatre, Czech theatre was the richer for it.

Indeed, the record of Radok and Krejča, especially in the 1950s, testifies to the flashes of diversity and creativity within the generally monolithic system that oppressed culture and society. The same was true of much of Frejka's work, and some of Burian's and Honzl's.[21] Obviously in the debt of their predecessors, Radok and Krejča evolved the work that the former were no longer in a position or psychological state to do. By the time Radok and Krejča entered their mature creative years, from the late 1950s on, the balance between oppression and controls vis-à-vis freedom to create was less unequal: there was enough restriction to challenge and focus one's energies and creative talent, and yet enough relative freedom to operate within the explicit and unspoken parameters. In this sense, perhaps the dehumanizing, contra-artistic era of 1948–1956 could be viewed as a cruel test which, although destroying or crippling many, also energized and motivated others (perhaps tougher or luckier) to significant creative efforts. In this sense, too, despite strong differences, the era was something of a variant of the 1935–1945 era, when prewar fascism and wartime nazism were the challenges.

Aeschylus spoke of wisdom through suffering, and it is likely that a rather special wisdom did develop in those enduring the blackest years of the 1950s. In most people it probably took the form of survival tactics, but in some it may also have sparked a special effort to inject their art with the distillation of their will to resist, to counter the ego-destroying force of a "socially engineered" system by the nonmaterial means at their command. The oppressive dogmas and directives created a special bond among most genuinely creative theatre artists and workers. They could not overtly denounce the system, but they could be passionately dedicated to condemning it indirectly through their art. In other words, may there not have been in the 1950s an ironic but serious relation between profound vicissitudes and creativity? Not only wisdom, but also creativity may have been produced through suffering. The deformative and even deadly force of the powers that then prevailed may ironically have prompted the very motivation, heightened concentration, psychological bonding under duress, and total focus to generate a determined though covert resistance of the mind and spirit. And the legacy of this resistance contributed vitally to the creation of the indisputable achievements in the Czech theatre of the late fifties and sixties.

5

The Dynamic 1960s, Part One
Significant New Plays

The 1960s represent the high-water crest of Czech theatre of the twentieth century. The many repressed talents of the postwar generation began to assert themselves as the contra-artistic ideology and practices of the Communist regime entered a slackened phase after the death of Stalin and other hardliners and, later, the official denunciation of the worst excesses of the Stalinist era. As already indicated, notable creative work began to appear in the late 1950s. It spread and grew in vitality in the 1960s and had the promise of a bright future embodied in the 1968 ideal of "socialism with a human face," the motto of the Prague Spring, the significant liberalizing movement from within the Communist Party which we associate most clearly with the name of Alexander Dubček.[1]

This liberalizing creative surge was cut off abruptly and harshly with the August 1968 invasion of Czechoslovakia by the Warsaw Pact armies under Soviet leadership. Fearful of the infectious spread of democratic ideas and projects throughout its empire, the Soviet leadership felt compelled to stamp out the Czechoslovakia experiment, as it had previously done in East Germany (1953) and Hungary (1956). For Czech theatre, the experience was a trauma similar to those of 1938 and 1948; once again, its organic evolution was, if not aborted, at least deformed.

The Czech theatre's achievements, which reached world-class status by the mid-1960s, were the products both of playwrights and of those who produced their works: theatre companies, directors, and designers. I believe that this rich period of Czech theatre and drama may best be discussed by focusing first on the new playwrights and then on those who embodied their work in the theatre. This chapter emphasizes the notable plays of this peak era, with only occasional attention to how they were staged.[2]

As already suggested, many playwrights as well as other theatre people were in favor of the socialist ideals underlying the 1948 change of regime, or at least sympathetic to the lofty moral ideals expressed by the Communist Party. Before long, however, the very humanism that prompted the intellectuals' and artists' rejection of a bourgeois capitalistic society with its seemingly inherent disregard for spiritual and cultural welfare led them to become progressively distressed by the realities of the new socialist order. The phrase that symbolized the liberating surge of 1968 known as the Prague Spring — "socialism with a human face" — implicitly condemned a regime that had lost sight of virtually all human-centered values. The efforts culminating in 1968 in Czechoslovakia were directed at restoring integrity and credibility to socialist ideals that had been increasingly ignored over the previous twenty years.

The year 1956 was decisive in marking the beginning of the reversal of the march of dismal years of forced social engineering. The denunciation of Stalin by Khrushchev at the 1956 Congress of the Communist Party of the Soviet Union sent powerful signals to the Czechoslovakian CP apparatus. In 1956, also, the Second Congress of the Czechoslovak Writers' Union was held in Prague, and for the first time several writers questioned or even spoke against certain policies and practices affecting their profession as well as against certain general social abuses. From then until roughly 1963 additional liberalizing measures alternated with arbitrary acts of repression: what was given with one hand was taken away with the other. Nevertheless, increased opportunities for artistic expression became available, and a degree of questioning of previously near-sacred sociopolitical premises was tolerated.

Coupled with these gradual, tentative improvements was a growing awareness of and interest in existential philosophy: the works of Søren Kierkegaard, Jean-Paul Sartre, and Albert Camus and the plays of Jean Anouilh, Eugene Ionesco, and Samuel Beckett became more available and could be discussed, although rarely performed before the 1960s. On a less intellectual level, increased interest began to be paid to the everyday personal problems of the ordinary individual as distinct from schematic figures derived from ideological formulae. Although some Czech plays began to reflect existential themes, the plays as plays still remained rooted in variations of traditionally realistic forms throughout the 1950s. A few novels at least partly critical of life since 1948 were published, and some Czech plays also reflected the growing spirit of questioning and skepticism, although direct criticism of the regime or Party, or even strong satire, was not yet a feasible option.

The plays of the late 1950s began to emphasize individuals rather than groups, and the individuals are presented in relation to problematic issues within an established socialist context in Czechoslovakia. Indeed, the characters are often

Otomar Krejča's production of František Hrubín's A Sunday in August, *with scenography by Svoboda, National Theatre, 1958. Photo by Dr. Jaromír Svoboda.*

identified as members of the Communist Party, and on more than one occasion we are introduced to the world of Party membership — its duties, conflicts of view, and internal stresses. Considerable *indirect* criticism is made of various aspects of life under socialism and Marxist-Leninist principles, but the issues are resolved by attributing faults and shortcomings to weaknesses of individuals rather than to the Party or its ideology. Chekhov's influence on the style of playwriting is strong, and a considerable portion of the meaning of these plays is to be found in their subtext.

This section focuses on aspects of theme, characterization, and structure in the plays, leaving detailed matters of staging to the next chapter. The Chekhovian mode is especially evident in a 1958 work, *A Sunday in August* (Srpnová neděle), by František Hrubín, a major poet and frequent critic of official policies affecting him as a writer. The play evolved in collaboration with the Krejča team at the National Theatre and was successfully produced in theatres not only in Czechoslovakia but elsewhere in Europe. A landmark in the revival of significant drama during the thaw following the official rejection of Stalinism, the play directs our attention to the private and personal lives of the leading characters rather than to ideology or class struggle.

Nevertheless, the play also touches upon larger social realities. The central characters are essentially misfits in the new socialist order, dilettantes who have subsisted on their feelings and their wit. It is a play very much in the Chekhovian manner, taking place by a pond in a small provincial town frequented by summer visitors from Prague. Essentially apolitical, the play has a calm, seemingly listless surface but considerable turbulence and intricacy beneath it. The ambience of a summer pond was captured impressionistically by Josef Svoboda's use of scrims, projections, and reflective surfaces. The main emphasis is on states of mind and spirit, the values and attitudes one lives by. By way of resolution there is perhaps a suggestion that youth and/or ingenuousness is more attractive and enviable than experience or even hard-won wisdom. In the late fifties the play's depiction of vulnerable humanity was like a breath of fresh air in a long-closed room.[3]

Josef Topol's *Their Day* (Jejích den), still another product of Krejča's collaborative team in the National Theatre, took up many of the issues of *A Sunday in August*. It was first presented in 1959 and was among the most performed and longest-running postwar Czech plays. The central concern is again the conflict between values held by different elements of society. In *Their Day*, however, values become polarized, and the tensions between the old and the new are harshly revealed. Topol creates a relatively complex web of relationships: the plot deals with two families and their offspring. Most of the characters feel alienated in a milieu of altered cultural values in the post-Stalinist era. The elders for the most part represent a bourgeois grasping for security even as their children grope uncertainly for ideals in the midst of disillusionment.

The play's fragmented structure of action and dialogue reflected an impulse to break away from familiar forms of Socialist Realism in playwriting. It was embodied scenically by Svoboda's innovative multiscreen projection system, Polyekran, which could almost instantly provide a cubistic variety of images of a given setting. Reminiscent of *A Sunday in August,* the dialogue is marked by a fresh contemporary idiom, broken discourse, and considerable subtext. *Their Day* catches the rhythms and currents of its time, a period of uncertainty and tentativeness as the dogmas of the establishment were increasingly questioned and youth was openly rebelling against the hypocrisies of its elders.

Otomar Krejča's production of Josef Topol's Their Day, *with scenography by Svoboda, National Theatre, 1959. Photo by Dr. Jaromír Svoboda.*

Another group of plays of the late fifties and early sixties involved wartime situations, as if to remind audiences of what they had to fight against and what they were fighting for. These plays contain no criticism of the Communist regime, but rather an indictment of human failures to live up to standards of honor and responsibility, failures still evident in all segments of society at the beginning of the 1960s.

Perhaps the most successful and well-known of this group of plays was *The Owners of the Keys* (Majitelé klíčů, 1962) by Milan Kundera (b. 1929), whose later novels were to make him internationally known a decade or so later. Another product of the Krejča National Theatre "workshop," the play was still in the National Theatre repertoire as late as 1965. The action occurs during the wartime occupation of a provincial Czech city. We are presented with a young married couple living with the wife's parents. The focus is on a crucial ethical dilemma: the choice that the young husband must make between a life of relative security and insulation and action that involves the sacrifice of others but serves a larger cause of the resistance movement, of which he was formerly a member. He must choose between protecting his wife and her parents or preserving the safety of his former comrades and their cause. Painfully, he chooses to rejoin the resistance. Contrasting with the positive values of dedication to a larger humanistic cause is the sharp depiction of the pettiness, greed, and instinct for self-survival of his wife, her parents, and their neighbors. Indeed, their very flaws defeat his desperate efforts to save his wife at the climactic moment of the play. The implication for the audience is the need to live according to demanding ideals rather than for creature comforts and the security symbolized by the set of household keys of the title.

Formally, the play is an example of straightforward realism with one striking exception — a series of expressionistic interludes representing the inner state of the hero at the moments when he must make critical decisions. Such moments were staged effectively thanks to Svoboda's use of special lighting effects in conjunction with mirrors to create a dreamlike interruption of reality. Even the realistic actions employed the theatrical device of simultaneous action in the two adjoining rooms of the setting; the rooms were placed on adjacent platforms that could be rolled up or downstage. The play is an effective melodrama with ethical overtones, but its positive values are offset by the schematic and predictable working out of its action and themes and (with the exception of its protagonist) by its pamphletlike characters.

In the mid- and later 1960s, the tendency toward a diversity of themes and subject matter was also evident in plays of ordinary people without direct reference to their political alignments or even to a socialist context.

Josef Topol turned to the one-act form after *Their Day*, writing three short works in addition to one other full-length play. The first short play, *Cat on The Rails* (Kočka na kolejích, 1965), was again directed by Krejča, but after he had left the National Theatre and opened his own Theatre beyond the Gate (Divadlo za branou) in Prague that same year. Two young lovers confront each other at a seemingly ordinary but actually decisive moment in their affair as they linger by a rural railroad stop. Finding no satisfaction in their societal roles, they focus almost exclusively upon each other but sense an ultimate sterility and emptiness even there. While embracing they flirt with the idea of death, and their caresses threaten to become aggressive, destructive. It is an emotional form of Russian roulette, in which each has a finger on the trigger. The play ends with no resolution, but with the distinctly existential suggestion that their lives are in their own hands, from which one might infer that no social system is finally capable of satisfying the complex, often tormented drives posed by the human condition.

Topol's sequel, *Hour of Love* (Hodina lásky, 1968), was also presented by Krejča at the Gate Theatre. A denser, less accessible play, it wrings the last variations from the encounter of two lovers who have reached a dead end in their relationship. Having sought an ideal in love only to have the inevitable sordid realities of life corrupt or frustrate that ideal, they appear to have nothing else to give meaning to their lives. There seems to be no middle ground between absolute fulfillment and bleak existential emptiness. The Anouilh-like theme would have been inconceivable a few years before, in the early period of the new socialist regime.

Topol's slightly earlier one-act play, *Nightingale for Supper* (Slavík k večeři, 1967), was a more abstract and overtly symbolic, absurdist-influenced study of the inability of the ideal to survive amid the materialism and cruelty of the everyday. The play begins with an ordinary incident, a young man's visit to his girlfriend's home for supper. As the visit progresses, however, the visit turns to a chill nightmare of the persecution and eventual destruction of the young man (whose name is Nightingale) at the hands of the girl's family, which comes to represent the forces of brutality and death in the world.

Alena Vostrá's (1938–1992) *When Your Number Comes Up* (Na koho to slovo padne) is similar to *Cat on the Rails* in its existential focus on contemporary youth. It was first presented in 1966 by the Drama Club (Činoherní klub), among the most outstanding of the new theatre ensembles formed in reaction against the relatively inflexible repertory policies of most of the large state or municipal theatres. Vostrá, one of the house playwrights of the group, depicted a rootless, disenchanted cluster of young people who feel cheated by life and so find a perverse satisfaction in playing rather malicious tricks on those less clever or perceptive than they are. Yet they are unable to hide for long their gnawing sense of boredom and insecurity. Significantly, the play does not moralize about the distinctly antisocial behavior of the young people but presents virtually without comment a freshly idiomatic, almost improvisational view of Czech urban youth of the mid-1960s.

This reluctance to render overt judgments marks several other plays produced by the artists of the Drama Club. For example, Ladislav Smoček (b. 1932), another house playwright and the actual initiator of the Drama Club, wrote *Piknik* (1965), an intense psychological study of the antagonisms among a number of American GIs on patrol in a Pacific island jungle during World War II. Far from being a propaganda piece, it is almost studiously apolitical, dealing with the dra-

Jan Kačer's production of Alena Vostrá's When Your Number Comes Up, *at the Drama Club, 1966. Photo from the Theatre Institute, Prague.*

matic possibilities of man-to-man confrontations under the stress of fear and battle fatigue.[4] In keeping with the Drama Club's focus on the actors, the performance took place on a virtually bare stage with a half-dozen bentwood chairs.

The Topol one-acts and these plays of the Drama Club focused on the unheroic, private lives of apolitical people. In Topol's plays metaphysical overtones emanated from concentrated, often elusive exchanges of feelings and attitudes which brought to mind the work of Marguerite Duras. The works of the Drama Club, on the other hand, created on stage a sense of the immediacy of eccentric life. At their weakest the Drama Club plays resembled acting exercises, appropriate enough in a theatre devoted to the policy of emphasizing the contributions of actors; at their richest, the plays provided suggestive, lively reflections of ongoing contemporary life in Czechoslovakia.

A distinct category of plays that emerged with the loosening of restrictions on theme and subject in the 1960s consisted of adaptations of seventeenth- and eighteenth-century folk plays with biblical subjects. Realistically textured, wryly humorous, yet revealing genuine faith, such pieces had the charm of primitive paintings and were another example of increased interest in apolitical materials, although many undoubtedly read political significance into the attraction to faith and things of the spirit inherent in these plays. The most popular of these folk re-

Ladislav Smoček's production of his own Piknik *at the Drama Club, the first production of the new company, 1965. The jungle scene was represented by green panels against a black backdrop; four rehearsal chairs made up the rest of the setting. Photo from the Theatre Institute, Prague.*

vivals were the work of Jan Kopecký (1918–1992), an influential critic, Ministry of Culture official, and university professor in the pre-1968 years: in 1965 *A Play of the Martyrdom and Glorious Resurrection of Our Lord and Savior Jesus Christ* (Komedie o umučení a slavném vzkříšení Pana a Spasitele našeho Ježiše Krista) and in 1967 *A Play of the Star* (Komedie o Hvězdě), dealing with the nativity story.

From 1963 to 1968 a growing momentum of broader cultural, artistic activity and increasingly critical reaction to the sociopolitical environment became apparent. The rigged purge trials of the early 1950s were formally exposed in 1963, and other absurdities of the regime revealed themselves, chiefly its use of bureaucracy to control, if not suppress, creativity and critical thinking. Moreover, the regime was exhibiting signs of uncertainty and even confusion. The eroding police state, no longer employing draconian measures, became a challenge to the conscience and social concerns of artists, inadvertently allowing them opportunities to present oblique, variously camouflaged expressions of their views. Writers' meetings reviewed the recent past and the guilt shared by all for the gross abuses of the Stalinist period. Franz Kafka and Karel Čapek were removed from the index of proscribed writers. Novels critical of life and society since 1948 came out in increasing numbers,[5] and the Czech film renaissance of the mid-1960s — built on the same critical view of the deformities of social and personal life created by the still-ruling establishment — included several thinly veiled indictments of the contemporary scene among its major works.[6]

Increasingly disillusioned by the realization that the dehumanizing flaws and evils formerly identified as fruits of bourgeois capitalism were not only flourishing but acquiring cancerous proportions in their supposedly enlightened state, more and more intellectuals and artists turned away from politics to art in order to express their sense of having been betrayed. The revolt of the writers culminated in the Fourth Congress of the Writers' Union, in 1967.[7] Speech after speech denounced new censorship laws, the culturally crippling isolation of the nation, and the deformations of power which had virtually destroyed traditions of trust, honor, and spiritual health in society. When Ludvík Vaculík (b. 1926), a leading writer and spokesman for liberalization, suggested that "not one human problem has been solved in the last twenty years" and that "our republic has lost its good name,"[8] he was expelled from the Communist Party, as were several others for similar statements, including the playwright Ivan Klíma (b. 1931). Other playwrights, such as Milan Kundera and Pavel Kohout (b. 1928), were formally reprimanded.

The middle and late 1960s also witnessed a return of inventive, frequently harsh and powerful satire as playwrights vented the frustrations and resentments of increasing numbers of the society. Another, less readily definable set of dramas also emerged at this time — more poetic, even visionary, employing a broad canvas for the development of their action, often turning to the past to comment indirectly on contemporary issues.

The outright satires usually employed grotesque, absurd models or parables of social actualities to underline the abuses of post-Stalinist Czechoslovakia, though their inventiveness and power carry them beyond immediate time and place. The extent to which they pinpointed specific deformations of socialist culture and doctrine varies, as does the critical detachment of their authors.

Václav Havel (b. 1936) became the best-known playwright in this group years before he undertook the overtly political activities that made him Europe's most notable dissident. In at least one broad respect, Havel's plays carried on the heritage of Karel Čapek. Like Čapek, Havel was drawn to clashes between humanistic values and twentieth-century phenomena: advanced technology, bureaucracy, materialistic positivism. His distinctive vision of the world as well as some hallmarks of his style were already evident in *The Garden Party* (Zahradní slavnost, 1963), the first of his major works. The play deals with a young man, Hugo, and

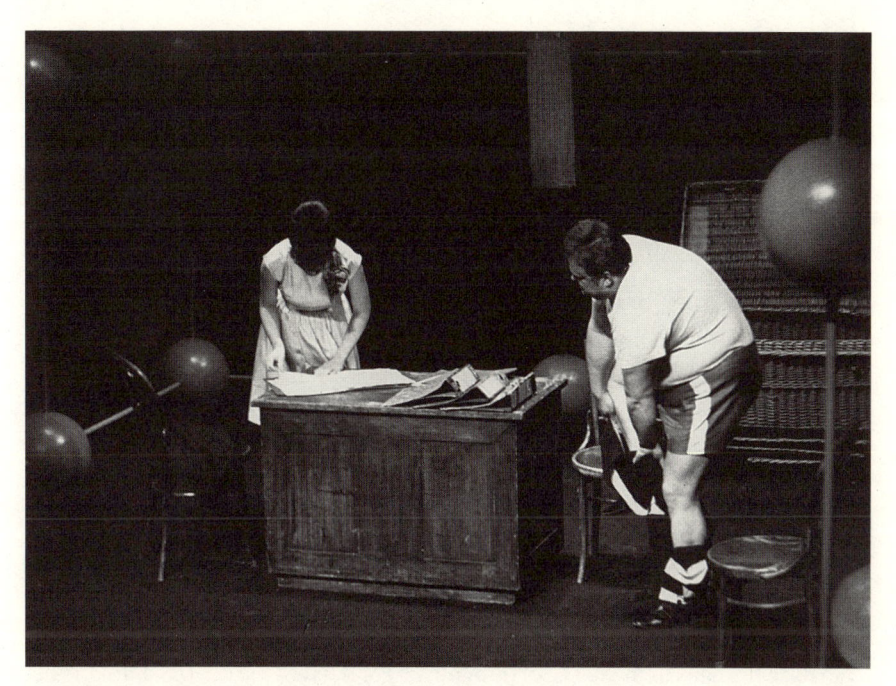

Krejča's production of Václav Havel's The Garden Party, *with a setting by Svoboda, at the Balustrade Theatre, 1963. Photo by Dr. Lubomír Rohan.*

his career. A seeming nonentity obsessed by chess, he acquires experience as he works his way through a nameless institution, finally reaching the top, but losing his identity in the process. The institution is a grotesque establishment dedicated to inaugurating and liquidating equally nameless projects. In doing so, it rejects logic and practicality in the name of tradition, authority, and empty phrases, its wildly irrelevant thinking represented by cant and shibboleths. There are incidental hits at routine bureaucratic follies and distortions of Marxist thought, but above all *language* here becomes a system in itself, symptomatic of a world that utterly dehumanizes people.[9] Sheer cant becomes a machine that jams, locks, or slips its gears; its infinite variations remain arbitrary signs. The master in this world is one who possesses a cybernetic brain and an absolutely interchangeable, componentlike identity — Hugo. Havel's use of language most nearly resembles that of Ionesco; what is stressed, however, is not the irrational absurdity of experience, but the deadly nature of sclerotic, dehumanized thought and feeling.

In *The Memorandum* (Vyrozumění, 1965), Havel once again used an institutional setting never precisely identified. The construction of the play involves a symmetrical arrangement of twelve scenes representing the fall, rise, and neutralization of the central figure, a bureaucrat of moderate status. Language is again a dominant element, but not quite in the same way as in *Garden Party*. The emphasis here is on the machinations of a power struggle within the institution over the introduction of a new "scientific" language (Ptydepe) designed for greater efficiency of operations. The center of Havel's concern, however, is not the power struggle, much less the individuals it involves, but the momentum of the apparatus of the institution itself, of which the new language is a symptom. Designed for maximum clarity of communication, the language is grotesquely unusable. The central figure, a self-proclaimed would-be humanist, proves impotent and ludicrous and is revealed as an unconscious hypocrite and phrasemaker. Once again there is considerable incidental satire of office types and behavior, and once again Havel maintains a cool detachment. Though *The Memorandum* is more farcical than *Garden Party*, the implications of its world are genuinely grim. Obviously, the implications were inspired by life in Czechoslovakia, but they can relate just as clearly to any technocratic society.

Havel's next play, *The Increased Difficulty of Concentration* (Stížená možnost soustředění, 1968), is a relatively more humanly oriented work. The satire is perhaps less sharp, its most evident object being the absurdity of scientific attempts to analyze humans in the name of humanistic goals. Here the central dramatic device is Puzuk, a sensitive, childish machine designed to interview people. Whimsically, the machine seems more delicate and temperamental than the human beings using it. The general theme is frustrated humanism in the context of banal domesticity as well as technology, but Havel also satirizes humanism itself when it is embodied in rhetoric more than in actions. The central character, a writer given to quasi-philosophical speculations about human values and needs, finally stresses somewhat lamely the need to have needs. The ironic embodiment of his abstract speculations is his romantic-sexual involvement with three women: his wife, his mistress, and his secretary. None of the involvements is satisfactory, but each seems essential to his sense of human identity. The play's action approaches conventional comedy more closely than the action in Havel's other two plays. Its structure, however, reveals Havel's signature. He presents the action in cubistic fashion to convey the fragmented consciousness of people. As scene follows scene, we realize that Havel juggles with time to make the scenes with the wife parallel those with the mistress. Although we seem to be progressing normally, we are actually jumping back and forth in time, witnessing deliberately repeated scenes with different characters. The process culminates in a wild, surrealistic, Ionesco-like scene in which all the characters concurrently enter and exit, shouting their lines in overlapping fashion. At the end of the play, with the repetition of the opening lines (as in Ionesco's *The Bald Soprano*), we have once again arrived at the very beginning. Havel denied that absurdist theatre was part of his theatre's "program," but added, "I have the feeling that, if absurd theatre had not been invented before me, I would have had to invent it."[10]

Several satires by other authors warrant mention. *King Vávra* (Král Vávra, 1964) by Milan Uhde (b. 1936) is perhaps most blatant in its use of a central grotesque model of the social scene. A king, who resembles Jarry's Ubu in his inherent coarse stupidity, has the special feature of donkeylike ears that he hides under long hair. National policy decrees that everyone must have long hair and that barbers are taboo. Gross deceptions and a corresponding ease of switching principles and political allegiances anger the playwright. The play has a more emotive, darker tone than those of Havel and gains immediate impact as a result, but the satire is not as consistent or as effectively controlled. The use of songs and a loose, almost improvised, revue structure is traceable to its director, Evžen Sokolovský of the State Theatre in Brno, who had a strong interest in Brechtian theatre.

At the center of virtually all these satires is power: its intricacies, its terror, and yet its seductiveness; its force of dehumanization, negation, and death. The environment of central Europe — and of Czechoslovakia in particular — has seemed conducive to the practice and study of power and the grotesque relationships to which it gives birth. As one observer noted, "In no other Communist country, not even Hungary or Poland, have so many key personages moved between power and prison and power again, between disgrace and rehabilitation and disgrace anew."[11] Many writers and other artists explored the fascination and horror of humans being mastered by brute, irrational power, especially the teasing suggestion that the victims may be responsible for the emergence of that power or for maintaining its viability through their acquiescence. The parallel to the attraction of many leftist artists and intellectuals to Communist totalitarianism is obvious, as Ionesco's *Rhinoceros* so imaginatively demonstrates.

Czech writers were of course familiar with Prague's best-known author, Kafka, and several darkly satiric plays of the 1960s present variations on Kafkaesque motifs on the workings of power. In Ivan Klíma's *The Castle* (Zámek, 1964) the title as well as the name of the central character, Josef Kahn, derive from Kafka. The work is a realistically presented parable of how power crushes anyone who is different or is an individual. The castle is occupied by what seems to be an academy of notable artists and scientists who are utterly sealed off from the general population and progressively reveal various aberrations and eccentricities bordering on madness. One of their number has been killed. An outsider, Josef Kahn, arrives and is invited to take the dead man's place. He ultimately becomes a new victim, primarily because he asks questions and does not fit in with the rest. Meanwhile, the previous death is officially investigated and solved. It was a joint murder by the great figures inhabiting the castle, but the cream of the dark, satiric jest is that the investigative process stops right there and no punishment is forthcoming — official procedure has been satisfied. Overlapping the completion of the investigation is a repetition of the killing, to which Josef Kahn willingly submits.[12] The play is straightforwardly realistic, but much of the action and motivation is deliberately vague, as if to suggest a controlled dream if not a nightmare.

A starker, more direct satire suggesting humans' complicity in their own destruction by a cryptic power is the one-act *The Maze* (Bludiště) by Ladislav Smoček, of the Drama Club. First presented in 1966, the play deals with a man who, despite ample warnings, virtually talks himself into entering a maze (seemingly with no exit) at a public park. Smoček successfully blends farce and fear, violence and sinister humor, in portraying the victim's fascination with the maze and the gatekeeper's ambiguous indifference to whether the man enters or not — until he virtually forces the man in.

Another satire focusing on the motif of power is Pavel Kohout's *August, August, August* (August is Czech for circus clown), which had its premiere in Prague in 1967. It is a rather long and belabored yet comic parable of a Chaplinesque circus clown who longs for a set of fancy show horses, which he naively assumes will assure his glory. To qualify for the horses, he willingly submits to a series of farcical public humiliations at the hands of a bored, sadistic ringmaster, only to be confronted at the final blackout with a cage of raging beasts instead. The play, which has an improvisational, revue format, is a dramatization of the thoughts Kohout expressed at the 1967 Writers' Congress (after which he was reprimanded by the Party). He feared, he said, that "man in this world, split by the interests of the powerful, is and will remain merely a walk-on who in various costumes of various times will be pushed around the scene in various ways, without most of those in the roles of walk-ons (as any director will confirm) knowing who wrote the piece and what it's about."[13]

As I have mentioned, the plays of the middle and late 1960s also included a number of more indirect, more speculative reflections of their time. Satire, if present at all, is secondary to a broader view of the world which is essentially poetic in nature. The sheer complexity and ambivalence of the issues and values in these plays are more pronounced than in the plays dealt with so far. Moreover, some of these plays raise relatively broader questions regarding the essence and the implications of the socialist revolution itself, as well as the society and culture to which it gave birth. In form, these plays employ what might be called a flexible realism, or impressionistic realism, and they tend to focus on groups of people rather than on individuals. While their structure tends to be more casual than that of most of the plays already discussed, they are not marked by any noteworthy departures from recognizable reality.

Josef Topol's *End of Carnival* (Konec masopustu) was first performed in Olomouc in 1963 as another product of the Krejča-Kraus-Svoboda team; in 1964 they restaged it in the National Theatre as Krejča's last production there. Arguably Topol's greatest play, it is especially interesting in its employment of myth and ritual elements. On its secular, realistic level, the play deals with the conflict between Frank King, a private landowner proud of his individuality and hard-won achievements with the land, and the new social order that is imposing a policy of collectivism of private property. Dominating the action are the masks and demonlike figures of an annual carnival that represents the end of the old and the beginning of the new, the death that insures revival and growth. A subsidiary theme lies in the groping attempts of several young people, alienated from their community, to find a certain solace and security in love. Still another dimension is added by the local barber who regularly stages the carnival entertainment; this rather cryptic figure suggests the seemingly inadvertent malice, if not evil, of one who derives satisfaction from manipulating the lives of others. All of these forces finally come together and contribute to the disaster crowning the action of the play — the accidental killing of King's retarded son by one of the innocent young lovers who happens to be one of the masquers. The play has no clear-cut meaning; its appeal and power reside in suggestiveness and various metaphoric levels of action involving the earth, death, and ritual enactment.

The second of these less readily classifiable plays is *The Heavenly Ascension of Saška Christ* (Nanebevstoupení Sašky Krista) by František Pavlíček (b. 1923), first performed in 1967. Based on stories by Isaac Babel, it is every bit as tentative, if not as ambivalent, as Topol's *End of Carnival* in its attitudes toward the sociopolitical realities of its time. The action occurs in 1920 in the interior of a Catholic church situated in a part of Russia where Bolshevik troops have been battling Polish troops in seesaw encounters along a constantly shifting front at a time when the Soviet system has not yet eliminated all resistance. At the moment, the church is occupied by the Bolsheviks during Easter week; the action spans Wednesday through Saturday. Nearly two dozen characters and a rapidly evolving, seemingly random series of encounters make us aware of the turbulence of the times, of the violence and cruelty accompanying the revolutionary spirit and its attempts to stabilize the results of the revolution. Concurrently, we are aware of the charity and sacrifices of individuals. As the action swirls on outside and within the church, a sense of incertitude about the ultimate values of the revolution prevails. The decisive additional element in this situation is an eccentric artist who, in the midst of the chaos around him, is painting a series of murals in the church depicting Christ's journey to the cross and His ascension. From his painter's scaffold, which hovers above the action, he observes and comments on what he sees, with his observations ranging from outright skepticism about the value of the Bolshevik movement to a speculation on its potential for the good of humanity: "God's scourge — for good or evil, who can tell?"

This is an unschematic, undidactic, truly ambivalent work with impressive imaginative scope — a genuine *teatro mundi*. The fundamental theme, expressed primarily in the observations of the painter, is the human obsession with raising oneself, an urge that forms the one immortal human element. As the painter says, "Onward — one more grave — one truth at the cost of a thousand bitter doubts — the eternal step between despair and hope."

Ladislav Smoček's *Cosmic Spring* (Kosmické jaro), first performed in March 1970 by the Drama Club, was probably the last notable original Czech work to be performed in Czechoslovakia after the August 1968 invasion, and its theme and perspectives are among the most all-inclusive of the works under consideration. I include it here because it is more representative of the 1960s than the 1970s. In tone and theme it is essentially an extended, open-ended "Essay on Man" in dramatic form, a speculative parable transcending easy categories, including satire. As its central character declares, "Everything that is, lies on the other side of optimism and pessimism."

A country house is about to be demolished to serve the dubious ends of progress: the countryside is being stripped for ore to feed a new foundry in the area. References to slag heaps and ash-laden smoke are frequent. The dying master of the house is devoting his remaining hours to a concentrated search for a rationale of life as he has perceived it. In the house (and suggesting a ship of fools) are a motley group of eccentric neighbors and random acquaintances who, along with the industrial cancer outside, seem to illustrate the humors, absurdities, and at times horrors of the world that the dying old man would attempt to define. The play is a rambling, overextended, at times confusing mixture of farce (the crowd) and metaphysical, poetic speculation (the dying man's soliloquies). Depth of characterization is distinctly secondary to the creation of a total, complex vision of human beings in relation to each other and to the cosmos. Reminiscent of *The Cherry Orchard* and *Endgame* in its sense of a terminal action, *Cosmic Spring* is also like *Heartbreak House* in suggesting faith in the sheer continuity of life and human efforts to persevere.

The dying man (who in the abstract might remind one of Karel Čapek) reviews human gullibility, greed, cruelties, and ignorance: "We reject God and know nothing, we believe in God and know nothing." He rejects the concepts of progress

Ladislav Smoček's original production of his own Cosmic Spring, *at the Drama Club, 1970. Photo by Vilém Sochůrek.*

and equality, all organized systems of brotherhood, and the human need for a "happy end." Seemingly alienated from utopian socialism or any other sociopolitical system, he does not settle for an easy nihilism. Rather, an attitude of sustained, uncommitted alertness is conveyed, a view of life with open eyes and mind, no longer credulous but not yet despairing — perhaps the most that might realistically be expected from a citizen of Czechoslovakia in the twentieth century, and perhaps of our world. In the epilogue, as a home movie of the old man is shown, his niece reads his last words, which end the play:

> Project the light and shadow as a witness that I actually existed, that I wasn't a phantasm, just as all history has not been a sham, and continue to search out

just what sort of creature I was. Perhaps we're rushing toward other worlds and eternity, who can say? Above me is a roof . . . beyond it, beyond clouds and away from earth in all directions is space. Light reaches all the way here from there. And I have light in me as there is light in a spider crawling over rough plaster, casting a shadow. It's imprisoned in us and doesn't emerge. While my hair grows and so do my nails, the air outside is cold as a mountain stream. Clouds are isolated, and you can see far into space.

Neither unqualified affirmation nor outright ridicule is expressed in this last group of plays. The transition from the unambiguous moral imperatives of the 1950s to the abstract, apolitical, even amoral ending of *Cosmic Spring* is a major one. Although the postwar Czech plays discussed in this chapter almost always communicated an awareness of the specific ideological and materialistic forces shaping the lives of their nation and its people, most of the plays remained humanistic in their broader implications. At an informal meeting of Czech writers several months after the climactic events of August 1968, Václav Havel made a statement that represented the attitude of most of his contemporaries:

What should theatre do, actually? According to my opinion it should awaken in man his authenticity; it should help him to become aware of himself in the full span of his problems, to understand the situation in which he lives, to provoke him to think about himself. Next to this true authenticity there exists, of course, authenticity that is actually obscurity, false, when theatre doesn't try to awaken in man a consciousness of his real problems but on the contrary helps his natural tendency to solve these problems superficially or actually to lie his way out of them or bypass them in the most varied ways. . . . At most, I can only help the spectator to formulate problems, which he must solve himself.[14]

6

The Dynamic 1960s, Part Two
Key Productions in New Studio Theatres and Elsewhere

The surge in provocative new plays in the late 1950s and the 1960s went hand in hand with new vitality and imaginativeness in their staging, as already suggested in the previous chapter. All Czech theatres, from the National Theatre to smaller regional theatres in the provinces, began to do much more interesting production work in the 1960s, but the most fresh and innovative work could be seen in a number of newly established small theatres in Prague. I saw much of the work of these theatres during extended residencies in Prague in 1965 and in 1968–1969, as well as a brief visit in the fall of 1970, by which time most of the creative flow of the 1960s had been shut off as a result of the August 1968 invasion and its aftermath.[1]

Before focusing on the new ensembles, some attention should be given to notable production work in established theatres, beyond the productions already mentioned in the previous chapter. Krejča's 1964 National Theatre staging of Topol's *End of Carnival* was, of course, one major example, as was his *Romeo and Juliet* in that same theatre a year earlier, with two of his strongest young actors, Jan Tříska (b. 1936) and Marie Tomášová (b. 1929). In his scenography for each, Josef Svoboda worked variations on the principle of kinetic scenery, which entailed physical movement during the course of the action. The most celebrated example of this was a loggia in *Romeo and Juliet* that seemed to float upstage and downstage during the action; in *End of Carnival* three rectangular projection screens would swoop down from the space above the stage to form a full rear wall onto which projections would be cast, after which the screens would be lifted out. Two other important productions of the National Theatre in the early 1960s were *Oedipus the King* (1963) and the Čapek brothers' *Insect Comedy* (1965), both directed by actor-director Miroslav Macháček. A huge staircase filling the entire stage became the playing area in *Oedipus*, and two large tilted mirrors at the rear of a stage turntable providing a kaleidoscopic view of the teeming "insect" life on the stage floor formed the basis of Svoboda's scenography for *Insect Comedy*. Underlying most of Svoboda's scenography was a premise — both his and most of his directors' — that scenography is essentially an *instrument* that may have as expressive and dynamic a role in a production as the performers. The scenographer is the one responsible for the design, placement, and "action" of everything on stage other than the performers, which would include not only all manner of material objects and forms — realistic, abstract, or metaphoric, of whatever material — but also lighting and sound.

Beyond the work of the National Theatre, any consideration of creative work in Czech theatre during the 1960s must take into account the further distinctive contributions of Alfred Radok, who had left the National Theatre to head the newly organized Laterna Magika project in 1958. At loose ends after being dismissed from that post in 1959, he was fortunately hired by Ota Ornest for the Muncipal Theatres of Prague, an established producing entity comprising several stages. In these theatres between 1961 and 1965 Radok directed seven productions, several of which were among the highpoints of Czech theatre of that decade. For example, his 1963 version of Gogol's *Marriage* produced a scathing farcical image of boorish, primitive provincial life in Czarist Russia that was a thinly veiled comment on all things Russian as perceived by most Czechs after more than fifteen years of Russian Communist indoctrination.

But Radok's greatest achievement of the 1960s, and many would say of his whole career, was his adaptation of Romain Rolland's *The Play of Love and Death* in 1964, which I had the good luck to see in 1965. Dealing with episodes from the French Revolution, the production exhibited Radok's strongest talents, an intuitive perception of the paradoxes and ironies inherent in any human social situation and the ability to embody that complex perception on stage with maximum theatrical impact. Here his central conceit was the simultaneous juxtaposition of the two worlds of the play, that of the doomed aristocracy and that of the revolutionary mob, in the brilliant physical metaphor of a rough-hewn bear pit enclosing the hapless, still posturing aristocrats while the French mob mocked and abused them from their perch on wooden benches above the enclosure. It was a scenic metaphor employed throughout the many scenes of the play, totally invented by Radok and given stage form by his regular scenographer in those years, Ladislav Vychodil (b. 1920), a Moravian who worked mainly in Slovakia. An original musical score accompanied the action, much of which Radok deliberately staged as an ironic parody of operetta conventions, with some of the leading figures occasionally

Radok and Vychodil's The Play of Love and Death, *1964. Photo by L. Dittrich. Photo from the Theatre Institute, Prague.*

singing their lines. The flow of scene after scene was arresting as the problematic pathos and "theatre" of all revolutions were played out with implicit echoes, for the Czechs, of the impact on them of the Russian Communist revolutions of 1917.

Still another memorable production by Radok in the 1960s was his adaptation of Gorky's novel *The Last Ones* in 1966 at the National Theatre, to which he had just returned. In this production, which dealt with a corrupted officer and his family in Czarist Russia, he and Svoboda employed the Laterna Magika system for the first time in the staging of a traditional play. The offstage actions of some of the characters were shown as film projections on the rear wall of the set at carefully chosen moments, in deliberate juxtaposition to the onstage action, as often to ironicize the onstage action as to reinforce it. This use of dual perspective, one of Radok's signature methods, was symptomatic of his vision of human experience, a painfully learned skepticism of face values and surface ideals.

Visitors to Prague in the 1960s were also particularly impressed by the work of certain "small" theatres (malá divadla): relatively new and youthful ensembles that had broken away from some patterns of the permanent repertory system. The reputation of these theatres was further enhanced by their appearances abroad, for example, at the World Theatre Season at the Aldwych Theatre in London.

Radok and Svoboda's production of Gorky's The Last Ones, *1966, suggesting the implied interaction of filmed and living characters. Photo by Jaromír Svoboda.*

(Prague's National Theatre had already appeared at the Aldwych in 1966 with Macháček's production of the Čapeks' *Insect Comedy*.) Beginning in 1967, three of these new small theatre companies appeared there a total of four times, making Prague the best represented capital at this international festival. The three theatres so honored were the Theatre on the Balustrade, the Drama Club, and the Theatre beyond the Gate.

    These distinctive companies began to form in the late 1950s. They remained active despite the events of 1968, and two of them are still very much alive today, more than thirty years later. A consideration of their evolution, especially during their first ten years, provides insight into a variety of theatre concepts and methods familiar to us in other contexts. Theatre of the Absurd, Epic theatre, theatre

[114] MODERN CZECH THEATRE

as game and therapy, "engaged" theatre — such theatre phenomena assume new meanings and values when viewed in relation to the special sociocultural contexts within which these Prague theatres developed. Their choice of themes and forms as well as their special approaches to the art of theatre were, not surprisingly for Czech theatre, a reflection of the stresses shaping their society.

The small, artistically independent theatres of Prague did not emerge in a vacuum, nor did they lack prototypes. They began within the context of an extensive state-supported theatre system, although they were in strong opposition to most aspects of that system. Distinctly original in many respects, particularly in Czechoslovakia of the late fifties and early sixties, they also revived and followed a notable Czech tradition of small, unorthodox theatres most signally associated with the work of E. F. Burian, Jindřich Honzl, Jiří Frejka, and the comic team of Voskovec and Werich in the 1920s and 1930s. Indeed, even earlier prototypes may be found in some of the cabarets of the pre–World War I era, as described in chapter 2.

After the traumas and stresses of the war and of the new Communist regime, several needs became apparent in the 1950s, including the need for an outlet for creative talents that had been bottled up for the better part of a decade and the need to explore contemporary reality and its problems without illusions or evasions. The opportunity to satisfy these and related needs did not come about suddenly as the result of a few obvious circumstances. Nevertheless, as originally noted, conditions began to improve after the denunciation of Stalinist cult and dogma during the Twentieth Congress of the Communist Party in the Soviet Union in 1956, the reverberations of which profoundly influenced not only the sociopolitical life but also the cultural and artistic life of all Communist bloc countries.

In Czechoslovakia the lid was not completely off, but it became unsealed, and the pressure of accumulated artistic energies began to be released. Moreover, although the mechanism of suppression had run down and become relatively powerless unless directly challenged, there were still enough restrictions and obstacles to freedom to provide a target and to stimulate indirect criticism and subtlety of expression in the arts. What had been feared could now — given skill and wit — be examined, probed, speculated on, and not infrequently satirized, as it had already begun to be in the National Theatre in the Krejča and Radok era of the late 1950s. It was within this climate that the significant development of the new small theatres occurred.

Fundamental to the fresh urge in theatre was a rejection of the entrenched repertory system of the permanent state theatres, which ranged from the colossus of the National Theatre to the slightly less grand Vinohrady Theatre but also included smaller state or municipally supported repertory theatres. These "stone" theatres all had in common not only monumental architecture but relatively inflexible operations. The new small theatres sought a break from the model of a large company and elaborate administrative machinery (with its inevitable internal frictions and cabals), from a fixed number of premieres and reprises each season, which in turn virtually necessitated crowded, inadequate rehearsal schedules, and from a repertoire requiring a certain universality of play selection to guarantee adequate attendance, thus forcing both actors and directors to work on many productions of limited challenge and interest to them. Instead, the ideal became a small group of kindred artists working together in small, manageable quarters with a drastically reduced production machinery, selecting works to which they could genuinely commit themselves, rehearsing until they felt the production was ready, and playing for an audience composed not of "average viewers," but of those attuned to their special kind of theatre, whatever it might be. (Actually, this comes close to describing what Otomar Krejča had already been working toward with his team *within* the grand frame of the National Theatre starting in 1957.)

In the early phases of the new movement, traditional theatrical form based on a tightly structured dramatic text was put aside in favor of a looser assemblage or montage of literature and music, consisting of "small forms" such as stories, anecdotes, songs, poetry, mime, and dialogue. Part of the rationale behind this change was the belief that such brief creations were less subject to the inflated, schematic, and ultimately hollow treatment associated with the more traditional theatre against which the movement was reacting. Implicit in many of the observations of both practitioners and theorists of the new theatre movement was a sense of theatre as a game, of theatre as play. At the very least, the creation of informal, open communication between stage and audience was vital: a shift from one-way proclamation to dialogue, to a form of mutual participation in the act of theatre, to a sharing of experience. In this, of course, the new wave of these theatres was to some extent parallel to similar tendencies in the West, especially in the United States in the Beatnik era and beyond (e.g., Caffe Cino, La MaMa).

The seedbed of the "small forms," assemblage type of production was in fact not a theatre at all, but a wine tavern, the Reduta, which featured jazz performances in the mid-fifties. Beginning in 1957, Jiří Suchý (b. 1931), a lyricist and popular singer, invited Ivan Vyskočil (b. 1929), a psychology and philosophy major as well as a graduate of the Theatre Academy (DAMU), to join with him in a number of casually structured entertainments that became known as "text appeals" to stress their literary component as distinct from more popular nightclub or musical cabaret entertainment. The programs consisted of Suchý's songs and Vyskočil's witty, topical monologues, later augmented by poetry readings, brief sketches, and other informal, semi-improvised theatrical elements marked by intellectual bite as well as amiable clowning. Deliberately undidactic, casual, and individualistic, consciously cultivating a degree of imperfection and lack of finish, the small forms embodied in rather pure form characteristics long absent and sorely missed in Czech theatre.

Subsequently, the model of the Reduta "text appeals" evolved in two directions. In one (what came to be the Semafor model) it retained its essential small-forms features, and in the other (the Balustrade model) it blended with more conventional theatre elements, thereby losing its own distinct features but continuing to provide stimulus and flavor to the work of many smaller ensembles in Prague and in the provinces.[2]

The overlapping stories of the Balustrade and the Semafor need sorting out. In the fall of 1958 Suchý and Vyskočil, in a move to expand and provide more order to their irregular performances at the Reduta, founded the Theatre on the Balustrade (Divadlo Na zábradlí) in a former storage warehouse near the banks of the Vltava in the Old Town section of Prague. Under their leadership during that first season of 1958–1959, the productions were rooted in the Reduta pattern, but with the difference that they incorporated the small-form, text-appeal features into somewhat more conventionally staged works and laid more stress on the literary elements. The first production, in October 1958, *If a Thousand Clarinets* (Kdyby tisíc klarinetů), was essentially a fully staged text-appeal with a strong musical component as well as mime, the work of Ladislav Fialka (1931–1991) and his youthful troupe. Soon after, within the first season, a takeoff on *Faust* already possessed certain features of straight drama.

During the first season, however, Suchý decided that he might put his special musical talents to better use in another organization or production format. He joined with a young composer, Jiří Šlitr (1924–1969), to launch the Semafor Theatre in October 1959, leaving Vyskočil in charge of the Balustrade. Because its chief element is music, the Semafor falls outside the central focus of this study, but one or two of its features are worth noting, as discussed below. Like Suchý, Fialka split from the core group after the first season, but he and his troupe remained as a self-contained unit at the Balustrade, alternating their own series of mime performances with those of the drama ensemble. Since Fialka's troupe toured a great deal, the Balustrade became primarily a drama theatre, with occasional musical elements.

Following Suchý's departure and Fialka's severance to form his own unit within the Balustrade in 1959, Vyskočil continued his experiments with original satirical, offbeat works based on an assemblage of elements and a program that focused on the actor-audience relationship: the appeal of the performance was primarily through its performers, and central to the appeal was the creation of a relaxed, playful mood between performers and spectators.

A retrospective article about the early years of the small theatre movement made a particularly astute observation about a characteristic already noted: the early efforts of the Balustrade were not a move toward increasingly polished, sophisticated work but had significance precisely in their devotion to seemingly imperfect forms. "The postulate of seeking an adequate form for an urgent message doesn't apply, because more conspicuously than in any other art or genre the form here is itself the message — precisely in its lack of finish, incompletion, and . . . lack of finality."[3]

By the 1960–1961 season, *Autostop*, the theatre's fifth production, revealed a relatively more unified, coherent dramatic form, though still not that of a traditionally structured play. It consisted of monologues, direct address to the audience, and satirical sketches presided over by Vyskočil and unified by a demonstration of automobile mania — grotesqueries displaying the obsession of many Czechs with possession of an automobile. It was, as Vyskočil pointed out, intended to show the unnaturalness and absurdity of such materialism from the point of view of socialist humanism. The work was done on a bare stage with black drapes, a few chairs, a table, and minimal props. The actors were advised not to play characters but to play about the characters; in short, to adopt an approach we tend to associate with Epic acting, including a frank orientation toward the audience.

Autostop marked the culmination of the Vyskočil era at the Balustrade, three years notable for experiments with actor-audience relationships, stemming from Vyskočil's interest in psychology and anthropology. By 1961 Vyskočil apparently felt that he had taken his work as far as it would go at the Balustrade. Perhaps preferring the more flexible, individualistic format of the earlier years, he returned to the Reduta, where he presumably felt more at home.

Meanwhile, Suchý and Šlitr's Semafor had been evolving a life of its own since 1959. The name "Semafor" is composed of the initial sounds of the Czech words for "seven little forms" (i.e., song, dance, instrumental music, mime, poetry readings, skits, dialogues), thus suggesting the essential nature of their productions, which proved to be of immediate and lasting popularity. The team of Suchý and Šlitr stayed together until Šlitr's accidental death early in 1969. Suchý has continued the Semafor Theatre to the present.

The cultural significance of the Semafor and its basic small-forms pattern was well expressed by a Prague critic describing what this type of theatre provided:

"an escape from the emptiness of big words to small, ordinary ones . . . full of real life. From serious, celebrational lies to jokes that capture truth with the hook of absurdity . . . a theatre that didn't programmatically insist on anything."[4] The theatrical significance of the Semafor lay in its implicit rejection of conventional dramatic and theatrical forms as well as in its reappraisal of professionalism in theatre. Suchý's attitude was indicative: "In the Semafor we ask for professionalism of work, not professionally trained actors . . . because they are trained for a different type of theatre and a different kind of acting."[5] The Semafor entertainment places special demands on the self-creativity and the distinctive personality of the performer, not on skills in creating the illusion of fictional characters.

After Vyskočil's departure, the Balustrade moved more decisively toward a more conventionally ordered dramatic form accompanied by a shift of emphasis from the personality of the performer toward the theme or ideas of the total presentation, both tendencies already observable in *Autostop*. Moreover, the mixture of absurdist and Epic elements found in *Autostop* developed into the single most distinctive theatrical feature of what came to be known as the Grossman-Havel era, from 1961 to 1968.

Jan Grossman (1925–1993), who had been a dramaturg under E. F. Burian after the war (and later an important critic), became head of the drama wing at the Balustrade in 1962. Václav Havel, who became the most widely known of the Czech postwar playwrights, was first a stagehand at the Balustrade before collaborating with Vyskočil on *Autostop*.[6] Havel, who moved into the position of dramaturg at the Balustrade when Grossman became head of drama, set the tone of the Balustrade's peak years, 1963–1966, with his two plays *The Garden Party* (November 1963) and *The Memorandum* (July 1965). These original works were complemented by a repertoire stressing modern Western drama with absurdist motifs: Jarry's *Ubu Roi* (1964), Ionesco's *Bald Soprano* and *The Lesson* (1964), Beckett's *Waiting for Godot* (1964), and Grossman's own dramatization of Kafka's *The Trial* (1966). With the production of these Czech and foreign plays the Balustrade achieved international recognition, toured throughout Europe, and helped bring Prague theatre back into the mainstream of Western theatre culture.

Under Grossman and Havel, the Balustrade became program or concept centered. Grossman put it this way: a repertoire should emerge "not from a list of original, interesting, or unproduced plays, but from an attempt to analyze contemporary problematic issues and the typical conflicts and knots in which such problematics are snarled; only then ought we to search for [dramatic] material and methods of staging it."[7]

Central to the Balustrade's entire program were an elaboration and development of Vyskočil's concept of revitalizing the impalpable, nonverbal contact between stage and audience. Grossman and Havel referred to the Balustrade as an "appellative" theatre, meaning, in Grossman's words, "a theatre that elected a certain approach to reality, to the world in which we live and in which as its contemporaries we act — here and now for something and against something . . . a theatre that wants above all to pose questions to the spectator, often provocative and extreme ones, and it counts on a spectator who is inclined to reply to these questions."[8]

Implicit in these statements was a shift from the personal and psychological to the social, from interpersonal rapport between stage and auditorium to a challenging of the viewers' attitudes and values regarding the problematic relationship of the individual to society. The viewers were called upon to share an experience and at the same time to respond by comparing their frame of reference to the world presented to them by the stage. The stage presented a certain model of human social experience, more often than not a hyperbolic, grotesque, absurd one in which nonsense was juxtaposed with banality, the unnatural with the natural, the gratuitous with the logical. And the viewers were asked to confront these discrepancies, to evaluate them in the light of their own experiences. The combination of an absurd subject and the rational, purposeful — indeed, Epic — handling of it was provocative. This approach worked well with all the Balustrade plays mentioned but found its fullest realization, understandably enough, in the plays of Havel. "I know of no dramatist more exact and rational than Havel," Grossman observed, "and at the same time no plays in which the spectator participates more and in more varied fashion."[9]

The curtain line was not broken, and the spectators did not become fellow actors, but they were expected to participate — perhaps emotionally, but certainly intellectually. The Balustrade productions of that time, as Karel Kraus reported, "do not draw the viewer into the play but provoke him to take a stand, do not suggest a solution but count instead on his intellectual revolt. The center of gravity shifts from the stage to the space between stage and audience."[10]

Havel's *The Garden Party* and *The Memorandum* are both social satires with primary relevance to the sociopolitical and, indeed, psychic scene of contemporary Czechoslovakia, but their relevance extends to any technocratic, bureaucratic, amoral world of presumed efficiency but no humanity or purpose, the ideal symbol of which is probably the cybernetic machine. *Garden Party* and *Memorandum* are models of this unnatural world. The Balustrade productions of these plays were not intended to suggest that life is inherently absurd, but to challenge the audience. In short, Grossman viewed Absurd theatre not as a final statement of the world's condition but as a means toward possible salvation or, at least, therapy: "Absurd theatre is analytic and, if you will, coldly diagnostic. It offers no solutions . . . not in the certainty that solutions don't exist . . . but that no solution will ever, at any place, by any one, in any way, be given to us. . . . Absurd theatre takes on the function of devil's advocate . . . in order to reveal the devil."[11] It was Absurd theatre with a thoroughly non-Absurd, socially concerned, Brechtian-Epic purpose.

The Balustrade approach to staging *per se* was experimental only to a limited extent. Grossman's attitude toward experiment was expressed pointedly: "I believe in experimentation that is concrete, practical, technically communicable and expressible . . . the most important experiment to be done is in fact always done, but no one knows how to do it well — that is, rehearsal."[12] Grossman went on to explain that the Balustrade's two or three premieres a year allowed for a special approach to each play, as if it were an unknown country about which the artists had no preconceptions, about which they were uncertain. He found such moments of uncertainty, especially at the beginning of the rehearsal period, perhaps the most inspiring moments of the production work as a whole: "Uncertainty becomes a maximally long maintaining of 'open space,' which allows for the most varied sorts of approaches and decisions."[13] It was not that the productions lacked an overall plan, but that such plans were themselves always subject to testing and adjustment by the action of the company as a creative ensemble that included designers, technical personnel, the composer, and, of course, the author when possible. What is particularly noteworthy about this approach is that although Grossman introduced a program of works considerably more complex, more deliberately socially oriented and critical, and more professionally performed than those of the prior years, he did not reject the fundamental openness and flexibility of performance that marked the early Balustrade.

The sheer physical limitations of the Balustrade Theatre necessitated considerable inventiveness in scene design and staging. Despite subsequent reconstruction, they still do. The auditorium seated about 200 in a narrow orchestra and small rear balcony. The stage was perhaps 18 feet wide and 25 feet deep, with limited fly-space and virtually no offstage space at the sides. On a stage that was usually bare, a few basic platforms, perhaps scaffolding, a few panels or screens, a table and some chairs, and a few other properties were placed and shifted about quite openly, to suggest various locales and to assume various functions. Grossman's description of the *Ubu Roi* set applied to most Balustrade productions. He referred to a raked floor, terminating in an irregularly cut and cracked wall:

Jan Grossman's dramatization of Kafka's The Trial *at the Balustrade Theatre, 1966. Photo by Jaroslav Krejčí.*

Practically the only decorations are old brass beds, an iron fire escape ladder, three garbage cans, some crates and tin cans. All these objects are authentic, but at the same time technically adjusted for the greatest possible variations: the beds alternately change into tables, platforms for military parades, a staircase; the garbage cans also act as wardrobes . . . or serve as execution machines and armor.[14]

The acting at the Balustrade during Grossman's era and beyond was dynamic and competent, but it would not be accurate to refer to the Balustrade as an actors' theatre. A half-dozen or fewer gifted, skilled actors formed the core of the ensemble; others were brought in as occasion demanded. The Balustrade's priorities, certainly under Grossman, were a socially oriented concept encompassing a blend of the Absurd and Epic (the latter sans ideology), followed by the text, the director, and only then the staging and acting.

The Grossman-Havel era at the Balustrade culminated in 1966 with the production of Kafka's *The Trial*, dramatized and directed by Grossman. To present the facts of Kafka's story in a chillingly ordinary way, the interpretation avoided any suggestion of expressionistic, nightmarish distortion. On a scaffolded, cage-like turntable, the action was presented as if seen through K's eyes. The premise of Grossman's interpretation was that K's guilt is simply his inadvertent complicity in the process that finally eliminates him. As Grossman said, the absurd is not the basis of the action, but its result.[15]

After the success of *The Trial*, the Balustrade's reputation began to exceed its accomplishments. Although European tours and acclaim followed for several years, no new work of significance emerged. New productions were staged but were repetitive of earlier work; what had been fresh and relevant now seemed mechanical, clichéd, and prefabricated. Even Havel seemed to run dry. His last play at the Balustrade, *The Increased Difficulty of Concentration*, in April 1968, essentially retraced familiar paths: the dehumanization of life in a schematic, technocratic civilization; the plight of the well-meaning but self-defeating intellectual. These were viable themes but they were by now familiar, for the Zeitgeist had evolved and the Balustrade company was left behind. Internal personnel problems of the theatre simply added to the tensions. The second era of the Balustrade ended with the departure of both Havel and Grossman at the end of the 1967–1968 season, before the August invasion. One is tempted to infer some connection between their departure and the political events of that period, but apparently the timing was purely coincidental.

The third era of the Balustrade lacked a clear outline. The new head of the drama wing, Jaroslav Gillar (b. 1942), formerly Grossman's assistant, was a young man who saw a need for a broader, fresher repertoire policy. He would have liked, he said, to work toward a more full-blooded theatricality with poetic, perhaps romantic and, indeed, metaphysical overtones without losing touch with the classic vaudeville tradition. The goal, in Gillar's words, was a *teatro mundi*.

Gillar's first production, a highly stylized, savage interpretation of Shakespeare's *Timon of Athens* (February 1969), was clearly a response to the trauma of the Soviet-led invasion of August 1968. The production underlined the corruption, decadence, and treachery inherent in the play. Gillar introduced masks, choreographed fights, surrealistically distorted speech and movement, and a great deal of incidental business to underline the sheer morbidity of the world that Timon rejects. It was a vivid, powerful production, but it suggested a degree of excess straining after sometimes gratuitous effects, although it resonated with the dislocated times of the 1968–1969 season.

The Drama Club and the Theatre beyond the Gate (hereafter simply Gate Theatre) were the most recent of the special, drama-oriented small theatres of Prague. Both were established in 1965. To find two theatres with more radically different features would be difficult, yet both reacted against the fixed, institutionalized repertory operations of the permanent "stone" theatres and both endeavored to view people and society inquiringly and freshly, without habitualized conceptions.

The Drama Club comprised the most tightly knit "family" of artists among all Czech theatres of the time and was also perhaps the most self-contained of all Czech theatres because of its several resident playwrights and the multiple talents of its leading personnel. In its first six years of existence, it retained virtually all its key acting ensemble. Its chief actors were classmates at DAMU in Prague before going as a group to one of the regional repertory theatres (the Bezruč Theatre in Ostrava), where they worked together for several seasons. They were brought to the Drama Club by their director, Jan Kačer (b. 1936), who joined the two original founders of the Drama Club at their invitation in the first year of its existence. Ladislav Smoček and Jaroslav Vostrý (b. 1934), the two founders, had varied talents, as did Kačer. Smoček, who initiated the concept of what became the Drama Club, was both director and playwright; Vostrý both director and theorist-critic; and Kačer both actor and director. (Vostrý's wife, Alena, like Smoček, was one of the leading young playwrights in Czechoslovakia.) The three directors had been fellow students at DAMU in Prague in the mid-fifties, and they remained the guiding force behind the Drama Club for the first decade or more of its existence.

The physical quarters of the Drama Club were the most restrictive of any of the theatres under discussion. Like the Balustrade, the Drama Club was not originally a theatre; the building first housed a women's club. Then as now, like the Balustrade, it also seated about 200, but in a shallower, broader seating arrangement, and had a narrow, three-sided balcony. The small stage lacked adequate flyspace and was wider than it was deep. Offstage space was virtually nonexistent, and dressing room facilities were limited. In most respects it would be thought utterly unsatisfactory as a production space, and yet its very smallness and intimacy were in complete accord with its style of performance, specifically its acting. Nothing was lost, every gesture and facial expression counted, and the acting could be low-keyed when necessary and still project clearly. Moreover, the very intimacy encouraged a kind of implicit rapport with the audience, the vast majority of whom were the theatre's long-standing devotees. Like the Balustrade, the Drama Club did not indulge in direct communication or physical contact with the audience; the fourth wall was always there. But it was distinctly permeable, and the persons on each side had an unspoken amiable relationship with those on the other. There was no mistaking the actors' alert, albeit indirect, awareness of the audience, and, in turn, the audience's agreeable acceptance of this awareness.

Of the three small theatres being described, the Drama Club performed the largest number of original Czech plays; in fact, nearly half of the fifteen plays that it produced from 1965 to 1969 were written by its own members. Smoček wrote four, Alena Vostrá two, and one of the actors, Pavel Landovský (b. 1936), one. Although one might take this as an indication of an author- or script-oriented theatre, the Drama Club was in fact an actors' theatre par excellence.

The dominant position of the actor in the Drama Club was integrally related to the conviction that a theatre ought to explore the "possibilities of man" by presenting "man in play" (the phrases were Vostrý's). The term "play" was central to the Drama Club's rationale and carried several meanings: play as action, as distinct from the static; play in the sense of game; and play with all its theatrical connotations.

The repertoire of the Drama Club reflected the actor-centered philosophy of the theatre's operation. Plays were chosen for themes relating to questions of human freedom and responsibility, particularly with reference to the individual and society or, as Vostrý expressed it, "encounters of individual human possibilities with actuality."[16] In contrast to Grossman's program at the Balustrade, the Drama Club's program was not focused on rational, ideational issues related to organized contemporary society, but on depicting people within a sphere of more generic forces, tensions, and moods and on observing their behavior patterns, their psychic pressure points. Tacitly questioning any system that accounts for human behavior on the basis of positivistic, materialistic, or economic categories (e.g., Marxism), Vostrý's approach involved no analysis, formal critique, or even tentative conclusions, other than that people were complex, unchartable beings whose attempts at realizing themselves often conflict with similar attempts by others. The original plays at the Drama Club deliberately accentuated these motifs, and other plays in the repertoire, such as *Crime and Punishment*, *The Cherry Orchard*, and *The Birthday Party*, certainly lent themselves to such an interpretation.

The entire issue of actor-human, play, and possibilities was succinctly expressed by Vostrý: "The discovery of the actor's possibilities is . . . the discovery of the 'possibilities' of humanity — and after all, that's what theatre art is concerned with first."[17] To facilitate the exploration of these "possibilities" the Drama Club addressed itself to the relation of the actors to the text. The actors' temperaments, their egos, received priority and were valued in themselves; only then were they adapted to the demands of the text. It was not that the actors played themselves, but that they achieved a full realization of themselves in their roles. They drew upon and projected their personalities as part of the creative process.

This theoretical basis of the Drama Club's view of theatre and of the actor most nearly found its fulfillment in the plays of Smoček and Vostrá. Smoček tended to concentrate on the interplay of distinct individuals in situations of stress. His characters are not made clear at the beginning of a play but define themselves in action, by their reactions to specific incidents. Aggression and violence are recurrent motifs in Smoček's work, sometimes seriously (*Piknik*, 1965), sometimes in a farcical context (*Dr. Burke's Strange Afternoon* [Podivné odpoledne doktora Zvonka Burkeho], 1966), sometimes more implicit than overt (*The Maze*, 1966), but in each case the limits of human freedom and the relation of the individual to other members of society are the center of attention.

Even more richly provocative in their embodiment of the rationale of the Drama Club were the plays of Alena Vostrá, especially her first to be presented there, *When Your Number Comes Up*, directed by Jan Kačer in 1966. The self-conscious games the characters play on others and among themselves give them a sense of being in control, of manipulating others. The relation to the exploring of human possibilities, human freedom, and responsibility is obvious. In a joint note published with the play, the Vostrýs offered an elaboration of the basic theme of the play. I expand on the translation (in brackets) in order to approximate the ambiguities inherent in some key Czech words and their syntax:

> In this comedy we're dealing with a play [in the sense of game] within a play ... an activity with no purpose beyond itself.... In the play of people with other people, it is not unusual to have victims. In fact, the victims in this sort of play [game] may be its very own creators: the situation that they provoke may develop in a variety of unexpected ways. It is, if you will, a play-model of every human activity, the risks of which always reside in an encounter with the "counter-activities" of all the agents that become drawn into the play [game].[18]

The authors go on to refer to additional significances of "play" in this play, such as illusion and reality, role playing, chance and fate. Their note then concludes with the following revealing comment:

> Yes, this is a play of the Drama Club, some of whose themes and principles it reveals in its own way. As the saying goes, it was written in the theatre, not for a theatre that would then proceed to adapt it to its own ends; in fact, we have here a play that was to an extent "made to measure" for certain actors — in the literal as well as figurative sense: it counts on actors who can perform not only with their souls but also with their bodies — with complete actors and their own potential motifs, not with acting in the abstract. In this sense, also, the play is inseparable from the context of the theatre in which it was realized.[19]

The intricate convolutions and organic relation of concept and creation, art and life, stage and world, underlying the philosophy of the Drama Club could hardly be put more tellingly.

What were the overt features of the acting style resulting from this approach? Observers tended to note its vitality and freshness, its exuberance and acrobatics, qualities most fully displayed in productions such as Machiavelli's *Mandragora* (1965) and *When Your Number Comes Up*. But equally central was a kind of casual authority, a mastery of smaller, subtler, highly revealing physical actions. The acting was often called cinematic; as a matter of fact, most of the Drama Club's actors appeared in many films, often as a group. Moreover, some of the more celebrated Czech film directors, such as Jiří Menzel (b. 1938; *Closely Watched Trains*) and Evald Schorm (1931–1988; *Courage for Every Day*), directed at the Drama Club: Menzel staged *Mandragora*, and Schorm staged *Crime and Punishment* (1966) and Landovský's original play *Rooms by the Hour* (Hodinový Hotelier, 1969).

The acting was based on a sense of inner reality, but without the curse of excessive internalization; that is, it was realized in interplay with other actors, in an unusual degree of ensemble coherence. The plays and the acting stayed within the mainstream of realism, inclining toward enrichment of character rather than any distortion of character. Each actor created a sensuously graphic, textured reality — not like a fabricated, strained mask, but like a comfortable set of old clothes, if not a second skin. At the same time, such enrichment did not preclude selectivity, economy, or a fine sense of timing.

The acting appeared to best advantage in two types of plays: those of traditional psychological realism (*Crime and Punishment*, 1966; *The Cherry Orchard*, 1969) and farces relying on colorful characterization and inventive business (*Revizor*, 1967 — a brilliant mélange of secondary characters — and *Mandragora* — acrobatics and rich physical byplay between the lines). The Drama Club's production of Chekhov's *The Cherry Orchard* was characteristic in several ways. In general, the emphasis was on a material, physical interpretation played on a virtually bare, carpeted stage. Gone was the traditional attenuated lyricism, the creation of a soft-focus atmosphere, muted passions, and fragile ideals. Instead, the characters were sensuously real and frequently unattractive. Ranevskaya, for example, was not unusually sensitive, but a strained, near-hysterical woman of considerable sensuality. Trofimov was here less an idealist than an impotent failure thinly disguising his bitterness. The ludicrousness of the lesser characters was stressed, and the cherry orchard itself was more a concrete piece of real estate than a transcendental symbol.

Although usually effective, the acting could sometimes encounter difficulties. For example, the obverse of the advantages gained from relying so thoroughly on the actors' distinctive attributes was that one inevitably became aware of certain personal mannerisms and idiosyncrasies not always sufficiently adapted to the character or play as a whole. In the Drama Club production of Harold Pinter's *The Birthday Party* (1967), for example, the acting created a set of credible characters but ignored Pinter's carefully structured rhythms and precisely indicated pauses, thus throwing a substantial portion of the play out of alignment and generally sacrificing its elusiveness and eerie menace.

On another level the Drama Club actors, superbly adjusted to the dimensions of their small theatre and extremely effective in cameolike details, would probably have been less effective in roles demanding definition and color on a larger scale, in a considerably larger theatre, or in, say, Greek or Shakespearean tragedy. In the latter case, no doubt, the Greek or Shakespearean work would be adapted to the Drama Club's approach and strong points, rather than the other way around.

In summary, of the three drama ensembles under consideration, the Drama Club was the least overtly engaged in or responsive to the topical issues and tensions of the world outside the theatre. Implicitly rejecting any ideologically slanted view of humanity, it was, rather, extremely responsive to what it viewed as the complex interpersonal realities of human behavior underlying that world and to the embodiment of those realities by means of actors whose distinctly personal creativity was nurtured and given priority in the total production process.

The Gate Theatre, besides being the youngest of the successful breakaway theatres, was distinctive in having its roots in the established, permanent repertory system. As previously noted, Otomar Krejča had already been moving in a direction similar to that of the small theatres during his tenure at the National Theatre from 1956 to 1964. It was a tribute to his stature and clout that, despite his sometimes controversial productions there, he was given his own theatre. Moreover, when he began production at the Gate Theatre in November 1965 he brought with him from the National Theatre several key actors, including Jan Tříska and Marie Tomášová — his Romeo and Juliet — as well as Europe's most celebrated designer, Josef Svoboda. Although Svoboda and some of the actors still continued to work with the National Theatre, they formed the core of Krejča's strong production team at the Gate, which also included Karel Kraus, a close working associate of Krejča for years, as dramaturg and Josef Topol, playwright in residence.

In striking contrast to the Drama Club, the Gate Theatre was the most director-centered of the theatres being described and the one most clearly dominated by one man's artistic vision. Krejča, who directed or supervised all seven of the Gate's premieres, was a man of strong convictions and possessed the will to make his convictions prevail. By the end of the 1960s he had become acknowledged as a leading director not only in Czechoslovakia but abroad; his Gate ensemble toured throughout Europe, and he guest-directed in such centers as Brussels, Vienna,

Stockholm, and Salzburg. His productions ranged from flamboyant, large-cast spectacles to intimate, sonatalike duets, but they always provided evidence of a strongly conceptualized, many-layered interpretation as well as an inherent theatrical sensibility. The Gate Theatre, in short, produced a wider spectrum of theatrical entertainment than either the Balustrade or the Drama Club, and it carried the most theatrical voltage.

Although the Gate Theatre was a latecomer to the small theatre movement, Krejča himself had already battled long and hard to reform the "stone theatre" system. His significance was analogous to Vyskočil's in launching the Balustrade Theatre, even though the two approached the problem from radically different angles and favored radically different methods of production. In an era of dogmatic abstractions and formulas, Krejča probed the complexities of human social behavior. Moreover, while the heavy-handed marks of Socialist Realism still prevailed in much Czech staging, Krejča encouraged designers like Svoboda to create boldly expressive scenic designs such as the kinetic, poetically evocative scenography of *Romeo and Juliet* (1963).

Krejča's reasons for leaving the National Theatre were made clear in his own words:

> I don't believe in a theatrical colossus, in a theatre factory, in a theatre with several ensembles and buildings, with a dozen premieres each season, with a dozen performances a week. All of that contradicts the essence of theatre.... It seems to me that today's theatre ought to resemble a research institute for dramatic art rather than a production factory, a hand-craft workshop rather than an establishment for producing confectionery.[20]

Krejča sought a theatre in which he and others could do what they liked. A preliminary project in line with these sentiments was Krejča's guest-direction of two productions at the Balustrade Theatre in the early 1960s at the invitation of Jan Grossman: Claus Hubalek's *No More Heroes in Thebes* (1962) and Havel's *The Garden Party* (1963), with Svoboda designing both. His direction of the Havel play was particularly interesting because it was not the sort of work one associates with Krejča, yet the play's intricate, rational absurdities must certainly have appealed to him.

From its inception the Gate Theatre shared the facilities of Prague's Laterna Magika Theatre, which had opened in 1959 in a former subterranean movie theatre. Like the Balustrade and the Drama Club, it had to accommodate to quarters essentially unsuited to maximal staging opportunities. Although the theatre seated 450 in comfort, its stage was designed for the cinematic features of Laterna Magika: more breadth and less depth than is desirable for staging, and no fly space.

For a director with Krejča's penchant for a broad, fully orchestrated *mise en scène*, the physical limitations of the theatre were a constant tribulation. Adding to the difficulties was the problem of scheduling performances in alternation with the Laterna Magika, a problem somewhat like that of the Balustrade, where drama alternated with mime. Easing this scheduling problem and perhaps as a result of it, the Gate Theatre toured Europe extensively. Moreover, Krejča preferred not to perform steadily. Part of his ideal theatre program was freedom from regular quantitative norms of production, freedom permitting time to work toward maturity and ripeness of production. Accordingly, compared to the Balustrade and the Drama Club, his theatre mounted fewer productions and had longer rehearsal and tryout periods — an average of at least six months for each production.

As leader of the theatre, Krejča demanded total commitment: his regular actors were discouraged from doing film work, if not forbidden to do it (quite the opposite of the practice at the Drama Club). His company consisted of a small core of actors who consistently performed the major roles, actors with whom he had worked for ten or more years; several had been students under his tutelage at DAMU. These half-dozen or so were supplemented by fluctuating numbers of others. Characteristically, and in contrast to the more permanent arrangement at other theatres, every regular actor at the Gate Theatre had only a one-year renewable (and cancelable!) contract. The difference was probably traceable to Krejča's aversion to the tenure system as he knew it at the National Theatre, which resulted in a considerable amount of artistic deadwood. Krejča did not seek especially versatile actors, but rather those with distinctive traits that he could employ to maximum effect in his interpretations. He had little use for improvisation or what he would consider the vagaries of intuitive, subjective acting. It was, indeed, difficult to imagine a greater contrast than the one between his creative method and the one practiced at the Drama Club.

Krejča's belief in centralization of production under a strong director was carefully reasoned: "Every theatrical work (perhaps more than any other form of art) resists its own totality, flees from its unity, and this constant breaking away can be corrected only by the organizational power of the director. Where this is lacking, the disintegration of productions and theatres is imminent."[21]

Not surprisingly, Krejča insisted that the actor accept entirely those directions necessary for the production to emerge as an entity. According to him, such subordination of the actor's will did not limit creativity:

> Extensive preparations for a production ought to be a protection against uncertainty and chance, a guarantee that the production will emerge as a whole, that it will have its own, theatrical identity, and its characters, situations, points

will obey fixed relations. By a detailed system of single "points," we pin the actor in his proper place in the production. From this place he can soar to the clouds, but only from this place.[22]

Krejča's "extensive preparations" included hundreds of detailed notes made before rehearsals began, testifying to a long and painstaking study of the text. By the time he was ready to begin rehearsals, however, he had usually formulated and identified with a complex, many-stranded interpretation or vision of the production. His densely annotated *Regiebuch* became, as he put it, the text of the production. Although he denied that it was a fixed and formal chart, and although he undoubtedly made allowance for adjustments and the evolution of shading and details, the basic spine and configuration of the production were settled in advance. (Again, the contrast to both the Balustrade and the Drama Club was noteworthy, even though it was not an absolute one.)

During rehearsals, Krejča concentrated intently on every detail. Even while actors still had scripts in hand, he hovered over the slightest bits of business — coaching, urging, demonstrating, asking that a given reading or action be repeated until it achieved what he felt was the necessary rhythm or form, for even the slightest errors at this stage of the work, he believed, might lead to major misinterpretations later.

Krejča's elaborate preliminary study of the text and his attention to detail were consistent with his concern for the complex relationships inherent between people as individuals and people as social beings. Krejča was, moreover, always sensitive to his times, to the world in which his work was done, as is evidenced by his involvement with the sociopolitical activities of various cultural unions and deliberative bodies. Never overtly apparent in his productions, such concern nevertheless underlay and guided his work.

All these tendencies in Krejča found embodiment in productions distinguished by their profusion of motifs, their dense scoring, their multiple layers of suggestion and implication. As he said: "I don't believe in the quality of plays and stage works that are easily described, easy to analyze and compare."[23] His staging was notable for its synthesis of theatrical elements, its surging, dynamic movement, its intense physicalization in gesture, color, and choreographed patterns, its sustained inner tension even in calmer moments. A production for Krejča became a theatrical metaphor of a complex human and social situation, with varied though not obvious echoes of the world outside the theatre.

Krejča's method worked superbly with pieces of broad scope and inherent theatricality. Michel De Ghelderode's *Masquers of Ostende* and Arthur Schnitzler's *The Green Cockatoo* were good examples. The De Ghelderode piece was an extended, large-cast mime-ballet dealing with the juxtaposition of carnival revelry and death. Grotesque masks and costumes, acrobatic dance, and insistent, driving music combined to create a hyperintense, ritual-like event, which Krejča intended as a theatrical warm-up for the much more inwardly oriented play following on the same bill, Topol's *Cat on the Rails*, a long one-act play for two characters. The two works formed the opening production of the theatre in November 1965.

Schnitzler's *The Green Cockatoo* (1968) is a classic example of a play within a play, with pre-Pirandellian themes of illusion and reality, set during the storming of the Bastille. It allowed Krejča to give full rein to his instinctive theatrical bravura as well as his speculative, analytical working over of multiple themes. The appropriateness of treatment to script was near perfect. At other times, however, Krejča's method could produce an effect of overdirection, as if he were reluctant to let even a moment go by that was not loaded with significance or dramatic effect; scenes became hyperexpressive. Intensity and animation guaranteed that the result was never dull, but it might become fatiguing. With plays inherently more intimate and reflective, such as Chekhov's *The Three Sisters* or Topol's extended one-acts, *Cat on the Rails* and *Hour of Love*, the effect might be undue strain, excessive complication, or the overburdening of a fragile situation. Krejča's treatments were always challenging, but questions might arise about the balance between text and production.

Two productions that marked a culmination of Krejča's work in the 1960s, Chekhov's *The Three Sisters* and Alfred de Musset's *Lorenzaccio*, vividly illustrated the spectrum of Krejča's art: its masterful theatricality and challenging concepts as well as its potentially overloaded embodiment.

Krejča's production of *The Three Sisters* (1966), a profound reassessment of the play, formed an interesting contrast to the Drama Club's treatment of *The Cherry Orchard*. Allowing for the differences between the two plays, it is worth noting that both productions rejected the soulful, nostalgic accretions marking many Chekhov revivals and that neither production was concerned with making the characters attractive or appealing. But whereas the Drama Club's essentially low-keyed approach devoted itself to a close-textured, ostensibly casual study that stressed the banality if not vulgarity of the lives depicted, Krejča's Gate Theatre production was shrill, brittle, and jagged, its movement consistently dynamic and intricately patterned. The characters were presented as highly agitated, tense, essentially neurotic, and in varying states of desperation. Krejča's predilection for rich physicalization of emotion was most evident in a series of unforgettable, nearly expressionistic images that ended the play: the sisters resembled birds trapped in a cage, swooping and darting in frustration and despair. The dashing of their dreams and

Krejča's production of de Musset's Lorenzaccio *at the Theatre beyond the Gate, 1969. Photo by Dr. Jaromír Svoboda.*

hopes was rendered in powerful, absolute theatrical terms. Although the interpretation was questioned as being excessive and spastic, the consensus was that it was profoundly exhilarating.

Lorenzaccio (1969), by far the most ambitious, demanding, and provocative of Krejča's productions at the Gate Theatre, also provided the most complex yet indirect comment on the human and political forces implicit in the tragic events comprising the birth and death of the Prague Spring of 1968. De Musset's plot of a frustrated revolutionary idealist in Renaissance Italy and his seemingly inevitable defeat in a decadent, malevolent world was a starting point for Krejča. At the top of his form, he used de Musset's plot as an armature for dense, interwoven, many-layered patterns of theatrical images that created an overpowering sense of the world's deceit, corruption, and, indeed, bestiality. It was a world suggesting a montage of Hieronymus Bosch's nightmarish monsters and the morbid elegance of a Renaissance court. It was, moreover, a world of the stage, taking on a life of its own, with multiple levels of awareness and significance.

The total effect of the production was created by the interaction of a variety of elements, including Josef Svoboda's scenography. Even before the play began, we saw the bare stage enclosed by an irregular border of semitransparent mirrors reflecting multiple images of the stage and also the audience, pulling us into the world of the stage and later, once the action was under way, indirectly suggesting our complicity in what followed.

The theatricality at the very beginning of the play was essentially heightened when all the actors (approximately thirty) entered in solid-colored tights and leotards, frankly comporting themselves as actors, now and then staring at the audience before dressing themselves in costumes and masks already placed on the stage. The seemingly casual action was actually intricately choreographed. The masks were of several types. At first we were mostly aware of carnival masks that presented the wearers' features in enlarged, exaggerated form and monstrous, surreal animal masks — heightened versions of what might have been figures in a contemporary court masque. Later we became aware of other masks, tightly fitting ones reproducing the wearers' faces but projecting a colorless, deathlike image.

All the actors remained on stage throughout the play, overhearing, whispering, constantly shifting with greater or lesser motion, a living, dreamlike, ominous background suggesting a totality of involvement, an interpenetration of private and public life. Each scene was demarcated by a major shifting of this background, yet an overall rhythmic flow and coherence were maintained. As we watched the protagonist, Lorenzaccio, weave around and among the figures and spectres of his real and inner world, we also became aware that Krejča had introduced a double for him. Silently observing him at a distance or hovering close by, the figure reinforced certain scenes and provided an ironic perspective on others.

The action was not easy to follow. It was a difficult yet enormously suggestive production, offering no single, clear, conveniently accessible meaning, but rather a host of partial insights and impressions. The audience was left with deeply disturbing perceptions of relationships between inhumane forces and human contingencies, of innocence and deceit, power and impotence, despair and continuity. Equally strong was the perception of a challenging, autonomous work of art and of the incredible amount of preparation and work that must have gone into the integration of its countless, often simultaneous details.

The production recalled, to some extent, the Balustrade production of *Timon*.

Both seemed bent on presenting a monstrous image of the world's evil and unnaturalness, drawing on a variety of theatrical elements to underscore their vision. The profound difference between the productions was largely the difference between youthful excess and mature, conceptualized artistry: the *Timon* production was striking and inventive, but also forced, melodramatic, and strident compared with the controlled, intricately structured complexities and ambiguities of Krejča's *Lorenzaccio* production. *Lorenzaccio* was Krejča's master work to that time. It rekindled one's sense of the latent powers of theatre, and it stood as *the* Czech production bearing witness to the world that produced the events of August 1968 in Prague.

Krejča's observations on the relation between art and life (from a speech early in 1969) were especially relevant:

> Art ... detaches itself from everyday reality in order to encompass it. In its own fashion it has to ignore the present and its routine problems in order to question the very heart of the present. Hitting the bull's-eye gains significance the greater our distance from it. Art doesn't force its way, it infiltrates ... it doesn't scream, it persuades in whispers. It works slowly, patiently, and persistently. It doesn't plead for freedom because it itself is free and radiates freedom. It expands and strengthens the realm of freedom in everyone who opens himself to it. And at the same time it immunizes him against coercion, fear, and falsehood. Against cant and demagoguery. Against closed mindedness and barbarism. Free art fills that space in each of us into which unfreedom might otherwise insinuate itself.[24]

The events of August 1968 punctuated the evolution of Prague's small theatres, as they did all life in the nation. Fortunately, the punctuation was more a semicolon, or perhaps a dash, than a period. Life went on, and so did the activity of these theatres. Distinctive as they were, they now became assimilated into the total theatre spectrum of Prague. Some observers, in fact, saw dangers of a new institutionalism. Ivan Vyskočil, ever a purist, denied that any true small theatres existed by the end of the 1960s, his ideal being a theatre "small enough so that those who operate it are not financially dependent on it."[25] Certainly the political situation after the invasion clouded the future of these and other artistic enterprises.

In retrospect, the birth, evolution, and maturity of these small theatres of Prague provided a fresh perspective on the significance of theatre as a symptom and even as a contributory cause of sociocultural realities. Just as there was ample evidence of these theatres being products of their time, there was no denying that their distinctive work had also been in the vanguard of cultural forces contributing to the shortlived but memorably democratic society being created in Czechoslovakia during the spring of 1968.

What stood out as one reflected on these theatres (as well as work such as that of Radok in other theatres) was not a singular style or approach to experimentation — neither the modish shock of theatre of cruelty nor the carnival radicalism of guerrilla theatre evident on many Western stages, for example — but a number of deliberate, independent, strongly conceptualized explorations of humans and society, of the limits of people's humanity and their freedom, of fresh communication between stage and audience, and of the power of theatrical metaphor to capture and illuminate critical moments in the life of a people. Considered in this light, the small theatres of Prague represented a remarkably mature, artistically sophisticated, socially engaged art, justly comparable to the crucial work of their predecessors in the similarly challenged Czech theatres of the 1930s and wartime 1940s.

7

August 1968
The Trauma and Its Aftermath

Although reference to some plays and productions after August 1968 has been made in the previous chapters, the full effect of that event on Czech theatre in the following months warrants a more detailed account. The remarkable evolution of Czech theatre in the 1960s — as an art form sensitively responding to its time — suffered a crippling blow. Although the sheer energy and talents of that theatre carried it on for a surprisingly long time after August 1968, it eventually entered a decade or more of enforced blandness and subservience to political mandates. Exceptions existed even then, as we shall see, but they were oases in a barren landscape.

Nerve-wracking negotiations and brinksmanship between Czechoslovakia and its Warsaw Pact allies went on for weeks in the late spring and summer of 1968. At issue was the reform movement culminating in the Prague Spring and its motif of "socialism with a human face." Finally, during the early morning hours of August 21, the Warsaw Pact armies, led by the Soviet forces, invaded Czechoslovakia. The impact of that event shook the Czechs to the core but also unified them in ways reminiscent of the feverish days of the Munich crisis some thirty years earlier. I followed the crisis with special interest because I had earlier received notice of a grant to study contemporary theatre in Czechoslovakia. My research residency was to commence in September, and so I set sail with my wife four days after the invasion. After a temporary stay in England, we were informed by the American Embassy in London that we could proceed to Prague in mid-September because the situation there seemed stable enough not to pose a threat to our safety.

We spent the next ten and a half months in Prague. During that threatening yet exhilarating period we were in a position to observe the theatre season firsthand.

A remarkable psychic electricity was generated between stage and audience during most performances, even as Soviet troops still patrolled the streets (until late October, as I recall). Once again, as in pre-Munich days, theatre became a vital element in the life of the people, a source of catharsis and enlightenment; but whereas events in the thirties were building inexorably toward a mortal crisis, in the sixties the dreaded event had already occurred, and theatre and its audiences were experiencing the postimpact shock waves.

I wrote the following piece six months after the invasion, in February 1969, but it was never published. Keeping it in the present tense captures, I think, some of the special atmosphere of the time, which managed to prevail in varying degrees for some two seasons. A provocative balance of forces existed: lingering outrage and a will to resist, threats of serious reprisal, and yet enough slackness of surveillance to reduce the risks of punishment.

THEATRE AND LIFE: THEIR INTERACTION IN PRAGUE SINCE AUGUST 1968

Six months after the tanks of August clattered across the frontiers of Czechoslovakia, the nation's theatres at midseason 1968–1969 were not only alive but actively reflecting the times. Although the drama of real-life events since August has doubtless overshadowed the dramas on stage, the theatre has continued its traditional role as a cultural force acutely responsive to the shifting stresses in the life of the nation.

A performance of García Lorca's *The House of Bernarda Alba* on January 22, 1969, in the Tyl Theatre epitomized the continuity of Czech theatre culture and the stress of immediate public events during this nation's latest winter of discontent. The Tyl Theatre itself, nearly two hundred years old, virtually abuts the ancient Karolinum of Charles University in the Old Town section of Prague. It was in the Tyl Theatre that Mozart conducted the premiere of his *Don Giovanni* in 1787, that many plays in the Czech language were first performed, and that the song (with words by Tyl) which eventually became the Czech national anthem was first heard. In 1920 the Tyl became one of the three theatres housing the National Theatre, and as one of Prague's fifteen full-time professional repertory theatres it currently presents fifteen to twenty different productions each month.

On the evening of January 22, 1969, however, the Tyl Theatre did more than represent the tradition of one of Europe's most active theatre centers. It also participated, as so often in the past, in the drama of events outside the theatre. A remarkable cluster of forces intersected that evening in and around that space. Before the performance began, one of the actors stepped before the curtain to read two proclamations. One was issued by the Union of Czech Theatre Artists and the other by the artistic ensemble of the National Theatre. Both proclamations were in response to the death of Jan Palach and what it symbolized. Palach, a university student, had made a human torch of himself a week earlier in Wenceslaus Square to protest the military occupation of his country. Both proclamations asserted the necessity of continued, unified, and active dedication to the ideals that were beginning to acquire substance before August 1968, as well as the necessity of resistance to those forces in the government seeking to act against the will of the people. "Do not allow Jan Palach's sacrifice to be dismissed or made futile" was the repeated exhortation.

The proclamation gained even greater impact by being delivered from a stage less than one hundred yards from the courtyard of the Karolinum of Charles University where Palach's body lay in state for two days. Adding to the immediate relevance of all these circumstances, the director of the evening's Lorca production, one of the Czech's most celebrated theatre artists, Alfred Radok, was still absent from the country as a result of the August events. Having endured artistic repression during most of his creative years and refusing to face the possibility of similar experiences yet again, he fled to the West with his family within twenty-four hours of the invasion. His last production in Prague had been James Saunders' *A Scent of Flowers*, in the same Tyl Theatre.

The performance was notable for still another, happier event attesting to the continuity of a rich theatrical tradition: the ninetieth birthday of Leopolda Dostalová, the grand lady of the National Theatre, who began her career there in 1901 as a colleague of the great actor Eduard Vojan and went on to play leading roles for directors Jaroslav Kvapil and K. H. Hilar, as well as title roles in several Čapek plays. A brief celebration was held on stage during intermission, with speeches by dignitaries, colleagues, and Miss Dostalová herself, who was acting the role of the grandmother in Lorca's play that evening.

To return to the broader question of how the Czech theatre has functioned since last August, the answer would be, "Remarkably well, under the circumstances." The sheer quantity of theatre production has not diminished. Prague, a city of slightly more than one million inhabitants, has twenty full-time professional theatre ensembles, all state-supported (an average of 70 percent of their total expenses), playing a constantly alternating repertoire. In the four months from

October through January, for example, they mounted well over one hundred and fifty different productions, of which ninety were dramas (fourteen American), the rest being opera, ballet, operetta, mime, and marionettes.

Not only has the productivity of the theatres not flagged, but, even more remarkable, censorship has not been reestablished. Freedom from official preproduction approval of scripts, which began with the post-January 1968 reforms, has not yet been revoked. Theatres are at liberty to choose their own repertoire, each theatre usually staging eight to ten new productions per season, plus carrying over a half-dozen or so productions from previous seasons.

Although censorship does not formally exist, the choice of plays this season has been understandably influenced by the special circumstances affecting the country during the past year, especially since August. A tacit, self-imposed censorship has continued — perhaps "repertoire policy" would be a better term. In the first place, the repertoires do not contain plays that directly or explicitly confront, much less condemn, the present political-military realities. To do so would invite severe repercussions without improving the situation for anyone. Moreover, quite apart from the threat of an external clampdown, the Czech theatre is simply not one of inflammatory agitation or blatant "protest," neither by cultural tradition nor by national temperament. Its ways are considerably subtler and ultimately perhaps more telling.

Another characteristic of the present season is the virtually total elimination of plays and operas from the Warsaw Pact countries that entered Czechoslovakia last August. This policy, initiated by the theatres themselves, not only expresses obvious condemnation of those countries' aggression but also suggests an ironically tactful consideration for the authors of such plays; any author, especially a living one, whose work is performed today is implicitly assumed to favor the ideals and values inherent in the Prague Spring period. To perform their plays would imply their leaning toward the Czechoslovakian cause and, conversely, their criticism of the Warsaw Pact action, implications that would make problems for them in their native country. Actually, however, many Czech theatre artists find the elimination of certain classics, such as those by Chekhov or Dostoyevsky, an embarrassment, and the policy may shift before the season is over.

Positively speaking, this season has been marked by plays that illustrate the special social engagement on which the Czech theatre prides itself. The plays fall into several main categories and have different degrees of subtlety.

The first consists of native plays (mostly from the nineteenth century) with strongly nationalistic themes from Czech history and legend. Virtually all such works suggest one or more parallels to the crisis existing since last August and stress the fortitude and defiance of the Czech spirit in times of adversity. Perhaps the outstanding example of this relatively straightforward, inspirational type is J. K. Tyl's *Jan Hus*, depicting the Czechs pitted against the oppressive power of Rome in the fifteenth century. It has been performed by many theatres in the months since the invasion. The operatic repertoire has even more forceful examples of this type of work: *Libuše, Dalibor,* and *The Brandenburgs in Bohemia* by Smetana and *The Jakobin* by Dvořák. A modern play in this category is *Playing with the Devil* (Hrátky s čertem), by Jan Drda (1915–1970). A comedic satire written in 1945, it was pointed at the German invaders; revived a month after the invasion, it applied neatly to the Russians. The Devil, for example, bore a remarkable resemblance to Leonid Brezhnev, the Soviet leader responsible for the invasion. Karel Čapek's *The White Disease*, on the other hand, presents a more abstract parallel in its metaphoric picture of malignant force and aggression.

All these works, both operatic and dramatic, have provided a rallying point and a release, one of the few ways in which the audience may experience a communal and positive counterthrust of the spirit against the oppressive realities governing their lives in the world outside the theatre. These works continue to be performed, but their greatest impact was felt in the first month or so of the fall season when, still close to the shock of the August events, the people sought a form of cultural first aid. And it is also true that the intrinsic artistic merit of some productions in this group was secondary to their value as morale boosters.

A quite different type of play has been equally satisfying to the immediate emotive needs of the audiences. Several of the Voskovec and Werich comic satires-with-music of the 1930s have been revived. Originally composed in the face of the Fascist threat before World War II, they have proved to be remarkably on target in post-August Czechoslovakia.

Another group of mainly foreign works have subjects essentially parallel to the current Czech experience. The parallels may be close or remote and the tone emotive or rational, but they present a more complex critique than found in the works of the previous groups. Arthur Miller's *The Crucible*, Sartre's *The Flies*, Anouilh's *The Lark*, Ionesco's *Rhinoceros*, and Maxwell Anderson's *Barefoot in Athens*, for example, offer close analogies in their depiction of individuals uncompromisingly asserting their truth against the *diktat* of inflexible power. *Timon of Athens* underlines the treachery of presumed friends, and Edward Albee's *A Delicate Balance* is a ruefully accurate image of close friends becoming unwanted guests.

Explicit topicality and irony are found in Sartre's *Dirty Hands*, yet to be performed in any other Warsaw Pact nation. Its critique of the adjustability of means and ends under the stress of power struggles within the Communist Party itself relates to still another facet of the complicated realities experienced by the Czechs during the past twenty years, namely the multitude of evils excused in the name of a rosily defined but never materialized ideal.

What of *new Czech* plays and their relation to events outside the theatre? Of the half-dozen or so original Czech works produced by midseason, some have only the most tenuous connections with the political situation of the past year, but others provide fascinating and contrasting studies with obvious links to the ongoing national crisis. The first to be produced, František Hrubín's *Oldřich and Božena*, written in 1967 but produced in September 1968, presents an action drawn from Czech history and legend and centers on the frustration of alien stratagems against Czech sovereignty in semipagan Bohemia. An early Czech king, Oldřich, in defiance of powerful Germanic neighbors, puts aside his barren German wife in favor of a Czech maiden, Božena, who, as the play opens, awaits the birth of his child. Hrubín deliberately subordinates the traditional romantic tone of the story (Božena never appears) in favor of its themes of political conspiracy and the morality of violence and power. The play was written well before August and its themes are universal, but with only a minimal shift (for German, substitute Russian) its appropriateness to the central problems of the day is obvious, perhaps nowhere as clearly as in its opening line by the foreign envoy sent to coerce Oldřich: "I've come to Bohemia to prevent the birth of a child."

More interesting as a total theatre piece, although less literary and "finished," is a new play-with-music by Milan Calábek (b. 1940), *The Czech Christmas Mass*, which had its premiere in Ostrava at the Bezruč Theatre in December 1968. I saw it there in January. Mixing themes from traditional folk sources with biographical details from the life of the eighteenth-century Czech composer Jan Jakub Ryba (1765–1815), the play operates on several levels simultaneously and exploits the inherently theatrical impact of a play within a play somewhat in the manner of *Marat-Sade*. The "real" action depicts Ryba's staging of a Christmas play after the repressive Habsburg, Roman Catholic establishment of his village has denied him permission to perform his Christmas Mass. Blending with the traditional biblical narrative of the play within a play, in Genet-like fashion, are Jan Jakub's personal life as well as certain political-military realities in Habsburg-dominated Bohemia of the late eighteenth century.

The Czech Christmas Mass was the first new Czech play written after August to be staged (shortly before Christmas), and much of its basic action expresses the post-August climate. Pointed reference is made to alien troops standing by in readiness to occupy the town in which the action takes place, as well as to mock trials and other oppressions of liberty. Responding to a disenchanted speech by the priest of the local church — a speech cataloguing the obverse and negative aspects of liberty — Jan Jakub says simply, "Even one second of freedom makes it all worth while."

Another play opening in December was Alena Vostrá's *On Knife's Edge* (Na ostří nože), in Prague's Drama Club. An ironic semifantasy presenting a cross section of life in a small apartment house, it is a much milder and subtler response to the discomfort and hypocrisy attendant on the invasion events. The custodian of the apartment house has the hallucination of having a knife in his head (symbolic of his difficulties in comprehending the world around him), but tries to behave as if nothing out of the ordinary had happened.

The most recent premiere of a new Czech play having marked relevance to contemporary realities is Milan Kundera's *Birdbrainia* (Ptákovina), or in its alternate title, *Two Ears, Two Marriages* (Dvě uši, dvě svatby), first presented in January 1969 in Liberec and later at the Balustrade Theatre in Prague. It deals with issues antedating last August and is reminiscent of such earlier works as Havel's *The Memorandum* in its sardonic depiction of an absurd bureaucratic world in the microcosm of an institution, here a school. The staff maneuvers for power, the students are informers, and confession and punishment rituals for even trivial infractions are a daily occurrence. The difference between Kundera's world and previous Czech plays of similar genre is the degree of revulsion lying under the surface comedy of the piece as it traces the ultimate effects of bureaucratic idiocy and ideological sclerosis: a perversion of natural instincts and the debasement of both ruler and ruled. Kundera presents a series of grotesque comic scenes dominated by sado-masochistic forces recalling the submerged savagery in Ben Jonson's bitter farces. The tone is best suggested in one of the concluding speeches, delivered by the temporary victor in a running struggle for power: "Power is sweetest when it's completely incongruous. When the idiot rules the wise man . . . the loathsome the beautiful." The play echoes the worst excesses of the era of deformation in the 1950s and early 1960s, which is still fresh in the memory of the nation and helps explain the stubborn refusal of the people to slide back to the period before January 1968.

A completely different presentation deserving special mention is hardly a play but more a recital in the tradition of chamber readings of literature accompanied by music. Originally produced last autumn in Gottwaldov (formerly Zlín) and titled *A Concert for Mr. Masaryk*, it is a solo performer rendition of selections from the speculative and critical writings of Czechoslovakia's first president, integrated with taped portions of a Dvořák quartet and taped selections from two critiques of Masaryk, one hostile, the other tolerably favorable. What is remarkable about the presentation is the insight and prescience of Masaryk's observations, some written over seventy years ago, about the political, psychological, and philosophical aspects of the "Czech question" in the context of European superpowers, both Western and Eastern. Writing with a rare humanism, Masaryk expressed a world view astonishingly close to the ideals guiding Czechoslovakian policy for the past year. Less than five years ago, Masaryk was a nonperson in Czechoslovakia, and a performance devoted to his writings would have been inconceivable as recently as 1967.

That such original works and revivals are being performed at all in Czechoslovakia today is noteworthy in itself and suggests the complexity of the present situation, in which traditional concepts of freedom and repression, sovereignty and vassalhood, become problematical and relative. But even more striking are the existential moments of performance in the theatre as the audience members, alert to the slightest allusions, keenly respond to those lines or to unspoken bits of business that touch their deepest anxieties and resentments. In its indirect fashion the Czech theatre today speaks of those things that cannot be said by other public media. In effect it provides a catharsis, even though not in the traditional classic sense. Whether with relatively blunt simplicity or with complex subtlety, it renews the fundamental solidarity of the people during the shifting stresses and crises dominating public and private consciousness here since last spring. Czech theatre today is practicing a remarkable balance between artistic autonomy and social responsiveness, a model of "political" theatre in the best sense of the term.

POSTSCRIPT, 1999

The "high" described in the previous pages inevitably declined in the following months, but for almost another season or two a suprising tolerance for provocative theatre seemed to coexist with the inexorable dismantling of the Prague Spring reforms. Recent history began to be rewritten, and a newly restructured and externally controlled, politically correct regime was installed, evoking echoes of former takeovers. But in contrast to the relatively rapid and harsh "new order" imposed by the Nazis in 1938–1939 and the Communists in 1948, the post-August transition was relatively softer and took years, though the decisive actions and protocols were in place within three months of the invasion itself.

Before the first anniversary of the August events, several crucial steps were taken: the agreement to have the Soviet military remain in the country "temporarily but indefinitely"; official renunciation of the 1968 liberalization program and a strong implication that it had been provoked by Western imperialism; a purging of the reform leaders, climaxed by the removal in April 1969 of Alexander

Dubček as first secretary of the Party and his replacement by Gustav Husák, a firm even if not notorious hard-liner; and a program of "Normalization," which prevailed for almost two decades. Both Dubček's ouster and the imposition of Normalization were triggered by mass celebrations of the double defeat of the Russians by the Czechoslovakians in World Championship hockey matches in March. The festivities in Prague's Wenceslaus Square rivaled those of Times Square on New Year's Eve. Ironically and regrettably, they also provided a rationale for stepping up repressive measures, chiefly because the windows of the Russian Aeroflot offices were smashed during the revelry, whether by enthusiastic Czechs or by agent provocateurs was never determined. That same March also marked the final performance of any play by Václav Havel in any Czech theatre until late 1989.

Normalization meant total censorship of news media, elimination of freedom of speech, denial of free political assembly, and de facto one-party rule. And yet within such parameters Czech theatres (as well as other arts) still managed to operate without too many overt restrictions if they were sufficiently astute about what would or would not be tolerated by the authorities. Much also depended on whether a theatre was in a large city, especially Prague, and therefore under close scrutiny, or in outlying regions. Two realities resulted: an increasing shift of morale from spirited, hopeful resistance to increasingly sullen, soured hostility and resentment, but concurrently the irrepressible urge to keep creating and producing despite disenchantment with "causes" and increasing official pressures to control the repertoire and personnel of all theatres. The erasure of the Prague Spring reforms took as long as it did because it was a different age than that of Hitler or Stalin; even militant ideologues were now sensitive to world opinion and public relations. Implementing Normalization in theatre also took longer because the new regime put first things first: consolidation of its power was obviously more important than close monitoring of stage entertainment, no matter how irritating.

Some other key moments and events in Czech theatre and the world outside the theatre during the 1960s–1970s watershed illustrate the transition. To summarize key political developments and to start with one of the most striking, by February 1972 conditions were such that Czech President Ludvík Svoboda (who had been adamant in denouncing the August 1968 invasion) bestowed the highest Czech decoration, the order of the White Lion, 1st Class, on Leonid Brezhnev. Some transitional milestones preceding that symbol-charged ceremony included the hard crackdowns and investigations that followed attempts to mark the first anniversary of the August invasion with written or public protests against the Normalization process. After his removal as first secretary of the Communist Party in April 1969, Dubček was removed from the Central Committee of the Party in

September 1969 and ousted from the Party entirely in June 1970. Meantime, January 1970 saw the beginning of official individual screenings of *all* Communist Party members, resulting in thousands being purged from the Party; and in May 1970 a new treaty of friendship was signed with the Soviet Union.

In theatre, as in all public or otherwise sensitive enterprises, key administrators considered liberal were replaced by conservatives, that is to say, ideologically "reliable" personnel according to their track record and credentials; a precondition was their approval of the August invasion. It was a rollback to the fifties, but in a lower key and with reduced zealotry. The regime was less concerned with a theatre leader's convictions than with his or her political practices.

Productions with some claim to resistance gradually became tamer or more cryptic, with memorable ones becoming less and less frequent. One of the last original post-August Czech plays with some real bite was Ivan Klíma's *The Jury* (Porota). Staged in Prague's municipal Chamber Theatre in April 1969, it was a thinly veiled comment on efforts to legitimize the 1968 occupation of Czechoslovakia. The action centers on a state trial of a man who has already been executed: the regime wants post facto justification of its action. All the jurors but one eventually fall in line to condemn the dead man, even though the evidence is full of holes. The exception, an engineer who is a rather timid intellectual, cannot bring himself to support the outrageous distortion of justice even though he is virtually sure that his refusal will mean his own liquidation. But the final irony is that the state welcomes his defiant stand because it provides a semblance of independent thinking and nonconformity in the judicial process while in no way affecting the final verdict or the *fait accompli* of the execution. For theatre people, it was a painful reminder of the quixotic nature of their own efforts.

Another outstanding work after the first season, Krejča's production of *Lorenzaccio* in October 1969 (I saw it in previews in June, before we left), has already been discussed. As a Party member, Krejča still carried some weight; moreover, the production, for all of its relevance to evolving events, was obscure and ambivalent enough to prevent its being attacked as hostile to the status quo. Smoček's *Cosmic Spring* (March 1970), also previously discussed, was inherently more universal and detached from current events, less likely to be viewed as bearing on hard realities of the moment.

In January 1970, it was still possible for Radok and Svoboda to collaborate on a production in West Germany, Heinrich Böll's *The Clown*, but it was their final joint effort, as conditions progressively hardened. Radok had been hired by the municipal theatre in Göteborg, Sweden, and occasionally directed in other European theatres. Svoboda, who remained in Prague but could work abroad under certain restrictions, would not have been allowed to work with Radok after 1970. Concurrently, in the early 1970s, another major director, Jan Grossman, had to direct abroad for several years, mainly in Holland, before being allowed to return to work in Czechoslovakia.

The two chief theatrical periodicals, the weekly *Theatre News* (Divadelní noviny) and the monthly *Theatre* (Divadlo), were forced to cease publication in early 1970.

Russian classics were again being produced by the fall of 1969, particularly Chekhov and Gorky, but soon thereafter — in a neat tactical maneuver — plays by Gogol and the Soviet satirist Nikolay Erdman as well. Their works were ostensibly critical of Czarist society but could equally be seen as satires on Soviet society. By the fall of 1971, however, almost all theatres were obliged to include at least one unambiguously pro-Soviet or pro-Communist drama in their repertoire. And by November 1974 a festival of Soviet Dramatic Art was mandated in the whole country; on average, each repertory theatre was expected to mount two Soviet pr_____ a season, a far cry from the days when theatres had pledged not to p_____ Russian plays at all. But by that time Czech theatre was thoroughly Normalized and into its long period of gray mediocrity.

Krejča continued to direct in his own theatre until 1972. His conflation of Sophocles' Oedipus and Antigone plays in March 1971 was notable in its use of masks and other inventive staging, with scenography by Svoboda. Krejča's other productions included relatively "safe" classics: Shakespeare and Chekhov, but also the work of house playwright Josef Topol. In March 1972 Topol directed his own play for the Theatre beyond the Gate, *Two Nights with a Girl* (Dvě noci s dívkou); the production had a number of preview performances, but its April premiere was not allowed. Thereafter, as had been true for Havel, no Topol play was allowed anywhere in the country until the late 1980s.

In the spring of 1972 Krejča's Theatre beyond the Gate was a lonely survivor of the great days of the 1960s, a theatre which somehow seemed able to maintain its high profile and refused to present inferior work. Other theatres of the 1960s also survived and continued to do honorable work, but in various understandable ways most had been forced to make many compromises. The days were numbered even for Krejča and his theatre. Their last new production was Chekhov's *Sea Gull* in March 1972, and their last *performance* was of that play on June 10 of that year. Reliable witnesses claim that the audience, who of course knew it was the death knell of an era, would not stop applauding at the final curtain because, as they said, "It was our theatre, and as long as we kept applauding it was still alive." The theatre was officially dissolved that month. By a coincidence of timing, June 30,

Josef Svoboda and Otomar Krejča in 1970; behind them is the Oedipus-Antigone *model. Photo by J. Burian.*

1972, was also the date of Alfred Radok's official severance from the National Theatre, which, until then, had managed to keep him as a member on leave of absence. Normalization in mainstream theatre seemed nearly complete.

By the 1974–1975 season, when I was on another research grant in Prague for nine months, the situation had deteriorated even further. The dynamic resistance following August 1968 had ground to a halt. It seemed to me that the Czech theatre was doing penance and marking time, without direction or motivation. It was paying its dues by concentrating its repertoire on pre- and postrevolutionary Russian plays, plays from other Soviet bloc countries, and uncontroversial classics both native and foreign. In terms of repertoire, it was almost a throwback to the Stalinist years. Moreover, guest directors and actors from the Soviet bloc appeared regularly with Czech ensembles, a collaborative activity inconceivable a few years earlier.

The Czech theatre was mounting competent productions but had nothing to say. It spoke, it performed, but without purpose, passion, or vitality. Normalization meant the triumph of political orthodoxy over art. Most of the outstanding artists were either in exile (abroad or within their own country) or safely defused. Outstanding ensembles were either dissolved or muzzled by the knowledge that

Krejča's last production in his original Theatre beyond the Gate, Chekhov's The Sea Gull, 1972. *Photo by Dr. Jaromír Svoboda.*

the staging of anything provocative or controversial would mean suicide for any theatre foolish enough to hazard it. The result was a dispirited theatre that operated primarily by conditioned reflex.

Of playwrights whose names were common coin in Europe — Havel, Topol, Kundera, Kohout, Klíma — not one play remained in the repertoire. Of directors whose productions had attracted international audiences — Radok, Grossman, Pavlíček, Krejča — only the last endured, although his theatre had been terminated and he sat unemployed on the sidelines for more than a season. Other significant directors were either banished to the provinces (Jan Kačer and Miloš Hynšt) or allowed to direct only intermittently in their regular theatres (Macháček and Pleskot in the National Theatre).

It was impossible to do plays that adopted a critical attitude toward the realities of life in Czechoslovakia since 1968. It was equally impossible for Czech artists to present any justification for those realities without violating their consciences or arousing the derision of audiences. And yet ignoring the sheer existence of those realities — for example, censorship, the stationing of tens of thousands of Soviet military in the country, careers dependent on Party membership or approval — made most theatre productions seem inconsequential or pointless. That was the dilemma of Czech theatre in the mid-1970s. What was true of mainstream theatres in Prague could also be said for established repertory theatres in other large cities, such as Brno, Ostrava, Olomouc, or Pilsen.

There were some exceptions. Sporadic productions by force of distinguished acting, forceful direction, or sheer ensemble energy occasionally transcended the dilemma. Film's loss was theatre's gain when Evald Schorm was forbidden to work in Czech film after 1968. He had already directed a strong production of *Crime and Punishment* for the Drama Club in 1966, and in the 1970s he did some notable productions for the Balustrade Theatre, which had otherwise entered a prolonged fallow period. In addition to doing nomadic work at other regional theatres, he also became a scenarist and director for Svoboda's Laterna Magika starting in the mid-1970s, where one of his most successful, long-running productions was *The Magical Circus* (Kouzelný cirkus) in 1977, a production that is still in the repertoire.

Good work by others included Carlo Goldoni's *The Outburst at Chiozza* directed by Smoček at the Drama Club in 1973; an apolitical contemporary Hungarian work, *Catsplay*, at the National Theatre in 1974, starring Dana Medrická (1920–1983) and Vlasta Fabionová (b. 1912), which proved to be the longest-running production in National Theatre history (over 400 performances); the Semafor production of Karel Erben's *Kytice* in 1974, an occasionally surrealistic medley of traditional folk materials; and *Cyrano* (1973) and *Optimistic Tragedy* (1974) at the National Theatre, both directed by Miroslav Macháček.

Krejča's productions were a greater exception. After a two-year blank he was able to pick up his career in 1974 in a small suburban Prague theatre, the S. K. Neumann. The productions testified to his stature as a director and were a reminder of what Czech theatre had once been. They were marked by great charges of energy and a total expenditure of artistic force, as if to defy all circumstances alien to creativity. Krejča exploited the essential resources of the stage — time, space, movement, sound, and light — and made even the most banal or flawed scripts seem exciting. Working without elaborate or sophisticated technical facilities, and without his former actors, he filled the stage with complexly orchestrated *mises en scène* based on playscripts that he himself thoroughly adapted for his kind of staging (for example, Chekhov's *Platonov* in 1974). A pattern of intricately organized, multiple, simultaneous action demonstrated Krejča's painstaking study and revision of the script. It echoed his approach in some of his last productions at the

Theatre beyond the Gate, such as *Lorenzaccio* and *Oedipus-Antigone*, and in some ways was reminiscent of Radok's methods in adapting texts and strongly theatricalizing them. Regardless of his success, however, Krejča's period of grace expired; after two years at the S. K. Neumann Theatre, Krejča did not work in Prague again until 1990.

Although it was not widely apparent at the time, the biggest exception to the generally routine, flavorless repertoire and production quality of Czech theatre during most of the 1970s and into the 1980s was found in a new cluster of informal, unorthodox studio theatres initiated by young people reacting against what they perceived as a number of shortcomings in mainstream theatre, much as did their ancestors in the 1920s and 1930s as well as in the late 1950s and the 1960s. The new generation began to organize "alternative" theatres that implicitly rejected the patterns of institutionalized theatres with their relatively inflexible administrative and production apparatus, repertoires mandated by political considerations rather than genuine merit or relevance, and methods of staging that set up any barrier or gulf between performer and audience.

This new studio theatre movement had its own distinct additional motivation — to counteract the devastating social and cultural effects not only of life under Stalinist communism after 1948 but of life following the more recent Soviet-led invasion and subsequent occupation of their country in 1968. It was their implicit commitment to a purpose larger than their own artistry that imbued much of the work of these theatres with substance and point and prevented it from being merely self-indulgent or anarchic.

Each of these new generational theatres developed its own repertoire and production style, but they shared a number of characteristics which set their work apart from most of the earlier small studio ensembles of the 1960s, such as the Balustrade, Drama Club, and Gate theatres in Prague. However fresh and innovative the work of those earlier theatres may have been, it was based on traditional dramaturgy and staging: however fanciful some of their productions may have been, they almost always embodied a script created by a playwright; and their staging involved professionally trained actors concerned with presenting characters from a scripted play directed by a single artist, and doing so within a consciously designed stage set. There were two exceptions: both the early "text appeal" era of the Balustrade Theatre under Ivan Vyskočil and Jiří Suchý and the subsequent Semafor Theatre under Suchý foreshadowed the later studio theatres of the 1970s in their air of casual improvisation, their reliance on music and mime, and their establishing of a spontaneous, direct relation to the audience. Equally valid and earlier prototypes, however, could be found in some of the early revues of V + W in the 1920s and the scenario-based productions of E. F. Burian in the 1930s, or even in some earlier cabaret theatres, such as the Red Seven.

Reflecting postmodern tendencies of the late 1960s and the 1970s, such as reduced concern for traditionally scripted plays, the new small ensembles, especially in their initial work, put even greater emphasis on unstructured, improvisational work than did their Czech prototypes. Rather than start with an already written play, they would either work with nondramatic prose or poetry (or factual, documentary data) or else improvise from what was often a single human or social motif or at most a sketchy scenario. And if they did start with an existing script, they radically adapted it, simply using it as raw material, a starting point.

Such "irregular" dramaturgy was also a tactical matter: authorities had more difficulty in monitoring their inexplicit, nonliterary repertoire projects. In any case, the principle of improvisation was critical. Even though a production might eventually become "set," the suggestion of spontaneity and improvisation, as well as an ongoing, informal communication with the audience, remained important in performance, whether that communication was verbalized or not. Moreover, a lack of polished acting skills, the absence of what might be considered a professional presence, was valued; or to put it in positive terms, the actor's own personality and temperament, his or her authentic self — not the ability to transform into a character under the guidance of a director — was nurtured. This, too, was a reaction against the posturing and role playing evident in public political life for several decades.

Music became a significant component of most of their work, often performed by the actors themselves, as did mime and dance, or sheer physical byplay among the performers or with the audience. Scenery was usually minimal, while properties, costumes, platforming, and lighting were primarily functional or merely suggestive of a setting rather than illusional or atmospheric. It is with good reason that the work of these new groups came to be associated with medieval street theatre, elements of *commedia dell'arte*, naive folk theatre, and circus clowning. The purging of conventionally structured or literary elements, the unvarnished humanity of the performers, and the conscious inclusion of the audience to form a temporary community became prime values in and of themselves, essentially as a response to the flat, neutralized society established by Normalization.

Although some of these groups started performing before the decisive year of 1968, they did not achieve widespread recognition until the mid- and even late 1970s, primarily because they were located in relatively remote areas or, if in larger cities, they remained in the shadows of better-known traditional theatres. Because I did not see much of their work until the 1980s, I have reserved detailed accounts of the chief groups and their productions for the next chapter.

8

A Gradual Thawing in the 1980s

From today's vantage point (1999), the period 1975–1985 was probably the ebb tide of Czech theatre's significance as an artistic, relevant force. For undistinguished achievement, it was a decade rivaled only by the hard-line years of 1948–1958. In fact, the decade after 1975 was truly bleaker in lacking the exceptional, outstanding productions that occasionally appeared in the years after 1948 as well as the major personalities that created them: Alfred Radok, Jiří Frejka, E. F. Burian, Otomar Krejča. In the late 1970s and early 1980s these people were either dead or in exile, and their potential successors were mostly restricted to intermittent activity with provincial ensembles.[1]

The contrast of theatre in the two eras reflected the two respective regimes. As dreadful as the Stalinist years were in Czechoslovakia, they still included powerful people in important positions who were not only committed ideologues but also artists and intellectuals with a discriminating appreciation of art. On occasion, such people were able to shield certain artists and even productions from outright persecution. The post-1968 regime, on the other hand, consisted of reliable nonentities, apparatchiks, and careerists of varying administrative competence but minimal talent or cultural interest. The resulting climate of Normalization repressed all but the most tenacious artists in traditional theatres and in the new, mostly provincial — and therefore low-profile — studio theatres.

Some productions that formed exceptions to the general dreariness of the mainstream theatres from 1975 to 1985, beyond those mentioned in the previous chapter, should be cited: Miroslav Macháček's *Our Swaggerers* (Naší furianti, 1979), *The Duchess of Waldstein's Armies* (Vévodkyně valdštejnských vojsk, 1980), and *Hamlet* (1982), all at the National Theatre; Jan Grossman's *The Sea Gull* (1978) at Cheb, *Revizor* (1980) at Hradec Králové, and *Uncle Vanya* (1983) at the S. K. Neumann Theatre in Prague; and Evald Schorm's *Hamlet* (1978), *Brothers Karamazov* (1979), and *Macbeth* (1981), all at the Theatre on the Balustrade in Prague.

In any case, the Czech theatre that I experienced in the spring of 1988 was clearly in the process of rejuvenation and liberalization. In part this was due to an inevitable erosion of the regime's will to control all social and cultural matters and in part to theatres becoming progressively more adept at maneuvering within parameters of varying rigidity. More important than both, however, were the models provided by the Soviet Union's policies of *glasnost* and *perestroika* (political and economic openness and restructuring), which in fact were very close to what the Czechs had been advocating in the Prague Spring of 1968. In the 1980s, however, these measures were designed to postpone if not prevent the collapse of the Soviet empire. The Mikhail Gorbachev–inspired reforms begun in 1985 obviously influenced cultural activity in the whole Soviet bloc.

The breakdown of Communist Eastern Europe in 1989 now seems to have been inevitable, although in the spring of 1988 it was still but a hoped for, remote prospect. Nevertheless, in Czech theatre, gradual easing of repressive measures and policies for several years had been creating a climate within which even mainstream theatres could again be moving toward increased artistry and relevance. In this sense it was a time reminiscent of the early and mid-1960s, when a light could be seen in the distance.

During the 1970s and most of the 1980s those who remained in Czech theatre had to exercise unusual agility and stamina simply to keep functioning in the face of purges, labyrinthine bureaucracy, and de facto censorship. Those whose activities were severely restricted or entirely eliminated included most of the major playwrights and directors of the 1960s. A tally sheet in the mid-1980s would have shown that Radok had died in Vienna in 1976, Krejča was in exile, and others (e.g., Jaromír Pleskot, Jan Grossman, Evald Schorm, Miloš Hynšt, Miroslav Macháček, Jan Kačer) directed only intermittently in various theatres. František Pavlíček, director and artistic head of the Vinohrady Theatre in the 1960s, had in fact been banned from theatre completely since 1968. The plays of virtually all the major pre–August 1968 playwrights (e.g., Václav Havel, Pavel Kohout, Josef Topol, Ivan Klíma, Milan Uhde, Ludvík Kundera, Milan Kundera) were still forbidden stage performance; in fact, some of their very names were not to be found in public print. Several of the playwrights had even harsher experiences. Pavel Kohout was prevented from returning to Prague after traveling to Vienna in the late 1970s. Václav Havel was incarcerated several times, for a total of five years. As late as February 1989 he was again arrested and sentenced to eight months, this time for allegedly inciting people to participate in banned demonstrations relating to the twentieth anniversary of the self-immolation of the student Jan Palach.

Nevertheless, a slow revival began in the early and mid-1980s. One of its more piquant ironies was that it was signaled by Czech productions of contemporary Soviet plays. Outspokenly critical of problems in their society, the Soviet plays prepared the way for the Czechs themselves to initiate tentative modifications of their play-it-safe repertoires. Even in 1988, when new Czech plays were reintroducing allusions and themes long absent from Czech drama, Soviet plays on Czech stages still remained more frank and more accusatory in dealing with contemporary socialist society.[2] What was permissible for Soviet authors was still only aspired to by the Czechs.

And yet the situation was changing. In a political and cultural climate in which nuances can be critical, the changes were at times striking. Even simple references in public print to directors like Alfred Radok and Otomar Krejča, or to playwrights like Josef Topol, were signs that conditions were shifting, though reference to others was still taboo (e.g., Václav Havel or Milan Kundera).

As the 1980s were drawing to a close, a new generation of actors, directors, and designers was steadily replacing the old guard in all theatres. It was a tendency also evident in the administrative and dramaturgical sections of Czech theatres, as new personnel gingerly tested the waters ultimately controlled by ministries and party committees. Of greater importance to the identity of Czech theatre, new approaches to staging were developing in the newer young studio theatres that were less subject to official surveillance than the large, established repertory theatres or even the surviving studio theatres of the 1960s.

Moreover, young playwrights, and a few established ones, were appearing on stage and in print with plays that were provocative in theme, form, and spirit. These were not plays of defiance or of overt challenge, nor did they make explicit reference to contemporary Czech conditions, but in their several ways they indicated that the Czechs were beginning to feel freer to explore themes that had been tacitly declared off-limits for two decades. Not surprisingly, for example, the precarious relation between the artist (or in fact any exceptional individual) and authority became a recurrent theme in new plays. Equally encouraging was a proposed shift in official guidelines that would allow theatres much greater flexibility in selecting their repertoires and making changes in them without elaborate bureaucratic negotiations with higher authorities. Of course, the theatres would be held responsible for the results.

Against this background, a consideration of several productions of contemporary Czech plays seen in Prague and in the provinces in the spring of 1988 provides a reasonable survey not only of the drift of Czech playwriting at that time

Oldřich Daněk's You Are Jan *at the National Theatre, 1987; directed by Václav Hudeček, designed by Zbynek Kolár. Photo from the National Theatre.*

but also of various representative theatres, their artists, and their approaches to staging.

Two works of distinction were produced, respectively, by the largest, most traditionally oriented theatres in Prague, the National Theatre and the Vinohrady Theatre. In June 1987 *You Are Jan* (Vy jste Jan), by Oldřich Daněk (b. 1927), an established playwright since the late 1950s, premiered in the recently opened New Stage (Nová scéna) of the National Theatre. *Urmefisto*, by Jan Vedral (b. 1955), a young writer whose background was that of a dramaturg and radio playwright, opened in January 1988 in the Vinohrady Theatre. Although both plays were based on historical material, remote Czech history in one case and twentieth-century German history in the other, they bore strong relevance to the Czechs in the late 1980s.

You Are Jan, directed by Václav Hudeček (b. 1929) dealt with the prototypal model of the Czech ethos — the case of Jan Hus, the Czech Protestant burned at the stake in 1415 in Constance by the inquisition for his refusal to recant his allegedly heretic beliefs. The action of the play occurs on the eve of his execution, while he still has the opportunity to recant, but we never encounter Hus himself. Instead, Daněk's strategy is that we meet some fifteen "shadows," who are, with the exception of a few incidental fictional characters, historical figures closely related to the career of Hus. Only one or two were actually present at his martyrdom; the others are there by dramatic license (somewhat like the situation in the epilogue of G. B. Shaw's *Saint Joan*). The first half of the play establishes their identities, their often hostile relationships, and their realization that they have been summoned not to judge Hus but to be judged by him. The last half of the play focuses on the question of recantation as characters reveal their guilt or uncertainties while examining their conscience, often under attack by the others. Not really a dramatization of historical events, the play dramatizes personalities and points of view.

Throughout the play, issues of conscience and fidelity to truth in the face of power politics and sheer human weakness are probed and debated in a series of encounters and solo confessional speeches. The play reexamines many problematics of the Czech character and, by tacit analogy, very recent Czech history. Particularly biting are allusions to the Czechs' tendency to be heretics but never to follow through with potentially painful actions, to step aside and let someone else play the martyr. Daněk presented us with a cross section of Czech humanity with whom we in the audience were progressively brought to identify. "You are Jan" became "we all are Jan," which is to say that we all had to measure ourselves by him.

Referring to the work as a "theatrical fugue," Daněk imbued the play with theatricality that was moderately Brechtian. Thirteen modern chairs that mirrored the chairs in the auditorium were arranged in a shallow arc on a curtainless stage that was bare of everything except a flight of stairs extending the width of the stage behind the chairs. The core characters were on stage throughout the play; they were supposedly outside the cell of Hus (the dialogue locates it at the rear of the auditorium) and were thus able to address him directly. The onstage characters made full use of the stage space in their various confrontations and solos, but at other times they simply occupied the chairs. The numerous units of action were provided with brief titles announced by the prison keeper's daughter as she rang a tiny bell. At various moments in the action a phalanx of red-robed cardinals, who judged Hus, silently mounted the steps from the rear in a show of strength. Organ music and dramatic changes of lighting from a U-shaped batten of high-intensity spotlights suspended above the acting area emphasized peak moments of tension.

The play built to its thematic climax as the historical characters unobtrusively stepped out of character, turned to the audience, and with powerfully affecting simplicity alternately spoke the final testament of Hus to his Czech compatriots, which called upon them to maintain their integrity, sense of justice and truth, and love for one another, qualities that many felt had been in short supply for twenty years.

The reading of this text led to the theatrically powerful conclusion of the play: as the cardinals appeared en masse and slowly descended toward stage level with intimidating force, those loyal to Hus joined hands to form a chain confronting the cardinals, as if protecting the audience from them. One of the Hussites cried out the penultimate words of Hus: "Let the fire be lit before me! Had I been afraid of flames, I would never have come to Constance!" As the two ranks were about to clash and the organ music reached a crescendo, another of the Hussites (one who had been witness to the event) turned to the audience in a sudden silence and *"slowly and ardently"* cited from the actual historical account of the last moments of Hus: "And when he wanted to sing the third stanza, the wind arose — and turned the flames toward his face. And so he fell silent." Slow blackout.

Ethical issues in a historical context also marked Jan Vedral's *Urmefisto* at the Vinohrady Theatre. It was a play based on the career of Gustaf Gründgens, the celebrated German actor and director whose career flourished during the Nazi regime.

Vedral went a bit further than Daněk in employing a Brechtian mode in order to distance and politicize a fundamentally emotive, psychological study of an actor. The protagonist, Henrik Höfgen, was observed from the 1920s to the 1960s in fifteen episodes plus a prologue and epilogue. Guiding us through these units was a female narrator named Mefistofela, who functioned as a mistress of ceremonies and ironic commentator and occasionally assumed a minor role in some of the scenes. This theatrical approach was also evident in the *mise en scène*, which centered on a stage (and backstage areas) within the stage, as Höfgen's rise to power and acclaim was paralleled by the disintegration of his conscience and the perversion of his original values. The distancing effect was strengthened by Vedral's flexible, sometimes casual blank verse.

Vedral concentrated on Höfgen's obsessive, consuming desire for fame as an actor, for which he was all too ready to sacrifice social and political convictions, personal friends, and his own integrity. Each scene took us forward in time while showing the corruption, fear, and breakdown of Höfgen and all of Germany. By publicly renouncing his early leftist leanings he was able to maintain his position as leading actor with the state theatre when the Nazis come to power in the early 1930s. He reached his greatest success as Mephisto in Goethe's *Faust*; later he became *intendant* of the theatre and, after various acts of moral cowardice, self-abasement, and artistic compromise, a member of the Prussian state council. By calculatingly helping to save the life of another actor threatened by the Nazis in wartime, Höfgen saved his own neck and prolonged his career after the war. The epilogue revealed a sick and broken figure finishing his career abroad as a member of a second-rate touring company.

The issues of ethical choice and moral responsibility, as well as the interplay of artistic ego and political involvement, lent themselves to application far beyond

Urmefisto *at the Vinohrady Theatre, 1988, directed by Jan Kačer, with Viktor Preiss as Henrik Höfgen/Mefisto. Photo by Martin Poš.*

Höfgen (Gründgens) in Germany of the 1920s–1940s. They had an understandable resonance in Czechoslovakia, where the issues of art vis-à-vis political ideology and morality vis-à-vis careerism had been a rarely absent fact of life since 1948, as had the more specific theme of the emigration of artists. That the Czechs were now, after nearly twenty years of "normalized" silence, dealing with such issues in a relatively frank though still indirect manner was one of the most significant indications of the gradual loosening up of conditions in Czech theatre. A play like *Urmefisto* would not have been tolerated even two years earlier.

The director of the production, Jan Kačer, was one of the original members of the Drama Club. After leaving the Drama Club, he was briefly a director at the National Theatre in the early 1970s before being terminated there; subsequently he spent several seasons at provincial theatres, chiefly in Ostrava, before being able to return to Prague and work at the Vinohrady Theatre in 1986. His dislocated career was not unlike those of many other leading artists since 1968.

Other critical themes were found in a drama of contemporary Czech life produced by the Laterna Magika Theatre, whose hallmark was the combining of live action and filmed images. *Vivisection* (Vivisekce, 1987), written and directed by Antonín Máša (b. 1935), was essentially an outgrowth of his earlier *Night Re-*

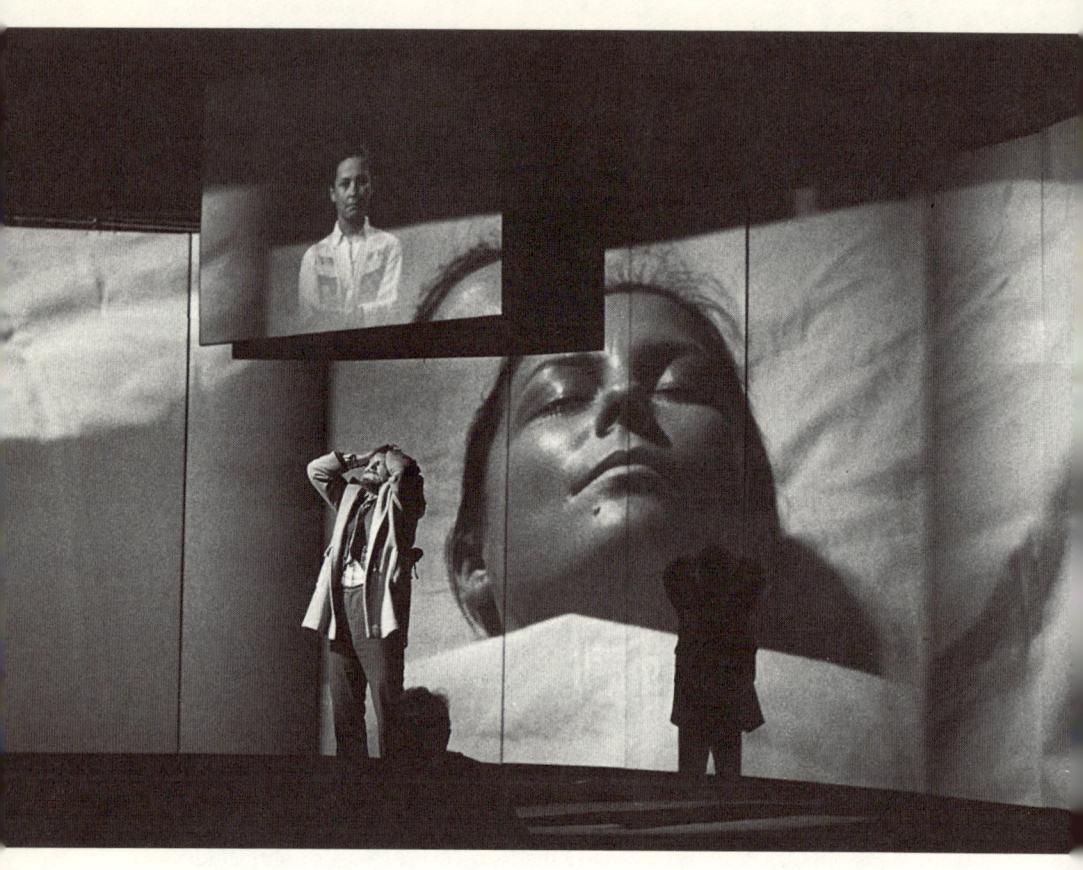

Laterna Magika's production of Antonín Máša's Vivisection, *1987. The vertical panels rotated to reveal an upstage area; the small screen lifted out. Photo by Vojtech Pisařík.*

hearsal (Nočni zkouška, 1981), which was the first Laterna Magika production based on a traditional dramatic text, written especially for Laterna Magika, and directed by Evald Schorm. Both were tightly scripted chamber plays in small-scale productions focusing on contemporary issues with similar strong themes — the need for social responsibility, for *caring* about one's work, one's environment, one's colleagues and loved ones. Also similar were the inherently theatrical settings.

Vivisection takes place in a television studio, which is preparing a dramatized documentary about a prosperous farmer of independent spirit whose life is in ruins as a result, he believes, of the irresponsible chemical spraying of the countryside, which led to his wife's contracting a deadly illness. Intensifying his grief and rage is the incompetent treatment his wife received while in the hospital for surgery, from which she did not recover. We never learn whether the farmer's accusations are valid, but that is secondary to the critique of current society and, by

[160] MODERN CZECH THEATRE

implication, its leaders. Thematically, the work condemns the dehumanization and callousness that lead to the waste and spoliation of natural resources as well as to the destruction of human potential. The combination of documentary drama technique and strong social criticism involving credible individuals in the *present* created an arresting theatre experience.

Maintaining a critical though veiled stance toward contemporary realities in Czechoslovakia has traditionally been a function of smaller, less institutionally dominated studio-type theatres. Outstanding examples were the Liberated Theatre of Voskovec and Werich and the D34 theatre of E. F. Burian in the 1930s and the Balustrade, Semafor, Drama Club, and Gate theatres of the 1960s. Carrying on this tradition in the 1980s were several more recent studio theatres, all of which came into existence earlier. Although they were similar in having rejected traditional scripts and traditional modes of staging, as well as in being more provocative than traditional theatres in choosing their repertoires, each nevertheless developed distinctive qualities.

The earliest of the new groups to come to prominence and sustain a substantial public life beyond a few seasons was Studio Ypsilon, founded during the 1963–1964 season in Liberec, in north Bohemia. Its core ensemble were members of a marionette theatre there known as the Naive Theatre, and their leader was — and still is — Jan Schmid (b. 1936), whose training was in glass, sculpting, and graphics before he became a designer and director in marionette theatre. (While pursuing advanced technical and crafts studies in the late 1950s in Prague, he asked Alfred Radok if he could be his assistant, but was advised to complete his nontheatre training.) The name Ypsilon resulted from the prior existence of a Theatre X in Brno when Schmid launched his own theatre in Liberec.

Not yet completely professionalized, the Ypsilon nevertheless had staged eight productions before the August 1968 invasion and by the late 1970s had mounted over forty more. Its growing reputation led to its being invited to move its entire operation to Prague in 1978, where it has performed ever since. It moved to its own quarters in the heart of the city in 1984, with performance facilities two floors below street level in a limited space accommodating at most two hundred people. The space allowed for a small but flexible acting area. The resident designer, Miroslav Melena (b. 1937), with the group since its founding, made ingenious and often witty use of platforms or other constructions, including some suspended from the ceiling.

The essential mode of an Ypsilon production was cabaret, a spritely and at times consciously naive cabaret, but always a thinking person's cabaret. Topicality, informal, even playful rapport with the audience, a strong element of music,

The tight quarters of the Ypsilon Theatre in Prague during the 1970s and 1980s; in most productions, the action occurred between two banks of audience seats. Photo by J. Burian.

an air of *commedia*-like improvisation, and a prevailing emphasis on good humor marked its productions. In many guises and styles — dramatizations of prose fiction, biography, historical data, or adaptations of existing plays (and even operas: *Carmen, La Traviata*) — Ypsilon usually rejected the option of conventionally producing an already existing, finished play. Instead, in the tradition of E. F. Burian, it assembled a scenario based on writings of varied genres. For many years, its most celebrated productions had strong elements of journalistic, historically based, and socially oriented material, to offset, as Schmid put it, the distortions and sheer gaps in information available to the public. But later the theatre began devoting itself to issues confronting individuals and the moral, ethical implications of their choices.

Paradoxically, in light of Schmid's dominant role in Ypsilon's identity for almost thirty years, the earmark of an Ypsilon production was the emphasis on the individuality of its dozen performers, most of whom had been with the company for ten years or more. The actors were expected to incorporate their distinctive temperaments and personalities even when portraying historical characters. It was all part of the larger aim of providing an alternative to the gray routine, the leveling of quality, and the lies — in life and art — that were associated with the era of Normalization since the early 1970s. Almost all the work at the Ypsilon arose from a process of collective improvisation under the guidance of Schmid. The emphasis was on maintaining one's own identity and point of view while respecting the personalities of the other performers. This approach resulted in a focused montage of individual performers.

Although a production finally became set in its overall form and main themes, details and even certain sequences were open to modification at each performance, though quite clearly under Schmid's control. Indeed, at times Schmid made directorial adjustments during performances while on stage as one of the performers. Other earmarks of an Ypsilon production included colorful, considerably physicalized clowning and a consistent disregard of sustained illusion: asides and friendly byplay with the audience marked each performance, as did songs, mostly original compositions by the several actor-composers in the ensemble, usually self-accompanied on guitar or piano. No particular attempt was made to integrate such numbers with the plot; they simply provided supplemental, often incisive lyrical comments on the main action, which was casually suspended. Many productions also opened and closed with musical numbers.

In a nutshell, the distinctive ambience of Ypsilon productions arose from their integration of the cabaret method with subject matter and themes that involved penetrating comments on the Czech national character and contemporary realities, often in the guise of personalities and events from Czech history or literature.

One such work still in the repertoire was *Honest Mathew* (Matěj poctivý; 1985), an adaptation by Schmid of a Czech play written by Arnošt Dvořák (1881–1933) and Ladislav Klíma (1878–1928) in the early 1920s. It is a fantasy-parable of a saintly simpleton into whose hands falls the state treasury, which he proceeds to guard from greedy tempters. The larger question of what to do with the treasury and how to assure happiness is provided with two potential answers. One, offered by the Devil, is a rationale of bourgeois pragmatism: the right of a strong personality to be free of moral responsibility and to acquire all one is capable of acquiring. The other, urged by Mathew's girlfriend (who ultimately vanquishes the Devil), is to thumb one's nose at the world, a world which is not to be taken seriously. The relevance of the Ypsilon production in the 1980s lay in its witty allusions to the bourgeois corruption within the socialist regime and to the blatantly acquisitive self-centeredness of much of the population at large.

The serious satiric thrusts of the work remained implicit; on the surface the production was a provocative, ambiguous farce with musical numbers, byplay with the audience, and *commedia* horseplay on a very small stage between two banks of the audience. Two distinctive Ypsilon embellishments were noteworthy: an interpolated sequence during which the actors dropped their lightly borne character identities to discuss spontaneously — as actors and as citizens — some of the ethical questions posed by the play; and the curtain call, which took the form of a choreographed roundelay in which the lyrics identified the entire production ensemble.

Among their other outstanding productions (which often created problems with the authorities) were a 1983 documentary collage of the life of Jaroslav Hašek (1883–1923), the author of *The Good Soldier Schweik*, a similar collage based on the Czech avant-garde movements of the First Republic (1972), and original scenarios by Schmid relating to other significant moments of Czech history. For example, *Thirteen Scents* (Třináct vůní, 1973) dealt with the 1930s and the years of wartime occupation; *Blacksmith Stelzig* (Kovář Stelzig, 1975) focused on the leader of a seventeenth-century peasant uprising; *K. H. Mácha* (1978) explored the career of the great nineteenth-century Czech poet of the Romantic era who epitomized the tensions between artist and society. At the other end of the spectrum were adaptations of satires by others, such as *The Suicide*, by Nikolay Erdman (1988), or *Evenings Under the Lamp Post* (Večery pod lampou, since 1973), impromptu evenings of chat and musical numbers with artists or public figures as guests.

A younger but very well established and extremely popular studio theatre was formed in Brno in 1967 by a number of graduates from the Theatre Academy (JAMU) in Brno under the guidance and leadership of their teacher, Bořivoj Srba (b. 1932), an admirer of Brecht and E. F. Burian. Inspired by an important avant-garde, leftist Brno author of the 1920s, Jiří Mahen (1882–1939), the new group took their original name from a collection of his writings called *A Goose on a String* (Husa na Provázku), but this caused considerable problems for the theatre in a few years because of the potentially explicit satire in the closeness of the word "Husa" to "Husák," the name of the Communist first secretary and de facto leader of Czechoslovakia from 1969 to 1987. "Husák" means either a gander or one who tends geese, neither very complimentary. With its new name, simply Theatre on a String (Divadlo na Provázku), it turned professional in 1972 and became the experimental studio of the State Theatre of Brno in 1978, although housed in largely improvised quarters of the municipal House of the Arts.

In addition to Srba, the founding members included three directors, Peter Scherhaufer (1942–1999), Eva Tálská (b. 1944), and Zdeněk Pospíšil (1944–1993), and composer Miloš Štědroň (b. 1942). The dramaturg since the early 1970s was Petr Oslzlý (b. 1945), also a sometime actor. He, Scherhaufer, and Tálská formed the core of the ensemble after 1975. The performer Boleslav Polívka (b. 1949) was also a charter member of the group but then for years devoted primary attention to his mime work, for which he gained international recognition.

The Theatre on a String did a good deal of touring, including visits abroad and to Prague, and aspired to be more than a theatre. According to Oslzlý, although the focus of the theatre was on creating artistic productions relevant to its public, the larger "program" was that of a cultural center or movement that would provide an alternative to official, institutionalized culture. It was an organized effort with various facets: a repertoire striving to project a sense of the world's complexities, ambivalencies, and contradictions; joint productions with other theatres; guest productions by other Czech and international theatre groups; design exhibitions, concerts, and a youth theatre studio. The all-embracing goal was to sustain and enhance Czech and central European culture in view of the effects of World War II, the Stalinist postwar era, and the trauma of August 1968 and its aftermath. In this and in other respects, the Theatre on a String was similar to Ypsilon but on a larger scale and with more extensive components.

In working toward its goals, the Theatre on a String practiced what it called "irregular theatre" (*nepravidelní divadlo*), a deliberate rejection of orthodox dramatic texts, illusionistic acting, conventional staging, authoritarian directing, and traditional stage-audience relationships. Instead, like the Ypsilon, it sought a more informal, communal encounter with its audience, productions built from scenarios or texts assembled from writings other than plays (or from major adaptations of existing plays), acting in which the personality of the actor was not hidden behind the character, and staging that took place in close proximity to an audience in almost any space — the streets, odd spaces within buildings — other than that of a traditional curtained stage. In various interviews and program notes, the Theatre on a String explicitly alluded to its debt to the prewar theatre of E. F. Burian and his efforts to create a cultural center, but unlike the Ypsilon, which prided itself on its made-in-Czechoslovakia identity, the Theatre on a String also consciously drew inspiration from the work of Meyerhold, Brecht, Jerzy Grotowski, and the Bread and Puppet and Living theatres.

Further differentiating it from the Ypsilon theatre, the Theatre on a String placed less value on the individual personalities of its performers and more on a relatively integrated, structured production. In fact, it was more nearly a traditional director's theatre rather than a theatre of individual performers under seemingly casual supervision. A Theatre on a String production was also likely to be larger, more dynamic, and more fully orchestrated than a typically intimate Ypsilon production. More emphasis was placed on visual composition and choreographed group movement in a Theatre on a String production, whereas the dialogue was relatively more important in an Ypsilon production. Music in a Theatre on a String production was more likely to be an organic part of the action as offstage recorded accompaniment or onstage performance, rather than take the form of live, personalized individual numbers. Similarly, some Theatre on a String productions consciously worked toward bridging the boundaries between drama and dance, drama and opera. Both groups sought contact with their audiences, but the Theatre on a String approach was usually less personal and less chatty and involved a greater degree of staying in character; audience intimacy and byplay was central for the Ypsilon, secondary for the Theatre on a String.

One of Theatre on a String's later works was yet another production commenting on the present, though based once again on Czech history, *Betrayer and Betrayed* (Prodaný a prodaná, 1988), a play on words relating to the Czech national opera, *The Bartered Bride* (Prodaná nevěsta). Typically, it was an internally generated production, text and music included. Developed from a scenario by Peter Scherhaufer and Petr Oslzlý, the director and dramaturg, respectively, *Betrayer and Betrayed* was originally produced in Brno in January 1987. It toured to Prague in February 1988, where it played a few performances before a capacity crowd seated on temporary bleachers in the very large, high-ceilinged ballroom of a peripheral hotel. The performance I saw was packed to the point of surely breaking existing fire and safety regulations.

Betrayer and Betrayed dealt with the enigmatic, controversial figure of Karel Sabina (1813–1877), a talented writer, revolutionary, and librettist of several operas by Bedřich Smetana, including *The Bartered Bride* (1866). Unlike Jan Hus, the heroic martyr of the Czechs, Sabina came to represent all that was counter to the Czech cause when he ostensibly sold out to the forces suppressing the Czechs' nationalistic aspirations, the Habsburg regime of the nineteenth century. And yet Sabina had been in the forefront of a militant wing of Czechs who urged nationalistic aspirations during the 1848 uprisings and had been jailed for eight years for his efforts. Within two years of his release from prison, however, he became a well-paid police informer, a secondary career that he followed from 1859 to 1872, when his activities were uncovered.

The production began with the dramatic confrontation of Sabina and his accusers, a group of prominent nationalistic Czech professional people, who accused him of his betrayal with conclusive evidence. In some twenty-five short flashback scenes that followed in a fluid, dynamic fashion, crucial incidents from Sabina's checkered life were vividly presented by ten actors who played some thirty roles. Intermingling with the action, and typical of the Theatre on a String's highly theatrical, imaginative staging, was a supplemental but interwoven singing and dancing chorus performing excerpts from *The Bartered Bride*. Their spontaneous appearances in the midst of many scenes with the regular actors, who ignored their presence, formed a striking accompaniment to the main action, the lyrical joy and innocence of the chorus ironically juxtaposing with the harsh and often grotesque realities of Sabina's career. Especially effective were the implicit parallels between the selling of the bride and Sabina's selling of himself to the police.

The energetic drive and tempo of the production were helped by purely functional scenography. The performers openly moved multipurpose furniture, and a rear two-level wall of doors opened up to reveal a variety of inner acting areas. Also characteristic of the Theatre on a String style was the tone of mixed comedy and seriousness. Rarely was the harshness of a scene not undercut by one or more capricious or satiric touches, but equally rarely did an ostensibly comic sequence not have a darker undercurrent. The Theatre on a String performers were particularly effective at projecting a Dickensian eccentricity just below the surface of most scenes. Sometimes this distracted from the serious theme of the play, but more often it created a special tension that contributed to the production's distinctive appeal. Although both theatres disdained a sober, businesslike approach to performance, Theatre on a String was relatively more straightforward than the Ypsilon, relatively less personalized.

Apart from its entertainment values, the production was another instance of the Czech theatre's probing of moral choices and ethical values in the context of Czech history and national character. As in *Urmefisto*, the focus was on an artist in relation to society and to a regime, but here it was a Czech artist, as it was in the Ypsilon production of *K. H. Mácha*. Moreover, parallels between the Habsburg regime and the Czech regime since 1948 were not too difficult to perceive. Finally, the freshness and inventiveness of the Theatre on a String staging were yet another sign of the relative vitality and resiliency of Czech theatre in the late 1980s.

Two later Theatre on a String productions warrant at least brief attention. *Shakespearománie*, another scenario jointly created by Scherhaufer and Oslzlý, was to be an extended, three-part homage to Shakespeare's vision of the world. I saw the first part in Brno in the spring of 1988: *Their Majesties, the Fools* (Veličenstva blázni), a crazy-quilt montage of scenes from the English history plays, *Midsummer Night's Dream* (which served as the frame), *Twelfth Night*, and *Romeo and Juliet*. Themes of power struggles, intrigues, and aggression predominated, and the staging was strongest in its dynamic choreography of battle scenes and general visual imagery. Offsetting this was an inherent incoherence in the continuity of the action, and a weakness of character depiction, but this seemed to be a conscious choice of its "authors," who were mainly concerned with the projection of themes. The second and third parts, respectively, focused on *Hamlet* and *King Lear–Tempest*.

I saw a performance of both the second and third parts during one evening in

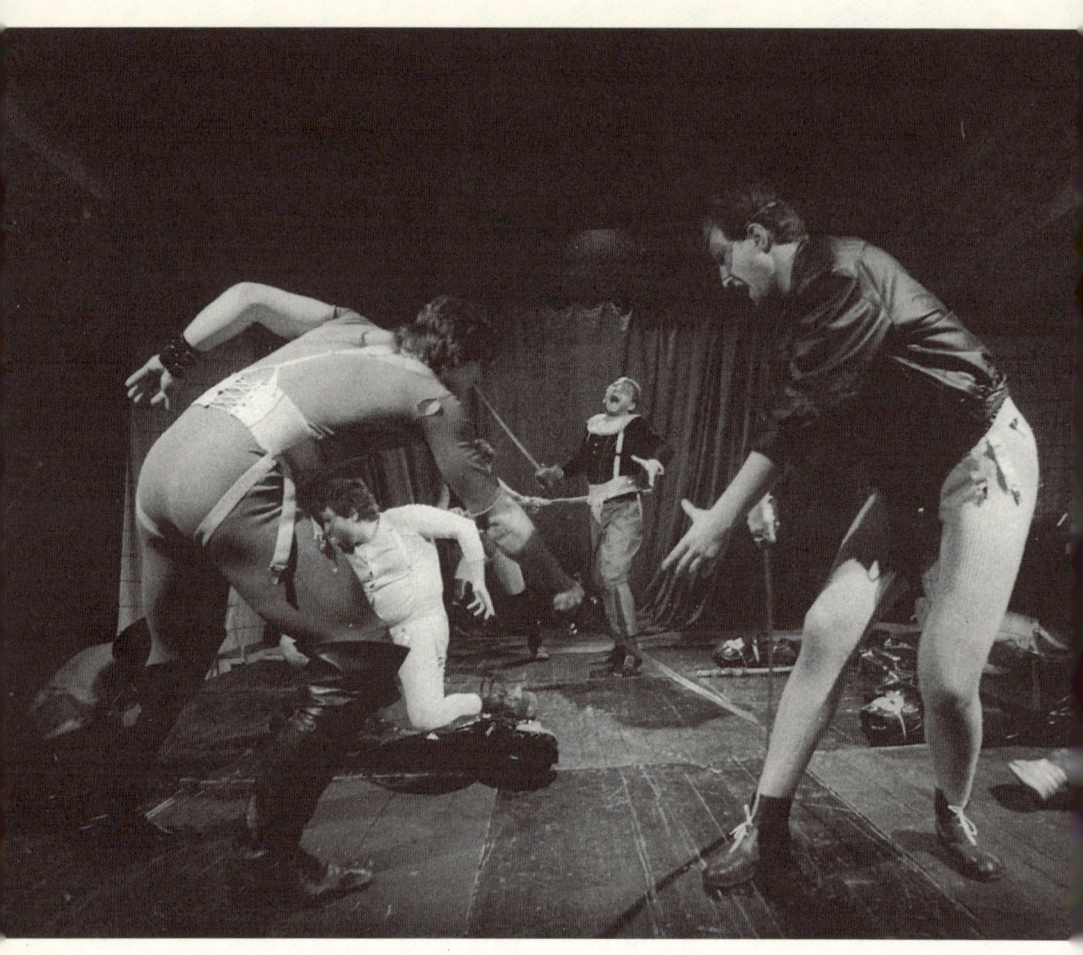

The Theatre on a String production of Shakespearománie I, *1988. Photo by Vladislav Vaňák.*

the fall of 1993: *Hamlet People* (Lidé Hamleti) had opened in 1990, *Man of Storm* (Člověk bouře) in 1993. Seeing both plays together produced a confused impression. The overall effect was a prodigal montage of Shakespearean themes, characters, and images on an epic scale. Some of it was brilliant in concept and execution; some of it seemed mere sound and fury, arbitrary editing, and shock-foolery. Most successful for me were the interwoven elements from *King Lear* and *The Tempest* in the final play, especially as presented through the characters of Lear-Prospero and Cordelia-Miranda. *Hamlet People* restricted itself to the *Hamlet* characters and incidents, whereas *Man of Storm* comprised elements not only from *King Lear* and *The Tempest* but also from *Hamlet, Macbeth, Midsummer Night's Dream, A Winter's Tale,* and flashback moments of some fragments from *Their Majesties, the Fools. Hamlet People* had four actors alternatingly playing

Hamlet, Claudius, one of the Players, and one of the Gravediggers. Both plays had characters from one play giving the lines of characters from another play; for example, the Macbeths gave Prospero's speeches on mercy and forgiveness. Both plays, moreover, went further with self-conscious theatricalism than did the first play of the trilogy, such as stopping the action to comment on what was happening; *Man of Storm* even had a contemporarily clothed Critic in the audience stop the action to berate the actors (e.g., Macbeth and Lady Macbeth) for their incompetent acting. Later on, the same critic was whipped out of the auditorium by the Lear figure. And yet some sequences were played straight, and others — however distorted — had flashes of insight into a spectrum of human follies, cruelty, compassion, and love. To make further sense of the plays, or to perceive a more coherent pattern to the stream of action, was beyond me on the basis of a single viewing with no access to the script. In any case, the trilogy as a whole demonstrated both what is best and also what is at times problematical about many Theatre on a String productions.

Eva Tálská, Theatre on a String's other current chief director, was usually associated with lyrical, poetic pieces that were adaptations of nondramatic writing, but she also had a penchant for fantasy and humor, such as her own dramatized adaptations of Lewis Carroll's and Edward Lear's "nonsense" writings. *Tales of a Long Nose* (Příběhy dlouhého nosu) opened in 1982 and was still playing in 1988, when I saw it. It was an elaborate collective improvisation on Lear's nonsense limericks, with a great deal of direct audience involvement, creating a sense of jovial community. Because a lot of water and bread was tossed about as well as consumed, much of the performance became messy but never uncontrolled. Medieval mimes and popular entertainment came to mind, or an adult version of theatre for grade-schoolers. Increasingly in the late 1980s and into the 1990s Tálská worked on theatre for young people.

HaDivadlo, a third important studio theatre, developed later and was smaller than the Ypsilon and Theatre on a String. Its roots, like those of Theatre on a String, extended back to 1967, when it began as an amateur group devoted to stagings of poetry in Prostějov, some forty miles northeast of Brno. Under Svatopluk Vála (b. 1943), the group had become semiprofessional by 1974 and taken the name HaDivadlo from the Hana region, where Prostějov is situated.[3] In 1980 the group was administratively incorporated into the State Theatre of Brno, where, like the Theatre on a String, it was considered a self-contained experimental studio. The change of status also meant complete professionalization, but the company itself remained in Prostějov until 1985, when it moved to Brno and settled into very small quarters seating only a hundred spectators.

The HaDivadlo acknowledged drawing inspiration from both the Ypsilon and Theatre on a String, especially in its rejection of traditional dramaturgy and staging, but soon established its own artistic identity. With a total staff of only sixteen, including nine performers, it was not only among the smallest of the studio theatres but also perhaps more flexible in its operations for that very reason. Its relative youth also contributed to its freshness; it did not have as much time to become settled in some of its practices. At a HaDivadlo performance (they maintain eight to ten plays in their ongoing repertoire), even more than at the Ypsilon or Theatre on a String, one felt a sense of experimentation, a feeling due not only to their improvisatory methods in rehearsal and the minimal production elements available to them in terms of space and materials, but also to the nature of their scripts.

In the late 1970s HaDivadlo began to give increased attention to dramas and dramatizations of prose. It was about that time that Arnošt Goldflam (b. 1946) joined the group as an actor and director, as did Josef Kovalčuk (b. 1948) as a writer and dramaturg. As the 1980s progressed, HaDivadlo became increasingly identified with scenarios and plays by Goldflam and Kovalčuk, usually directed by Goldflam, who had also become its artistic head.

More than either the Ypsilon or Theatre on a String, the HaDivadlo staged original, scripted plays rather than adaptations of prose or poetry or collectively created collages. Nevertheless, such plays, most of them written by Goldflam, were adapted to the actors' special characteristics and also subject to modification by the performers in the course of rehearsals. Moreover, some of the HaDivadlo productions went even further in the direction of actor-centered pieces for solo actor or duos that were custom-made, or other pieces arising from scenarios worked up by the actors themselves and finally given an overall coherence by Goldflam. Indeed, these peripheral productions sometimes approached the category of performance art, although the concentration was on acting rather than on a display of other varied talents.

Productions with an organized, shaped script by Goldflam as their foundation, however, brought most attention to the HaDivadlo in later years. From the early 1980s these scripts tended to deal with the inner life and moods of characters rather than with outward events or explicitly depicted social issues. Goldflam's strength as a writer was in a mixture of the intuitively lyrical and grotesque, with tragi-comic, often surreal, overtones that brought to mind Kafka and Chekhov or the paintings of Marc Chagall. Never strident or strained, his work had an elusiveness that left much for the director and actors to fill in and for the audience to interpret. *Sand* (Písek, 1988), like many of his works, was strongly autobiographical,

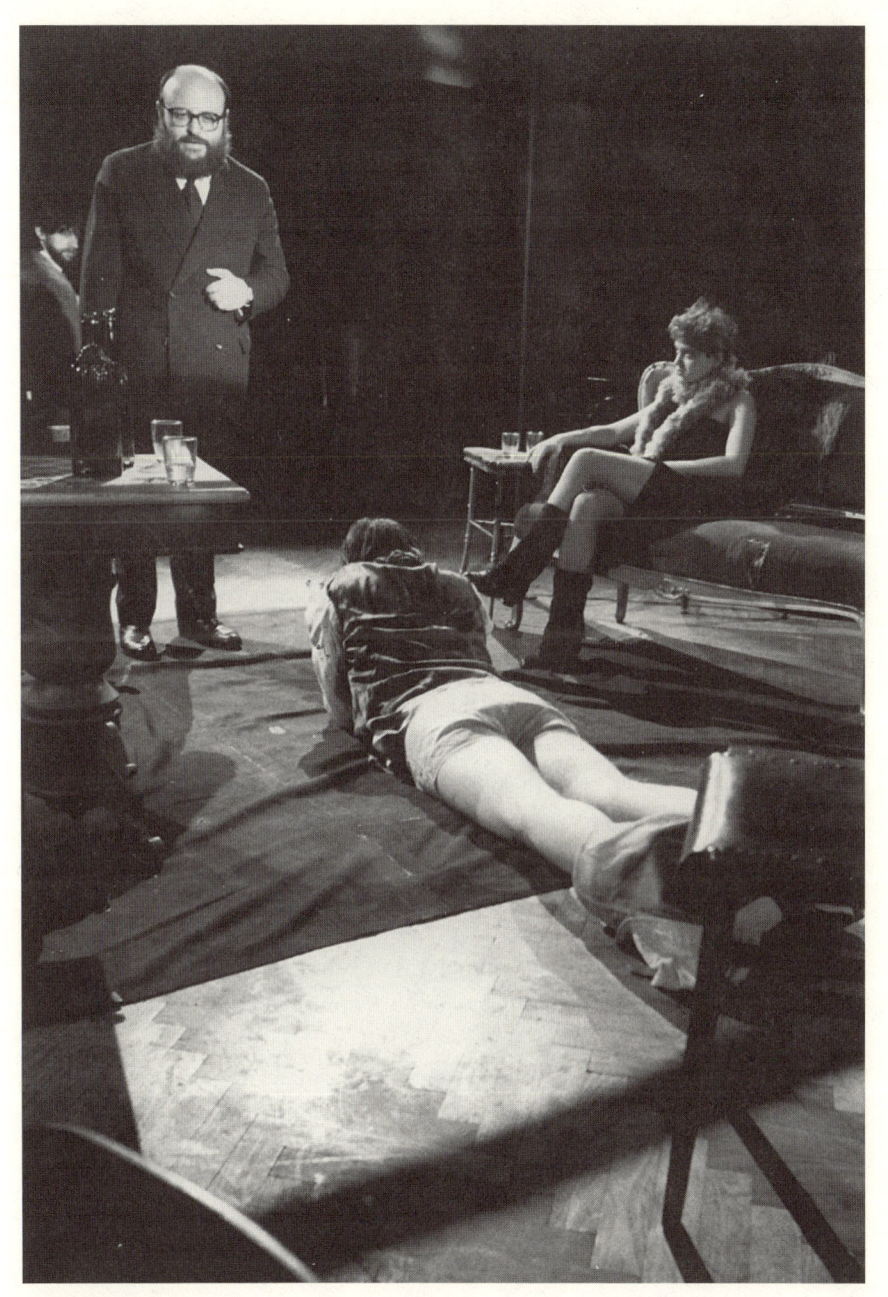

Arnošt Goldflam in a performance of his Fragments from an Unfinished Novel, which he directed and in which he played himself as the author of a "work in progress." Photo by Jaroslav Prokop.

dealing with three generations of a Jewish family in Moravia. In a dreamlike, bittersweet manner it blended tragedy, nostalgia, and the ludicrous in some twenty loosely related scenes that were played within a central space enclosed by ordinary wire screening and surrounded by the audience on three sides. The touring performance I saw was in a small cultural center in the outskirts of Prague, where the actors worked with only minimal platforms and props. Their style of acting — low-key, with great ensemble responsiveness, making the most of distinctive bits of gesture and business and very comfortable with the intimate presence of the audience — was well suited to the indirect, evocative nature of the play's action.

Accompanied by bits of narration, scenes flowed from one to the other, as fragments of memory-modified events and characters revealed a family's destinies from the turn of the century to the present. Images of fascination and fear from childhood recurred, often accompanied by musical echoes from earlier scenes. Historical events were evoked by stage metaphors: to the sound effect of a train coming to a halt, a group of people who had previously been sharing a family reunion removed their clothes and carried them offstage in an orderly manner, as we recalled several references to dreams of fire in preceding scenes. It was hard to avoid thoughts of the Holocaust — yet nothing explicit had happened or been said. Other fluid sequences depicted the humor and humiliations of a young man coming to adulthood: an Alice in Wonderland interrogation by a commission to test the protagonist's fitness to be admitted into a nameless organization; his discipleship in a cultural group lorded over by an unidentified would-be messiah of the arts. Every now and then veiled but pointed allusions reminded the audience that this was not some abstract, universal depiction of a young man's coming of age, but one rooted in the experience of growing up in postwar Czechoslovakia. Goldflam was born in 1946 to Jewish parents in Brno. Four of his father's siblings had died in the camps. Goldflam was and has continued to be a relatively rare phenomenon in Czech theatre, a Jew who deals with Jewish issues in his works. The long established tendency among Czech or German Jews toward assimilation in the dominant culture was modified in his case, but it must also be noted that explicitly Jewish subjects or allusions are the exception rather than the rule in his writing. *Sand* remained overtly apolitical and nonethnically centered. Avoiding direct comments that would underline the Jewishness of the characters and situations, presenting subjective, dream-shaped scenes with a nostalgic, emotive core, the play was nevertheless a witness of its time.

A few additional studio groups active in the 1980s deserve attention. The Theatre on the Fringe (Divadlo na okraji), a small young amateur ensemble devoted to staging poetry with music, was launched in Prague in 1969 by Zdeněk Potužil (b. 1947), who focused on texts and staging, and Miki Jelínek (b. 1950), whose interest was primarily in music. The ensemble turned professional in 1972 and shortly thereafter began to perform in the Rubín, a cramped cellar studio space in Prague's Malá strana section. In 1973 Potužil and Jelínek added an amateur ensemble, known as A-Theatre, and also shifted to dramatizations of prose texts. In 1979 they began to stage occasional works of dramatic literature, such as Shakespeare's *Othello* (1979) and *Romeo and Juliet* (1981), as well as Gogol's *Revizor* (1983). Nevertheless, their chief distinction was ingenious, poetically stylized staging of nontraditional scripts, as was evident, for example, in *Bitter Maxim* (Hořky Maxim), which I saw in 1988. A two-part performance comprising a collage of incidents from Gorky's life and a dramatization of a Gorky story, respectively, it was effectively staged in an expressionistic, choreographically stylized manner on a constructivist setting at one end of a low-ceilinged, vaulted room. Inner conflicts of flesh and spirit alternated with themes of morality and ethical choices in a context of revolutionaries and police agents in turn-of-the-century Russia, somewhat echoing the Theatre on a String production based on Karel Sabina's life. Despite many successful productions for its faithful limited audiences, the Theatre on the Fringe formally disbanded in 1987, not for political reasons but because its key members wanted to move on to other projects.

The Jára (da) Cimrman Theatre collective began producing literate, sophisticated, but deliberately low-key mystifications and spoofs in 1967. The entire repertoire became dedicated to a fictive legendary figure whose name the company bore. Several collaborators who conceived the figure of Cimrman and began the company also created the scenario-scripts and performed the central roles. Everything centered on Cimrman, a near-cult figure whom they depicted as a Czech polymath, explorer, scholar, and sometime theatre buff whose major achievements and adventures had to be chronicled. Each production had two parts: the first was a lecture or seminar on a phase of the master's experiences, the second an enacted demonstration of it. The tone was subtly parodistic: quasi-scholarly and relying heavily on wordplay, deliberately semi-amateurish, absolutely straight-faced but essentially tongue-in-cheek. The entire project was in the vein of Alfred Jarry's creation of Dr. Faustrolle and the science of Pataphysics, but was quintessentially Czech in that its whole point was an indirect critique of Czech history and national character, although some said that the Cimrmanians were at first also needling Russian claims of supremacy in all human endeavors. Mounting one or two productions a year, the Cimrmanians never lacked for audiences seeking sly entertainment with a literary, academic tilt. Some of the productions ran for hundreds of performances. Of all the more recent studio theatres, it probably had the least direct relevance to contemporary sociopolitical currents but was nevertheless a universal antidote to all institutional and national pretentiousness.[4]

Brief mention must also be made of the Prague Five (Pražská pětka), a loosely related group of five small, originally amateur performance ensembles that developed in the 1970s and formed a notable part of the indirect resistance to the Normalization era throughout the 1980s, during which time they became professional. Never overtly political or explicitly accusatory in their inventive, largely improvisatory work, they nevertheless formed a bright, youthful exception to the pall of routine production work in most regular theatres. The Cellar (Sklep) focused most nearly on plays, Forward (Vpřed) on recitations, Mimóza on pantomime, the Cramp (Křeč) on dance, and the Carousel (Kolotoč) on designer's theatre. Most of their activity began to dwindle in the late 1980s, but some activity persisted into the 1990s.

The final two distinctive productions of mainstream theatre which I witnessed in 1988 were the work of two younger Czech playwrights whom many regarded as particularly promising: Karel Steigerwald (b. 1945) and Daniela Fischerová (b. 1948), both of whom started writing plays after studying screenwriting at Prague's celebrated Film Academy, the seedbed of the creative wave of Czech films that dominated the 1960s. (Playwriting as such was not taught at the Theatre Academies, which focused on acting, directing, and design. In fact, playwriting was not a subject at any university-level school in Czechoslovakia.)

Three of Fischerová's plays had been well received: *The Hour between the Dog and the Wolf* (Hodina mezi psem a vlkem, 1979), a study of François Villon as an archetypal artist in conflict with authority; *A Legend* (Báj, 1982), her version of the Pied Piper theme, in which she explored the question of free will and drew parallels between the medieval and contemporary world; and *Princess T* (Princezna T, 1986), an adaptation of the legend of Princess Turandot and her many suitors, which had its premiere in the Drama Studio of the state theatre in Ústí nad Labem. I saw a subsequent production, in a peripheral but standard Prague theatre, the S. K. Neumann, in 1988.

Princess T is a highly theatrical, hard-edged melodrama that takes the Carlo Gozzi prototype and makes of that romantic fantasy a tightly knit study of varying degrees of evil. The context of Princess Turandot's deadly game with suitors becomes a universally identifiable crisis of power politics. Seemingly a remorseless and obsessive pursuer of ultimate justice, Turandot is implicitly revealed as a naive, sentimental dupe confronted with a horrific fait accompli as the play ends. Kalaf, the suitor with whom she finally falls in love, turns out to be a deadly enemy of China, who has been brought in by Turandot's father to crush the internal opponents of his foundering regime. Kalaf and the Emperor agree to slaughter thousands of each other's soldiers as the price of Kalaf's becoming Turandot's husband and the Emperor's successor. The world that Fischerová creates is a distillation of the absurdity and tragedy that have marked many times and places when survival is a matter of choosing between evils and humanistic ideals are irrelevant, if not actually mortal weaknesses.

As she drives the action forward through some twenty scenes of varying length, Fischerová writes terse, pointed dialogue that is literate without being literary, and vividly alive on the stage. Her background in screenwriting probably contributed to her talent for maintaining suspense with fine control and timing, frequently building individual scenes to a high pitch before sharply breaking the mood and cutting to another action without losing a beat. Simultaneous scenes with alternating dialogue provide an ironic reciprocal comment on each other and demonstrate her talent for integrating dialogue with visual effects that exploit the layout of the stage. Offsetting these virtues is her tendency to be too brief and elliptical in establishing key data, relationships, and motivations. Her successful suitor's true character and objectives, for example, remain ambiguous, even cryptic, until his climactic confrontation with the Emperor very late in the play, a scene which becomes a coup du théâtre rather than a meaningful revelation. On the other hand, these very characteristics may be appropriate for the dangerous, deformed world she created in the play.

Fischerová's strong theatrical imagination was most evident in her use of three *commedia zannis*, who moved in and out of the fictional stage reality. In addition to assuming various functional roles in the play (such as anachronistic newspaper boys shouting headlines), they introduced the play, shifted the scenes, created mood and atmosphere by embodying and speaking what would otherwise be stage directions, threw in frequent comments on a scene in progress, and provided very effective transitions between scenes. The *zannis* were only occasionally charming; most of the time they provided a sharply ironic, even cynical perspective on the action; their comments and actions often became grotesque and, at times, sadistic. They were apt agents in Fischerová's extreme, hectic vision, which was shaped with notable skill and an instinctive theatrical sense.

Karel Steigerwald had his most important association with the Drama Studio in Ústí nad Labem in north Bohemia, a successor to the Kladivadlo. The Drama Studio, headed from 1975 to 1983 by director Ivan Rajmont (b. 1945), was relatively more orthodox in its repertoire and staging than the other studio theatres mentioned here, concentrating on fresh, stimulating plays and very effective acting from its youthful ensemble.[5] In this theatre, in association with director Ivan Rajmont, Steigerwald developed a loose tetralogy of plays with a specifically Czech milieu, reaching back into the nineteenth century and extending forward to an unspecified postapocalyptic setting some thirty years after a devastating nuclear holocaust. The first play written, *The Tatar Fair* (Tatarská pout', 1979), deals with the period from the end of World War II to the 1960s; *Period Dances* (Dobové tance, 1980) presents events following the Czech nationalistic uprising of the 1848 era; *Foxtrot* (1982) is centered in the 1930s; and *The Neapolitan Disease* (Neapolská choroba, 1984) is a vision of the future. Only two of the four plays, *Period Dances* and *Foxtrot*, were allowed short runs in the Drama Studio before 1988. Both *Neapolitan Disease* and *Tatar Fair* had their premiere in Prague in the spring of 1988.

Neapolitan Disease, the more focused and powerful of the last two, was directed by Ivan Rajmont and presented as an *agentura* (agency) production, a method of producing plays and other entertainment that provided — relatively speaking — a considerable degree of free enterprise and free expression with the least official supervision. Official cultural offices were allowed to audition and book individual and group touring performances for dozens if not hundreds of cultural organizations throughout the country, with salaries keyed to attendance figures. Latest estimates revealed that the number of *agentura* theatre performances surpassed the number of regular theatre performances and that a great many actors earned more in their moonlighting *agentura* performances than they did from their resident theatres. As an *agentura* production, *The Neapolitan Disease* used actors from several Prague theatres as well as some from the Ústí nad Labem theatre. Before going on to one-night stands in other cultural centers in the provinces, it was performed a few times in a peripheral cultural center in the Žižkov district of Prague, where I saw it.

Like Fischerová in all of her plays, Steigerwald distanced his subject in *The Neapolitan Disease*. By dealing with the survivors of a future nuclear disaster, he was able to comment not only on the conditions that might have led to that disaster but, less directly, on conditions in Czechoslovakia during the previous few decades. Compared to Fischerová's tight control of every beat of her action, Steigerwald's method was relatively slack and almost meandering; certain scenes and speeches ran on beyond their optimal limits, and some situations and themes seemed unnecessarily repeated. The text consists of twenty numbered scenes in two parts; in performance, no break occurred between scenes. Although time and place clearly changed, such changes, even in the text, could be only tentatively inferred from dialogue and the sketchiest of stage directions. It is as if Steigerwald deliberately sought to estrange and abstract the details of his story while making his characters and their social, ethical implications as relevant as possible. The setting consisted of indoor and outdoor elements on a relatively bare stage backed by black drapes.

The plot involved a situation and characters who seem to be out of Gogol by way of Kafka. A makeshift hospital in a forest was dominated by an incompetent chief who was a physical education instructor before the disaster and could be alternately brutal and tearful. We gathered that life continued in remaining buildings and caves, while weeds and other vegetation covered the boulevards of the cities. At his own insistence, the Chamberlain of the still surviving regime was brought to this hospital because he had no trust in the hospital at the Castle. The Chamberlain was, if anything, cruder than the hospital chief. Originally a purveyor of false lottery tickets, he came to power with a few others after the disaster. Somewhat reminiscent of Jarry's Père Ubu or Beckett's Pozzo, but more amiable though less bright than the latter, he was actually suffering from acute and chronic diarrhea but insisted that he be treated for the "Neapolitan Disease" (i.e., VD) because he found the latter malady more appropriate to his macho self-image and his naive, picture-postcard fantasies of Naples. Other characters included an idealistic, relatively informed young medical aide and his medically inept counterpart, a malicious careerist. Characters outside the medical staff were survivors — rascals and innocents — who foraged in the woods but became part of the world of the field hospital.

In varying degrees, all the characters depended on grotesque fantasies and pathetic illusions, thus projecting one of Steigerwald's themes, the chronic, self-perpetuating lies at the core of society. Other themes related to the heedless, destructive incompetence of those in power and the tendency in all the characters to stifle conscience and suppress disagreeable aspects of the past in order to assure sheer survival and some degree of creature comfort. By the end of the play, partly through accident, partly through murderous though absurd ambition, the hospital chief, the Chamberlain, and the idealistic but weak doctor were dead, while the others remained hapless survivors. Steigerwald, commenting through the offstage, demented voice of the careerist medical assistant, provided a coda to the death and destruction amid the ruins; the gist was that, when the whole generation was finally weighed in the scales, it would be found to have been wanting. Steigerwald added a final, dark twist in this last, hysterical speech: not only was it delivered in German, but it was actually taken from a speech by Joseph Goebbels in 1933.

The production was rich in its imaginative plot premise, its tragi-comic grotesqueries, and much of its character interplay. Weakening its undeniable impact was an insufficiently edited and shaped action, in which clusters of incidents and speeches were more striking than the structure and sum of their parts. Another problem was the tone of the play, an often uneasy mix of grotesque satire and almost Saroyanesque sentimentality and bathos, especially in some of the secondary survivors. It was not easy to tell whether Steigerwald meant such moments to be ironic or to suggest that even outrageous and contemptible figures are still "human." In either case, the play's point became less sharply focused, although Steigerwald's confrontation of painful, problematic aspects of the Czech ethos demanded respect.

The underlying need to explore the peculiar realities of Czech character and Czech history formed the single most consistently present element in all these plays. Such realities included the memories of repeated defeats, humiliations, or simply mistaken choices, all of which led to life under various forms of subjugation (the loss of the First Republic at Munich, 1938, and the years of Nazi occupation; the Communist takeover of the postwar Republic, 1948, and the subsequent Stalinist era; the Soviet intervention and suppression of Socialism with a Human Face, 1968, and the following bleak era that was only beginning to alter). It was as if each playwright were creating variations on a theme arising from a basic question: How to account for the tragically repeated failures of a generally intelligent, productive, honorable people to translate their ideals into a lasting independence of national life and spirit, instead of being intimidated or coerced from without or betrayed by material, self-serving drives from within?

In these plays, in one guise or parable after another, we saw situations of victims and manipulative powers leading to deformations in social life and individual character. The emphasis could be on the victims (*Sand*), the manipulating intimidators (*You Are Jan, Princess T*, and *Neapolitan Disease*), or the victims' contribution to their own pain or humiliation (*Urmefisto, Betrayer and Betrayed, Honest Mathew*). Sometimes the analogies to the present were almost explicit (*You Are Jan, Urmefisto*), at other times more obscure (*Sand, Princess T*), but they were never missing. It was like an inmate or patient obsessed by his or her case. Like it or not, in the spring of 1988, it was difficult to imagine a contemporary Czech play or production not resonating, even if softly, with its nation's repeated traumas. Nevertheless, although the issues were painful, the sheer ability to address such issues after the long drought of Normalization was a welcome change.

The other chief impression created by these productions was that of a spectrum of *mises en scène* that ranged from familiar modifications of traditional forms and methods (*You are Jan, Urmefisto, Princess T, Neapolitan Disease*) to those that programmatically rejected traditional forms and methods (*Betrayer and Betrayed, Honest Mathew, Sand*). In no case was any of these productions radically innovative in the context of the day's world theatre. Even the work of the studio theatres represented variations of experiments seen in the West or in the Soviet Union or in the Czech theatre itself at various times since the 1920s. What was both impressive and special, however, was the extent to which these Czech works were able to wed vividly perceived and relevant issues with a variety of freshly theatrical approaches in playwriting (or scenario shaping) and staging.

To what degree was this work in Czech theatre noted in reviews and criticism of the time? Standard coverage of theatre in the regular press and periodicals had become innocuous: anything provocative was either totally ignored or treated blandly, often — ironically — because the reviewers did not want to call attention to such work for fear of having it and its creators get into trouble with the authorities. Serious contemporary theatre theory and criticism had lagged behind actual production practice for almost twenty years. Such writing was restricted to underground samizdat publications, but even the samizdat theatre publications to which I had access did not dwell on the specific, pointed sociopolitical issues underlying these plays and others like them. Rather, such publications seemed devoted to providing objective information and generalized criticism of a level not found in official publications since 1970. Primarily, one encountered comments on some recent playwrights, bibliographies of banned writers, or discussions and interviews with writers and other artists, who expressed their thoughts on the current state of theatre in broad philosophic terms that transcended the immediate realities of life outside the theatres.

One recurrent issue concerned the significance of the studio theatre movement vis-à-vis traditional theatre production. Supporters of the studio theatres regarded traditional theatre as an outworn, irrelevant relic of the past. For such people, the sheer existence of small, semiofficial groups that emphasized a sense of audience rapport, spontaneity, and nonconformity was in itself perceived as a form of liberation and progress. Even while acknowledging the freshness of dramaturgy and staging in some of the studio theatres, other critics faulted their lack of traditionally structured and shaped texts and their sacrificing of traditionally developed dramatic characters for the allegedly superficial values of audience involvement, improvisatory spontaneity, and gratification of the actors' egos, all of which were viewed as dubious virtues against the lack of powerful themes treated with dramaturgic complexity, distinctive language, and high theatrical imagination. The traditionalists looked to the production of plays like those of Fischerová and Steigerwald; those committed to new forms found their models in the improvisatory, collective creative processes of the Ypsilon, String, and HaDivadlo theatres. The unspoken ideal would have been a fusion of the best qualities of each approach.

Indeed, several classic revivals being performed in 1988 suggested that such tentative fusion may already have been occurring. Productions of Sophocles' *Oedipus* (1988) at the Vinohrady Theatre, *Hamlet* (since 1982) at the National Theatre, and Chekhov's *Ivanov* (1988) in the Drama Club demonstrated how traditional material could be staged with great freshness and audience appeal without indulging in superficial eccentricities in acting or directing. This was especially true of Macháček's *Hamlet*, with František Němec (b. 1943) in the title role. With no subjective directorial twists or quirks, the production simply had great immediacy, focus, and sustained dynamics. On the other hand, productions such as the Theatre on a String's *Balet Makabre* (1986) and the Ypsilon's *The Devil Who Promised the Moon* (1986) used improvisation and significant textual adaptation to shape substantive, coherent dramatic statements.

The Czech theatre in the late 1980s was not the theatre that produced such major international successes of the 1960s as Otomar Krejča's productions of *Romeo and Juliet*, *The Three Sisters*, or *Lorenzaccio*, Alfred Radok's productions of *The Entertainer*, *The Play of Love and Death*, or *The Last Ones*, Miroslav Macháček's *The Insect Comedy*, or Jan Grossman's *The Memorandum*. But despite the loss of some major directors and the exclusion of most of the playwrights of the 1960s, it was a theatre that was once again increasingly alive and, with new personnel, continuing to grapple not only with administrative restraints but with issues vital to its audiences. At the same time it was sustaining its own heritage of theatre that strives for a combination of mature artistry and fresh creative impulse. In the spring of 1988 it was experiencing a number of tentative breakthroughs toward a condition of freer expression that began to evoke memories of more creative, challenging days. Whether such progress would be able to continue remained to be seen.

9

1989
Annus Mirabilis for the Czechs and Their Theatre

In the space of a few short weeks toward the end of 1989, more than forty years of imposed ideology, inept social engineering, economic mismanagement, political repression, and cultural distortion were swept away as Czechoslovakia experienced its Velvet Revolution. What no one seriously anticipated but only hoped for in a distant future happened with almost startling ease. By the late 1980s the Communist system in Czechoslovakia was more vulnerable than anyone suspected. In retrospect, however, it was the severely weakened condition of the regime in the Soviet Union and in its other East European satellites, especially East Germany, that proved more decisive to the success of the revolution than the weakened Czechoslovak regime and the uprising of the citizens in late November 1989. No longer could the Czechoslovak leaders fall back on military intervention from the Warsaw Pact forces. The Czechoslovak Communist leadership was on its own, and on its own it was no match for the surge of the people's will to abolish it.

The excitement and euphoria of the liberation of 1989 equaled, perhaps even surpassed, the emotive power of the wartime liberations of 1918 and 1945. It was an immensely satisfying experience for the Czechs as a whole, but for Czech theatre people it was a unique triumph because they themselves were at the very heart of the events that led to the collapse of the Communist government and its replacement by a leadership embodying their own best selves. It was the climax and vindication of the Czech theatre's decades-long efforts to challenge and counteract the forces that had deformed the life of the nation since 1948.

Allowing for its slight hyperbole, the following comment at the time by the dean of Czech theatre scholars, Dr. František Černý, put Czech theatre's significance to the Velvet Revolution in proper perspective:

> What Czech theatre people did for Czech society after November 17 was a natural consequence of the best traditions of Czech theatre. Czech actors were never merely the paid entertainers of the nation, but, when necessary, also its tribunes, and the same applies to others bound to theatre, such as playwrights. Czech theatres during the days of November [1989] were transformed into political arenas — something that the history of theatre had not previously witnessed.[1]

In fact, the involvement of Czech theatre people was even more extensive than Černý suggested. For the full story, we must review the key events of the previous year as well as the host of changes that would follow from the astonishing events culminating in the inconceivable reality of Václav Havel's becoming president of Czechoslovakia in December 1989.[2]

In June 1988, a few days before I was to leave Prague after a six-month research residency, I bumped into Petr Oslzlý, dramaturg of Brno's Theatre on a String. He had just come from a meeting of theatre people from across the country which had been discussing the progress of the Soviet-inspired liberalizing movements of *glasnost* and *perestroika* in the recent past. Still flushed with excitement, he told me of the challenge he had flung into the relatively tame discussion: "Let's not talk of *glasnost* and *perestroika* until Havel is allowed to be played, until Krejča is allowed to direct, and until Radok is discussed fully and openly!"

Less than a year and a half later, not only had Oslzlý's rhetorical demands come to pass, but after more than twenty years of congealed grayness Czech theatre had shed its bureaucratic straitjacket and played a central role in the dramatic mass movement that ignited on November 17 and culminated before the New Year in the parliamentary election of Václav Havel as president.

Oslzlý's open challenge would have been impossible even one year earlier, and the same could be said of certain productions that I had seen in 1988, which had begun to address core questions of individual conscience and national morality that had long been ignored. Although nothing explicitly accusatory of the system could yet be staged, and the artists who had been banned were still banned, a tentative undertow was certainly evident in that spring of 1988.

During the following eighteen months, the undertow gathered strength. Before considering its key signs in theatre, we need to note some major incidents in life outside the theatre during this period, which had an indirect but powerful effect on what was evolving within theatres. Major public demonstrations and arrests occurred in Prague and elsewhere in October 1988 during attempts to mark the anniversary of Czechoslovakia's creation in 1918. Similarly overt manifestations of civic unrest occurred the following January on the twentieth anniversary of Jan Palach's immolation of 1969, and Václav Havel along with others was arrested yet again. He was sentenced to nine months' imprisonment, but international pressure contributed to his being released in May 1989, the same month that witnessed another foreshadowing, little noted at the time: the departure of a Soviet battalion from the Olomouc region, part of the USSR's pullout of 50,000 troops from East Germany, Hungary, and Czechoslovakia. In June a petition to redress a variety of wrongs and to allow free discussion of sociopolitical matters since 1968 began to be distributed; titled "A Few Sentences" (Několiv vět), it had gathered some 40,000 signatures by the fall. Also in June, a silent march of 1,500 activists for human rights was tolerated in Prague. Not tolerated were mass demonstrations on August 21 marking the anniversary of the Warsaw Pact invasion of 1968. Police used force, and hundreds were arrested.

One month earlier, in July, an exodus of East Germans had begun, crossing Czechoslovakia on their way to Hungary and thence to West Germany by way of Austria. By October, with the East German regime in a state of collapse, thousands of its citizens were flooding Prague, seeking asylum at the West German embassy. One month later, in early November, with the opening of the frontier between East and West Germany, the notorious Berlin wall began to come down. Meanwhile, in Prague and other cities huge demonstrations celebrating the 1918 birth of the Czechoslovakian Republic on October 28 were once again forcefully broken up. On the evening of November 17, against this background of historic public events, the drama of the Velvet Revolution in Prague began.

Meanwhile, two remarkably similar theatre productions one year earlier, in October 1988, signaled a major breakthrough symptomatic of the unraveling system of state controls and the increasing boldness of certain ensembles. In Brno, the Theatre on a String and HaDivadlo collaboratively staged *Rozrazil I*, a "stage magazine" or collage of documents, events, and scenarios unified by probing the theme of democracy.[3] Of major significance was the inclusion of a one-act play authored by Havel but not identified as such — *Tomorrow We'll Start It Up* (Zítra to spustíme), a version of events and key figures on the eve of Czechoslovakia's independence in 1918. The very title of the overall production, *Rozrazil*, was typical of the ambiguous titles often used by the two theatres: the word means both the flower veronica and "break or smash through."

At virtually the same time, in Prague's more traditional Realistic Theatre, headed by Karel Kříž (b. 1941), formerly of the F. X. Šalda Theatre in Liberec, an essentially similar anthology production opened: *Res publica I*, an assemblage of poetry, prose, and dramatic scenes of Czech life during the interwar First Republic. It included excerpts from the writings of T. G. Masaryk, the first president, and Karel Čapek, both of whom became nonpersons after the Communist takeover in February 1948. Some performances of *Res publica I* also included brief interviews with well-known dissidents, including banned playwright Ivan Klíma. Both *Rozrazil* and *Res publica I* resembled what the United States in the 1930s knew as Living Newspapers — critical journalism embodied in stage terms. After some skirmishes with the authorities, including a temporary banning of *Rozrazil*, both productions were allowed to keep playing, even if only once or twice a month.

On another level, starting in late 1988, the names and achievements of Otomar Krejča and Alfred Radok began to surface more often in public discussion and print. Although not allowed to direct in Czechoslovakia, Krejča was able to visit there while directing abroad, and he began to meet openly with students and theatre critics; in early 1989 interviews with him were serialized in a theatre periodical. Other key directors who had long been kept from important assignments began to reappear in major theatres with major productions. Jan Grossman, artistic head of the Balustrade Theatre until 1968, was invited by Ivan Rajmont (now head of the Balustrade) to direct a production there again in the late spring of 1989. His staging of Molière's *Don Juan* was regarded by most critics as the outstanding production of the season. The unlikeliness of Grossman's return to prominence was capped by his being designated a permanent director at the Balustrade Theatre early in the fall of 1989.

Jan Kačer, leading actor and director at the equally notable Drama Club theatre in the 1960s, had returned to Prague from the provinces in 1986. He proceeded to stage several provocative productions at the Vinohrady Theatre (*Urmefisto* has already been described), but his resurrection of Josef Topol was equally notable. Regarded by many as the most gifted literary talent of all contemporary Czech playwrights, Topol had been silenced since the early 1970s. A symptomatic shift in the winds was already evident in the January 1989 revival of his major play, *End of Carnival*, even though it occurred in provincial Cheb, remote from Prague. Kačer's move was bolder: he staged Topol's previously unproduced *Voices of the Birds* (Hlasy ptáků) in June 1989 in Prague's Vinohrady Theatre and in the fall of 1989 was preparing to stage another of Topol's unproduced plays, *Farewell, Socrates* (Zbohem, Sokrates), in the Drama Club, where Kačer had not directed since the 1960s.

In the late spring of 1989 the Realistic Theatre, producer of *Res publica I*, actually began rehearsing Havel's most recent play, *Urban Renewal* (Asanace), but was prevented from continuing once the authorities heard of the project. Building on its success with *Res publica I*, this same theatre presented *Res publica II* in late October as another homage to the anniversary of Czechoslovakian independence in 1918. Even more provocative than its predecessor, this production concentrated on the 1945–1968 era and included scenes from Havel's *Garden Party* and readings from the novels of two other banned authors: Milan Kundera's *The Joke* (Žert) and Josef Skvorecký's *The Tank Battalion* (Tankový prapor).

In retrospect, these events in and out of the theatre during the year preceding November 1989 indicated some basic changes in the fabric of Czech society and theatre, but no one foresaw the radical transformation that would occur before the year was out. Most people still expected that conditions might modify only gradually, perhaps when a new generation had completely replaced the old guard in the central seats of power of the Communist Party. But the dramatic volte-face that did occur now seems to have been inevitable, needing only the right spark, such as the one generated on November 17 by the harsh police suppression of a disciplined student march and demonstration commemorating the fiftieth anniversary of a student slain by the Nazis. A final spasm of a dying regime, this police attack became the shock that finally goaded the generally restrained Czechs to concerted, overt action. At the epicenter of the movement were students, primarily theatre and film students, who were the first to organize a protest and call for a strike, but professional theatre artists soon joined them. The dramatic, at times explicitly theatrical, action initiated by the Friday, November 17, clash is worth tracing in some detail.

The student-police confrontation occurred in the evening on National Avenue (Narodní třída), halfway between the National Theatre and Wenceslaus Square. Later that same evening the Theatre on a String and HaDivadlo theatres were jointly presenting an updated, revised touring edition of their *Rozrazil I* at an outlying studio theatre venue in Prague. Their performance was interrupted by the arrival of one of the bleeding students from the downtown site of the police attack. He was immediately incorporated into the loosely structured production and provided an eyewitness account of what was happening in Prague's center.

The alliance of students and theatre people became stronger the next day, Saturday, November 18. Representatives from virtually all Prague theatres held an emergency meeting at the Realistic Theatre that afternoon to consider their response to the mercurially shifting situation and to the demands of the quickly organized students for a strike. The choice of the Realistic Theatre (which had begun life in 1881 as the Švanda Theatre) was indicative of its leading quasi-dissident status among Prague theatres at the time. Urged by members of the Theatre on a String–HaDivadlo troupe, the Prague theatre people decided to call on all theatres to go on strike by canceling scheduled performances and instead opening their doors to the public in order to explain the stand of each theatre and then encourage informal dialogues with the audience on the rapidly evolving events beyond the theatres' doors. On that same Saturday, the Theatre on a String–Hadivadlo troupe canceled their afternoon performance and thus became the first theatre group to strike. National Theatre personnel, led by the current head of drama, Milan Lukeš, refused to participate in an afternoon TV presentation from the National Theatre, and evening performances were canceled. Actors and other personnel of the National Theatre were prevented from immediately organizing by being locked out of the theatre by its managing director.

Within a day or two, virtually all theatres went on a strike that was to last until December 10, by which time decisive changes had been made in the regime. Although there were no productions, most theatres (including the National Theatre after several days) remained open and were filled at performance times, for open meetings and spontaneous but disciplined discussion between theatre personnel and the public on the issues and implications of the historic events which they all were experiencing. At one such memorable meeting, on November 27, in the symbolically loaded National Theatre building itself, both Havel and Krejča discussed issues with the public. Back in Brno, the Theatre on a String and Ha-Divadlo theatres presented *Rozrazil II*: "open theatrical forms in which lectures and discussions alternated with enacted documents, songs, and parts of plays. . . . creations with theatrical elements."[4]

In the meantime, other Prague theatres became historic landmarks of the revolution in process. On Sunday, November 19, a hastily organized open meeting of leading dissidents and sympathizers was held in the Drama Club. Almost as if improvising a scene on stage, they designated themselves the Civic Forum and elected Václav Havel their leader. Other events that day included proclamations by personnel of the National Theatre condemning the attack on students, which many of them had witnessed from the National Theatre itself on November 17. Moreover, in protest against the subsequent closing of the National Theatre by its *intendant*, Milan Lukeš submitted his resignation as head of drama.

Hard-nosed, nontheatrical meetings and negotiations were developing nearly around the clock, but official media coverage was fragmentary. Therefore, teams of students and actors (who had the advantage of being familiar to thousands through their work in film and television, as well as theatre) sped to factories and outlying districts where news was not yet fully available or clear, to rally support for Civic Forum and its cause. Other actors and performing artists helped organize and moderate meetings throughout the country. On Tuesday, November 21, a huge demonstration was held in Wenceslaus Square and marked the first public appearance by Havel as leader of Civic Forum.

Wednesday, November 22, brought into play the final Prague theatre to be at the heart of the Velvet Revolution. Josef Svoboda announced the decision of the Laterna Magika personnel to offer their total facility as a command center to the Civic Forum. From that day onward, the Laterna Magika theatre became the cradle of the revolution. That same day the strike committee of the National Theatre formally announced the strike of all National Theatre personnel and their support of the principles of the Civic Forum. In the evening one of the most respected National Theatre artists, the actor-director Miroslav Macháček, as spokesman for the National Theatre, addressed a large crowd gathered at the statue of Saint Wenceslaus in the square bearing his name.

By Tuesday, December 5, a new government had been formed, including members of Civic Forum. On Sunday, December 10, Gustav Husák abdicated as president, and Miroslav Macháček announced on television the end of the theatre strike. On December 28, Alexander Dubček was chosen head of the Federal Assembly, and on December 29 Parliament elected Václav Havel president of Czechoslovakia.

The unbelievable had happened. The people had prevailed — not with bombs or guns or terror, but with the accumulated resentment and disgust of a people who had for most of fifty years swallowed one defeat or ignominy after another, from the Nazi occupation to Stalinist socialism to Warsaw Pact invasion to a domestically imposed Normalization for which they themselves began to feel culpable because of their growing indifference. They had had enough. More important, they had something to believe in.

The Velvet Revolution exceeded everyone's most extreme fantasies, and Czech theatre ensembles and individuals had expedited the process of the revolution itself during its month of glory by their personae and, equally, their actions. In some sense they became its star performers. As a front-page editorial comment in the leading Czech theatre periodical put it, "The fact that theatres by and large came to be the natural focal points of political life during those days that shook the world . . . is simply characteristic of the noble mission of theatre as the most vital laboratory of society," thus restating the leitmotif of Czech theatre for nearly two centuries.[5]

Havel himself put the achievement in a broader context in his New Year's address to the nation in January 1990: "The recent period — and in particular, the last six weeks of our peaceful revolution — has shown the enormous human, moral, and spiritual potential and civic culture that slumbered in our society under the enforced mask of apathy."[6] Now the Czechs had a playwright as president. Other significant early changes included the naming of the former head of drama at the National Theatre, Milan Lukeš, to be minister of culture of the Czech part of the federation that was Czechoslovakia. Lukeš, an O'Neill scholar, had formerly been a theatre journal editor and university professor. Taking his place at the National Theatre was Ivan Rajmont, who moved up from his position as artistic head of the Balustrade Theatre.

The specific effects of the Velvet Revolution on theatre repertoires and logistics in general remained unclear at the beginning of the new year, 1990. Censorship was abolished. The works of Havel and his silenced colleagues would obviously be performed. Svoboda offered Krejča the use of the Laterna Magika building, but Krejča was also offered performance space in the Palace of Culture. Other significant directors and actors were reappearing. The rest remained an open and exciting prospect.

Regardless of its considerable achievements, the Czech postwar theatre never had a chance to ripen to its full potential before being emasculated by the change of regime in 1948 and, after reviving in the 1960s, once again by the invasion of 1968. Now another opportunity existed. Czech theatre had managed to survive the marasmus of Normalization chiefly but not exclusively through the work of its new small, improvisational groups. By the mid-1980s it was again producing relevant works of vitality, fresh artistry, and thematic challenge to the actualities of the time. But the conditions that prompted this latest evolution were ironically wiped out in a matter of weeks by the Velvet Revolution, even as Czech theatre was at its pinnacle of national relevance. Enormous possibilities existed, but also unforeseen problems, as became evident before long.

10

Liberation and Its Pains
The First Year after the November Revolution

My first chance to visit Prague after the Velvet Revolution occurred during a one-semester sabbatical in the fall of 1990, just about a year after the event. For three months, I saw a variety of performances and interviewed many theatre people, while something of the revolution's momentum was still perceivable. The following is an account of my impressions then.[1]

One of the many observations by Czech theatre people describing the essence of their situation — and that of many other Czechs — during the first year after their Velvet Revolution seemed remarkably apt: "You rarely have a revolution in a tiled swimming pool where everything is nicely clean and contained; it's more like a lake where the wind and the waves bring up the mud from the bottom — that's what happened here."[2]

One year after the remarkably brief and essentially nonviolent transformation of Czechoslovakia from a conservative Communist state to a liberal democracy, Czech theatre (as well as its public) was experiencing an inevitable and painful process of transition.

A wave of euphoria prevailed in Czechoslovakia for several months after the parliamentary election of Václav Havel as president, while basic changes began to be made or at least planned not only in the social, political, and economic spheres, but also in the theatre world. Underlying all changes was a sense of unavoidable improvisation. No preparations had been made for the sudden freedoms that entered everyday life. Nor was it possible to halt time or postpone urgent demands for critical decisions in response to a broad spectrum of crises, including a devastated economy, one of the worst ecological conditions in Europe, and the necessity of restructuring complex state mechanisms.

Leadership was in the hands of people with integrity, intelligence, and imagination, but virtually no experience in political administration or economic management. For most of the previous half century, since 1938, almost all issues affecting the collective life of the nation had been in the hands of others: first during the German occupation begun even before World War II and then, after a brief interlude, in the Soviet-dominated Communist state established in 1948. Although there was no threat of a reversion to the old, abolished Communist system, the future was obscure and hazardous. Above all, everyone soon realized that harsh economic conditions and unemployment would be unavoidable before the country could begin to experience the full benefits of political, social, and cultural freedom.

Several other less tangible, more nearly psychological, factors cannot be ignored. Forty years of a totalitarian, largely inflexible, and corrupt regime not only ruined the nation's economy but also demoralized the work ethic of a formerly industrious, highly trained and disciplined work force. In his New Year's speech President Havel foresaw the problem in general terms: "Our main enemy today is our own bad traits: indifference to the common good; vanity; personal ambition; selfishness; and rivalry. The main struggle will have to be fought on this field."[3] To cheat or steal from the state had become almost fashionable; not to do so was regarded by many as stealing from one's family. A sense of responsibility for one's work or a commitment to values beyond the personal or familial became progressively rarer. Václav Havel and his core of idealistic, talented, often highly skilled advisors inherited all this, as did qualified and deserving new personnel put in positions of responsibility in most theatres. They also inherited an elaborate infrastructure of policies and personnel that could not be eliminated overnight if the state or a given theatre were to keep functioning at all. It was naive to think that sudden freedom and democracy would reverse the inertial flow of widespread ineptitude, apathy, and irresponsibility. Moreover, all too often people identified freedom and democracy with a spirit of "anything goes" and license to flout necessary regulations.

The question of Communist Party affiliation during the previous decades was yet another complex, ambiguous issue complicating the lives of many in and out of the theatre. Although the Communist Party was still legal in Czechoslovakia, it was clear that its members, even those who resisted many of its methods and programs, and who terminated their membership during the revolution or even earlier, were now experiencing various forms of bias if not outright prejudice, while other, more agile and opportunistic Communist Party members were still in positions of considerable power and authority.

On another level, in achieving a long sought freedom, the people — including those in theatre — were exchanging a host of familiar given circumstances and routines for new, untried equivalents. Most people relished the new freedoms, but, as time passed, more than a few sighed with at least some nostalgia for known parameters and predictable guidelines. Security and stability were often lost in discarding the old patterns and stepping onto unknown terrain.

Perhaps even more important, especially in theatre, a decades-long raison d'être and centripetal unifying force was lost, and no new one had yet developed to take its place. Within a few years after its installation in the beginning of 1948, the Moscow-controlled Communist regime became an *adversary* for most people in the arts — even for those who had initially been its champions. Many grievances and antagonisms among individuals and groups were subordinated or set aside in the unified front of resistance to a dogmatic ideology and repressive system imposed on the arts and to many deformations of justice and equity in the society at large. Complain as they rightfully did about the conditions under which they had to work, most theatre artists were by the same token prompted to outwit oppressive regulations and to produce excellent work in spite of the deadening policy of Socialist Realism. Theatre acquired the identity of a righteous underdog.

Moreover, a symbiosis was formed between theatres and their public: each reinforced the other's determination not to remain wholly passive or compliant in response to a faceless system that stifled independent thought or initiative. As had happened most notably during the wartime occupation era, and again for a year or so after the 1968 invasion, the theatre provided a means of legal assembly during which various abuses and complaints could be metaphorically addressed. It was a form of ventilation, of indirect therapy, of mutual trust between stage and audience which, tacit though it was, eventually proved invaluable during the Velvet Revolution as the audiences instinctively sought inspiration and guidance from *their* theatre people.

Now the "enemy" was gone. Václav Havel himself, after having won reelection as president in July 1990 by what was now a freely elected Parliament, expressed some of his subsequent intensely mixed feelings in a speech later that month at the opening of the Salzburg Festival in Austria: ". . . a sensation of the absurd: what Sisyphus might have felt if one fine day his boulder stopped, rested on the hilltop, and failed to roll back down. It was the sensation of a Sisyphus . . . whose life had lost its old purpose and hadn't yet developed a new one."[4]

The theatre world found itself disoriented and anxious. To celebrate independence and to honor their universally admired president, as well as to attract audiences, theatres rushed to put on all the plays of Václav Havel as well as those of other previously banned authors. But some of Havel's plays and many by other former dissidents, no longer having the appeal of forbidden fruit, no longer attracted audiences. Moreover, countless other Czech and foreign plays that previously resonated with conditions prior to the end of 1989 simply had nothing relevant to say in the new order of things.

In the turbulence and excitement of new freedoms contending with crucial political and economic issues that demanded daily debate and decisions, theatre suddenly found itself pushed from center stage to the wings. Theatre attendance had fallen off drastically by early spring 1990, as potential audiences eagerly sought information and commentary from a host of other sources previously banned or censored — newspapers, journals and, above all, television (including the Cable News Network [CNN] and televised parliamentary debates) — instead of going to the theatre.

Entire repertoires demanded emergency reexamination: What to perform? How to plan a repertoire that would sustain an adequate box office income while not selling out to purely commercial ends? State or local subsidies were not likely to disappear, but each theatre was to be increasingly on its own to sink or swim, especially until the enactment of new laws to allow tax deductions for support of the arts. There seemed to be no likelihood of such laws in the near future.

Reduced subsidies led to basic logistical changes. Tacitly understood lifetime tenure was scrapped. Every theatre was forced to plan reductions of up to thirty or forty percent of its staff, including its acting ensembles. In reaction against the pro-forma state-controlled union that comprised all theatre, film, television, and radio workers, separate unions for actors, directors and dramaturgs, and technical personnel were forming in each performance medium. If all their separate demands were to be met, most theatres would have had to close down.

The full impact of this crisis of shrinking subsidies, personnel, and box office receipts had not yet struck by the fall of 1990, but everyone anxiously anticipated January 1, 1991, as the date when new economic measures were to be announced. Such measures would define the extent of changes that would have to be implemented by the start of the new season in the fall of 1991.

Of course, there was much to celebrate in the new order, most satisfyingly in the rehabilitation and return to prominent position of many major artists who for years had been effectually prevented from practicing their art entirely or had been restricted to second-rate companies, chiefly in the provinces. Some of these welcome changes came about as a result of official "konkurses" or formal competitions that opened management and administrative positions in most business, educational, and cultural organizations during the first flush of reinstituted democracy after the revolution. Others were the result of committee decisions when the rightful leadership of a theatre was clear from the previous history of a given candidate and a given theatre.

The two most prominent examples of major directors who returned to leadership of major independent companies were Otomar Krejča and Jan Grossman. In 1976, after his work at the S. K. Neumann Theatre had been terminated, Krejča managed to get permission to work abroad without losing his citizenship or right to maintain residence in Prague. In the following years he directed successfully in many West European theatres, but he was cut off from his roots and prevented from any public activity in Czechoslovakia. As previously noted, his name could not even be mentioned in any public way. Now, fourteen years later, Krejča had not only returned but also revived his Gate Theatre under the direct sponsorship of the Ministry of Culture.

Known as Otomar Krejča's Theatre beyond the Gate II, the new ensemble was largely composed of members of the original company and was housed in its old quarters, the Adria Theatre, which it formerly shared with the Laterna Magika. Its first production was *The Cherry Orchard*, with an official opening scheduled for January 1991. The rehearsals and preview that I attended in the fall revealed a meticulously prepared, essentially orthodox interpretation that stressed the tragic elements in the figure of Ranevskaya (played by Marie Tomášová, Krejča's Juliet in 1963). Although the return of Krejča and his new production were obviously of enormous interest to the inner theatre world of Czechoslovakia, it was an open question whether Beyond the Gate II, born in a new time and facing a new and largely unknown audience, would achieve the significance and success of its predecessor.[5]

After 1968 Jan Grossman had been restricted to freelance work in several West European theatres and then a number of Czech provincial theatres before returning to full-time Czech directing in the mid-1980s in the same suburban Prague theatre that had employed Krejča in the early 1970s, the S. K. Neumann. As noted earlier, Grossman actually returned to the Balustrade Theatre before the Velvet Revolution to direct one production, Molière's *Don Juan*, in the spring of 1989. It was a brilliantly stylized piece accentuating Juan's total contempt for all values save his need for change and new experience.

Grossman was then hired as a regular director at the Balustrade in the fall of 1989 and immediately after the revolution was reappointed as artistic head. At the same time, he began to work on Havel's *Largo Desolato*, which opened in the spring of 1990. Grossman's direction of the work was notable for its relatively comic treatment of the autobiographical protagonist, an approach heightened by

The 1990 Balustrade production of Havel's Largo Desolato, *directed by Jan Grossman, setting by Ivo Žídek. Photo by Josef Ptáček.*

incorporating a voiceover of Havel himself reading the opening and closing stage directions to accompany the protagonist's very funny mimed actions. In the fall of 1990 Grossman worked on a new play with the unwieldy title *Woe, Woe, Fear, the Noose, and the Pit* (Hoře, hoře, strach, opratka a jáma), by one of the Czechs' most promising new playwrights, Karel Steigerwald. The play was a disturbing, fluid, but often cryptic montage focusing on refugees during several decades of central Europe's tragic mid–twentieth century history.

Examples of other established directors returning to work in major theatres, though not in charge of them, included Jan Kačer and Ota Ornest. Kačer, restricted to provincial theatre work after the mid-1970s, did work as a director in Prague again in the Vinohrady Theatre in the late 1980s, but in the new order he returned to the National Theatre as a senior staff director. Ota Ornest, for years

[194] MODERN CZECH THEATRE

the enlightened head of the Prague Municipal Theatres, but subsequently prevented from all theatre activity for over twelve years, returned as director, advisor, and head of the artistic council of the Municipal Theatres.

The case of Jaromír Pleskot was a disturbing example of the precariousness of the times. A major director with the National Theatre for decades, he had been prevented from directing there since the mid-1980s and managed to find only occasional assignments in a few provincial theatres. In early 1990, very soon after the Velvet Revolution, he accepted an invitation to become head of the E. F. Burian Theatre, which had been floundering without effective leadership for several seasons. (The depth of anti-Communist feeling surfacing in some quarters after November 1989 was evident: some members of the company seriously proposed a change in the name of the theatre because Burian, perhaps the most gifted of prewar directors, had been a Communist.) One of Pleskot's successes since his return was his direction in the fall of 1990 of a double bill of plays by Pavel Kohout, *Trifles and Troubles* (Lapalie a patalie). Within six months of the Kohout production, however, Pleskot resigned as head of the theatre because of budgetary and personnel crises, and the E. F. Burian Theatre company, whose roots extended back to 1933 and Burian's original D34, folded at the end of the 1990–1991 season.

Other notable administrative and personnel changes had less drastic results. The Drama Club, one of Prague's outstanding studio theatres since the mid-1960s, had been consigned to second-class status as a branch of the Vinohrady Theatre in the 1970s. After the revolution, it regained autonomy and once again came under the leadership of Jaroslav Vostrý, who had been prevented from working there for nearly twenty years. Even so, in the post-November reorganization, the theatre experienced some anxious times when a struggle for power developed between the technical personnel and the artistic ensemble.

Another studio theatre which had been subordinated to auxiliary status for years was the Ypsilon, headed by Jan Schmid. It, too, regained autonomy, but also had to endure an internal crisis after the revolution when its technical and administrative staff wanted to turn the culturally oriented theatre into a Western-style commercial enterprise. Fortunately, those members were outvoted, and the theatre planned to continue in its traditional role as a gadfly supporter of the positive values of a free society. In a simpler, more straightforward change, once Gustav Husák was removed from office, the Theatre on a String of Brno reverted to its original name, Theatre Goose on a String, and continued a project for building a new theatre and cultural center.

Nowhere did the stresses and strains of postrevolutionary Czech theatre become more apparent than in the National Theatre itself. Unlike smaller, studio-type theatres such as the Theatre on the Balustrade, Drama Club, Ypsilon, or

Ladislav Smoček and Jaroslav Vostrý reunited at the Drama Club in 1990. Photo by J. Burian.

Krejča's revived Gate Theatre, which were inherently more manageable and flexible because of the more limited scale of their operations, the National Theatre was a huge organization that found it very difficult to shift policy or initiate significant reform. One of the largest theatre organizations in the world, with well over two thousand personnel, the National Theatre comprised four distinct ensembles — drama (over eighty actors), opera, ballet, and the Laterna Magika — several orchestras, and four theatre buildings, at least one of which was often under reconstruction, thus overloading the demands and pressures on the others. Falling under the Ministry of Culture, it had in effect been controlled by the Communist Party for over forty years, a condition that led to extensive featherbedding, hiring of untalented but reliable Party personnel, and severe pressures on those in the company who deviated from Party guidelines for the arts. All things considered, it was remarkable that it continued to do work of generally respectable and sometimes high quality.

After the shakeup following the revolution, the new head of drama at the National Theatre became Ivan Rajmont, formerly a leading director of studio theatres, whose last assignment had been as artistic head of the Theatre on the Balustrade; it was he who managed to bring Grossman back to that theatre. Now faced with budgetary crises, stage shops that had been declining in productivity and quality for years, barrages of criticism, and demands from factions within the theatre as well as unsolicited advice from outside regarding this symbol of Czech culture and nationhood, Rajmont and the heads of the other branches of the theatre were being pressured to come up with plans and programs while under siege.

An issue aggravating the logistical and economic problems of the National Theatre was the artistic policy in the drama section relating to repertoire and to production modes. Antedating the Velvet Revolution was a conflict between those who generally favored large-scale works and traditional modes of staging and those who grew up in the context of studio or small theatre operations. The latter favored partially improvised scripts, a casual if not intimate relationship between stage and audience, and a minimalist, primarily functional approach to staging. Rajmont himself belonged to this movement, as did several of the younger directors and designers working in the National Theatre. The conflict remained unresolved in the fall of 1990, but it would be fair to say that the youthful antitraditionalists had yet to mount a production on the larger National Theatre stages that would persuasively demonstrate the appeal of their approach. A specific example of the inadequacy of a studio approach to a classic of large format was the production of the Čapek brothers' *Insect Comedy* at the National Theatre in April 1990; the action seemed lost on the large proscenium stage. In contrast to the last production of the same play on the same stage — the brilliant staging by Macháček and Svoboda in 1965 — the inadequacy of the present production was all the more blatant.

The several years before the revolution of November 1989 bore some resemblance to the years immediately leading up to the Prague Spring of 1968. At both times, a gradually more open, imaginative, and critical voice in the theatre reflected a weakening, less firm regime. In one sense, a certain ideal balance evolved between art and the regime. Artistic and critical expression, although still restricted from complete freedom, could use imaginative ways to make its statements resonate with the concerns of its committed audiences; and the state, though significantly softening its repressive measures, still posed a target that focused and unified the efforts of theatre artists and also attracted audiences for that most desirable form of entertainment — theatre with vital relevance to its public. In 1968 the invasion and attendant occupation stunted all creative work within a year or two and led to nearly twenty years of marking time, until a slow revival began in the mid-1980s. As in 1968, in late 1989 the Velvet Revolution — despite its wondrous liberation — also interrupted the gradual but positive evolution toward free expression, but rather than resulting in a suppression of creativity it abruptly threw off all restrictions. As I have described, this sudden freedom has also had its problems.

Given the Czechs' tradition of theatre as a culturally necessary force, it seemed unlikely that their model of imaginative, responsible theatre would founder at this critical time when, as one theatre artist said, "We are like children who have received a new train toy and become angry at it because we don't know how to make it work."[6] Many of the most distinctive achievements of the Czech theatre since World War II came about in times of adversity. It is ironic but perhaps inevitable that sudden freedom and democratization, a breaking up of old patterns and routines, in conjunction with a series of inherited crises, should produce temporary confusion and anxiety and an often painful searching for new procedures and goals.

11

Czech Theatre of the 1990s

The constituent elements of what had been Czechoslovakia — the Czech lands (comprising Bohemia and Moravia) and Slovakia — achieved a peaceful divorce in January 1993, after a union lasting virtually seventy-five years. Very few signs of the separation were evident when I visited Prague again several times in the 1990s, including the entire 1993–1994 theatre season. On the other hand, Prague was increasingly filled with tourists, and evidence of Western business and popular culture was everywhere.[1] John Updike's final lines of a short poem from 1997 neatly captured some of the new atmosphere:

> . . . all is freshened up,
> for sale. The trolley's squeal has been retuned
> for tourist ears; American voices haunt
> each archway. Habsburgs, Hitler, Russians — now
> the sleek brigades of Benneton and K-Mart
> besiege the Castle and its phantom lord.[2]

What Updike's sanitized account fails to note are some of the more disturbing aspects of the evolving transformation he describes, such as the sleazier elements of contemporary Western culture that are omnipresent: fast-food operations and their debris, hordes of boardwalklike shops full of kitschy Czech souvenirs manufactured somewhere east of India, and graffiti — crude and raw — everywhere, from billboards to walls of quiet parks to newly finished public buildings. And through it all, tens of thousands of tourists jam pedestrian and vehicular traffic where emperors once rode in state and Hussites confronted bishops. Nevertheless, Prague endures.

The tensions between past and present cultures have also been evident in the infrastructures of Czech life and its government since 1989. Although the new republic's democratic roots have held firm and the Czech state met the qualifications for North Atlantic Treaty Organization (NATO) membership (evidence of the country's stability and viability), the path has not been free of roadblocks, potholes, and detours in political, social, and economic terms.[3]

Czech theatre has also experienced mixed fortunes. Clearly, it weathered the turbulence and anxieties of the first two years after the Velvet Revolution. In those years, many theatre people envisioned major changes in the structure and operations of the theatre system that had been in place since the late 1940s, and in some respects much longer. But the crucial reality of Czech theatre almost ten years later, on the cusp of the twenty-first century, is that no radical changes have occurred. Despite some notable shifts affecting specific theatres and their personnel, the Czech theatre is still centered in an ensemble repertory system receiving considerable material support from a variety of sources. Moreover, it is still reflecting its time, although in less obvious and less sustained ways than during the Communist era.

The comfortable days of steady and relatively ample support and lifetime tenure are like the snows of yesteryear, but the dire threats of eliminated state supports or a blight of sheer commercialism were premature.[4] Czech theatre has found ways of operating within altered patterns of subvention from various levels of government (the practice for more than a century) as well as from other, primarily corporate, sources (something new since 1990).

In the first years after the Velvet Revolution, theatre people also anticipated a renaissance of playwriting and a flowering of fresh production styles as a natural consequence of sweeping new freedoms. By the end of the 1998–1999 season, however, it was clear that Czech theatre was still awaiting the appearance of an important new Czech playwright or even a notable new Czech play written originally as a play rather than as a scenario or a dramatization of other literary sources. There has not been a shortage of the latter; three of the seven productions to have won the prestigious Alfred Radok Award conferred annually since 1993 for best production of the previous year have been recent Czech dramatizations of prose fiction or poetry, and a fourth was a Baroque opera. The three *plays* to win the award were neither Czech nor even of the twentieth century.[5] Of the playwrights who showed strength in the 1980s, such as Karel Steigerwald, Daniela Fischerová, Antonín Máša, and Arnošt Goldflam, only Goldflam has continued to build successfully on previous work. Failures with audiences and critics alike have been Karel Steigerwald's *Nobel* (1994); Daniela Fischerová's *Fantomima* (1995); and Antonín Máša's *Strange Birds* (Podivní ptáci, 1996). The first and last were produced by the National Theatre. A rewritten version of Steigerwald's *Nobel* fared no better than the original. Only Máša's *Strange Birds*, a simplistic but at times theatrically effective attack on contemporary Czech gangster-style capitalism, remained in the repertoire more than one season. Older playwrights such as Josef Topol, Václav Havel, and Oldřich Daněk have been largely silent. Some new young playwrights have drawn attention, as I shall indicate, but not with works of broad appeal.

The shortage of important new plays may be traceable to the not yet fully stabilized Czech society and political processes. The old is gone, but the new has not yet fully formed. Stresses of political party feuding, ineffectual parliamentary procedures, graft and fraud in financial activities — all seemingly inseparable from the freedoms of capitalist democracy — have replaced the political and social stresses of totalitarian ideology as the context in which today's Czech theatre has been evolving. Moreover, Czech audiences today have available a much greater range of alternate entertainment than ever before. Theatres face enormous competition from film and from commercial television with its game shows, sitcoms, soap operas, and international sports.

For most playwrights and most theatres, the sheer quantity and the ambivalence of the new conditions fail to offer the clear target or motivation that inspired most of the outstanding work of the past. As a result, most theatres that wish to appeal to a general rather than a special, limited audience have been presenting eclectic repertoires that have few surprises or innovations. And yet exceptions have continued to appear.

More specifically, two patterns of theatre have dominated Czech stages of the 1990s. Although the center of gravity has remained in repertory theatres producing classic and modern works in essentially familiar ways, the cutting edge of Czech theatre has been found in certain departures from the repertory system and, even more, in iconoclastic, often cryptic productions created by young directors who came to professional stages for the first time shortly before or after the watershed year of 1989. These leading new theatre people have drawn increasingly from within themselves to create works that convey their personal visions and associations arising from their textual sources, and only then — indirectly, if at all — their responses to the new, rapidly changing society around them. The directors as postmodern *auteurs* who have been drawing most attention during the past decade are Hana Burešová, Petr Lébl, and Jan Antonín Pitínský.

No longer concerned with offering resistance to an oppressive regime, the new directors wished to express their own often eccentric impressions of whatever source material they were staging, which as often as not was prose fiction or poetry rather than an already crafted play; to convey what they regarded as the source's various subtexts; or simply to "play" with variations on motifs or characters for almost exclusively aesthetic, theatrical ends having little to do with the ideas and themes of the original work. The result, especially in the first half of the 1990s, was usually a highly subjective, often capricious mix of many styles and forms, the serious and the farcical but most consistently the grotesque, thriving on anachronism and anomaly and self-reflexive in its irony and its conscious theatricality. In short, these young directors made postmodernism an increasingly familiar mode to Czech audiences. Their very successes, however, seemed to go hand in hand with the attenuation of the characteristic symbiosis of stage and society in Czech theatre.

Nevertheless, traditional modes of staging were not abandoned, and even the more extreme forms of postmodern staging did not entirely lack relevance to the world outside the theatre. Moreover, a certain counterflow seemed to be developing in Czech theatre after 1994. Whether traditional or neo-avant-garde in forms and methods, such work began to seem less self-indulgent and more concerned with responding to the social and spiritual implications of the new society that has been evolving since the demolition of the Communist system.

These general tendencies of Czech theatre in the 1990s are anchored in specific theatres and individual artists, whose stories may now be considered. Because it is more difficult to maintain a sense of proportion and perspective in dealing with the very recent past, and to avoid restricting my observations to what I currently *think* has been most important in the 1990s, I shall be providing a more inclusive overview of theatre activity as it has been evolving in the 1990s than for most of the previous eras.

Highly indicative of the problems and shifting dynamics of Czech theatre in the 1990s was the case of Otomar Krejča. After reviving his former studio theatre in 1990 as Theatre beyond the Gate II in collaboration with his closest former associate, dramaturg Karel Kraus, Krejča proceeded to stage some half-dozen productions with mixed success between 1990 and 1993. *Cherry Orchard* (1991) and *Waiting for Godot* (1991) attracted the most attention but only limited praise. In 1992 he was rejoined by his former scenographic collaborator from the 1950–1970 era, Josef Svoboda. Their first two productions had middling success. A necessary spark seemed to be missing, as if the productions failed to resonate with the new society and new audiences. But in the spring of 1994 Krejča and Svoboda collaborated on Pirandello's *The Mountain Giants*, in which Krejča once again successfully demonstrated the talents that had made him famous thirty years before — talents which in the context of the 1990s were perhaps becoming unfashionable: deep study of text and characterization based on respect for the playwright, masterfully orchestrated, disciplined staging, and a sixth sense for touching the nerve of contemporary issues. Svoboda's use of a huge, mobile, semitransparent mirror helped reinforce the illusion-reality theme of the work.

The Pirandello production was a milestone for several reasons, some of them profoundly ironic. Not only was it Krejča's most effective production since his return, and not only did it celebrate the renewed collaboration of two great artists, but it was also the swan song for Krejča's Theatre beyond the Gate II and thereby became a paradigm of what has been troubling Czech theatre in the 1990s. The play itself culminates in a confrontation of theatre artists with indifferent sponsors and callous audiences. It paralleled the fate of Krejča's theatre and its 1994 socioeconomic context almost too painfully, reflecting the drastic reduction of monies to support the arts, a crisis intensified by the lack of laws from Parliament that would confer a nonprofit status on arts organizations or provide tax write-offs to encourage corporate support of the arts.

Late in the spring of 1994 the national Ministry of Culture announced that it would no longer fund a number of previously supported theatres, including Krejča's Theatre beyond the Gate II; only the National Theatre appeared safe, albeit with reduced support. Theatres such as Krejča's would have to find support elsewhere, but no such salvation occurred for Krejča, even though other theatres already being supported by municipal or regional public sources continued to receive some degree of subsidy, and some were even receiving a modicum of corporate funding despite lack of economic incentives for such funding.

In a disturbing echo of the fate of Pirandello's traveling players in *The Mountain Giants*, Krejča's Theatre beyond the Gate II closed down at the end of 1994, thus becoming the second major theatrical casualty of deregulated free enterprise in the post-Communist era of the Czech Republic (the first being the E. F. Burian company in the spring of 1991, as noted in the previous chapter). Efforts by Krejča's ensemble to carry on as Theatre beyond the Gate III proved futile.

Krejča's own saga was not finished, however. In 1995 he was among the finalists being considered for the head of drama at the National Theatre, the position he had occupied with great impact some forty years earlier, in 1956–1961. When the reappointment did not materialize, Krejča became engaged in negotiations for a return to the National Theatre as a director, specifically as director of Goethe's *Faust*, part one, in collaboration yet again with Josef Svoboda. I witnessed the production's first public performances at the end of the 1996–1997 season, in the Estates Theatre, prior to its official premiere in the fall of 1997. It was a large-scale, complexly orchestrated, technically demanding *mise en scène* that had the virtues of clarity and fidelity to Goethe's literary source despite considerable editing by Kraus and Krejča and despite technical problems in its first performances. The physical staging involved extensive use of projections in conjunction with a large circular mirror suspended above the stage to capture the tangible and spiritual dualities inherent in the work. The production's unusual length (almost four hours) and very fidelity, however, made its reception problematic at a time when audiences were becoming increasingly conditioned by sound bites, hard-rock video clips, and other theatre productions that may be closer to capturing the spirit of the times by flouting the traditional methods inherent in Krejča's approach. The Krejča-Svoboda *Faust* received mixed reviews. One extreme reaction was a dismissal of it as a Laterna Magika spinoff; on the other hand, several critics were impressed by the solid mastery of an extremely difficult text, noting that work of comparable scale was not evident in today's Czech theatre. Krejča's staging received several votes for the Radok award, and Svoboda's scenography won first prize in the category of stage design. He had won the prize earlier for his scenography in Krejča's production of Pirandello's *The Mountain Giants* (1994).

The production remained in the repertoire through the 1998–1999 season. When I saw it again in late May 1999 I did not find it to be an improvement on the original preview performances two years earlier except for being somewhat smoother in execution. Otherwise it seemed flat and routine. Krejča has not directed since the *Faust* production, although his achievements continue to be recognized. In January 1999 he received the K. S. Stanislavsky award in Moscow for his significant contributions to the development of world theatre. Previous awardees were Giorgio Strehler, Peter Brook, and Peter Stein.

Josef Svoboda's Laterna Magika Theatre represents a diametrically opposite example of the struggle for survival in Czech theatre today. Formerly a component unit of the National Theatre since 1973, it became an independent entity directly under the Ministry of Culture in the spring of 1992 (as did the newly configured State Opera in what had been the Smetana Theatre). Although the Laterna, like Krejča's Theatre beyond the Gate II, had also been subsidized by the Federal Ministry of Culture, and was also subsequently cut off from continued support, its box-office successes were such that it had been receiving only a token equivalent of a dollar a year of subsidy for several seasons. While still technically under the Ministry of Culture and performing in the National Theatre's New Stage (Nová scéna), for which it pays rent, it has continued to be self-supporting primarily by playing very effectively to the tourist market, as it had for years. Major new Laterna Magika productions in the 1990s have been Friedrich Dürrenmatt's *Minotaur* (1990), an adaptation of Mozart's *Magic Flute* (1993), *Casanova* (1996), and *Puzzles* (Hádanky, 1997), which is primarily a dance work with background projections. Most of the recent Laterna Magika productions have subordinated elements of text and characterization in favor of increasingly sophisticated choreography and spectacle and broad themes that cut across cultural and linguistic differences, tendencies doubtless influenced by commercial considerations, but not to the exclusion of high professional standards. In any case, the enduring profitability of the Laterna Magika Theatre, even in a marketplace environment, is an exception in today's Czech theatre. As for Svoboda, at seventy-nine in 1999, he not only still functions as artistic head of Laterna Magika but also continues to undertake a few limited scenographic projects in Prague, though rarely abroad. Svoboda's productions by 1999 totaled seven hundred. The latest Laterna Magika production, scheduled to open in the fall of 1999, is to deal with virtual reality in stage terms, which suggests that it will again emphasize spectacle over drama.

A more special, indeed unique, story lies in the death of one theatre and the birth of a new, very different one on the same site. The most radical and far-sighted change in Prague theatre operations after the Velvet Revolution involved Ondřej Hrab (b. 1952) and the Ark (Archa) Theatre, a brand-new facility occupying the space of what had been the E. F. Burian Theatre. The change of name to the Ark Theatre was meant to stress experiment and new beginnings.

Hrab, not yet forty, whose background lay in economics and sociology, was chosen by municipal authorities to be the chief on the basis of his proposal for the theatre's new identity and function. His plan was simple yet revolutionary. The theatre was to be completely renovated as a flexible, functional, hi-tech "production house," with a minimal administrative, technical, and dramaturgical staff — no directors, actors, or designers. Instead, already finished productions would be imported, or new production projects would be invited to create their work within the theatre. Hrab stressed that he was not interested in commercial entertainment but rather in nonprofit, innovative, experimentally slanted international work in dance, music, mime, film, and multimedia, as well as more traditional theatre. Whether Czech-made or imported, it would be aimed at Prague audiences rather than the tourist trade. Hrab was fortunate in obtaining the cooperation of the Commercial Bank, which owns the property and was willing to underwrite many of the theatre's expenses.

The opening performances in the theatre in June 1994 were avant-garde music and mime workshops and recitals, but these were topped by Robert Wilson's touring production of *Doctor Faustus Lights the Lights*, the first of his works to be done in Prague, under Wilson's on-site supervision. Subsequent performances and workshops have involved Kabuki and Bunraku artists, Meredith Monk, Peter Schumann's Bread and Puppet Theatre, Japanese choreographer and mime Min Tanaka, and selected Czech companies and artists, such as the touring HaDivadlo with its award-winning production of *Job* (1996) and the same group with *Oedipus* in 1999.

Several productions have actually been generated within the Ark Theatre, but the very first *drama* to be self-produced was Arnošt Goldflam's *Sweet Theresienstadt* (late 1996). It was in fact an international co-production between the Ark and En Garde Arts (USA) in terms of its funding as well as its creative personnel; supplementing its Czech author and actors, an American, Damien Gray, was the director of a rather overproduced staging with regard to some scenic effects that distracted from the primarily intimate aspects of the action. Goldflam's play itself deals with the Holocaust in terms of a few historically based inmates of the camp in Terezín, chiefly a former journalist who holds a minor supervisory position among the inmates and a former film director assigned to the propaganda project of idealizing conditions in the camp. As is usual for Goldflam, the focus was on the personal interrelations and illusions of the leading figures rather than on any explicitly stated or tendentious themes.[6]

The new physical theatre itself, designed by the long-time Ypsilon scenographer, Miroslav Melena, is another innovation for Prague. The former premises were stripped to the walls and an ultraflexible black box performance space was created. It contains a smaller and larger production area based on 4 × 4 meter lifts, something that Burian himself would probably have admired. On the other hand, there is distinct irony in Hrab's Ark, a product of free enterprise heavily subsidized by a bank, replacing a theatre dedicated to the Communist cause by Burian back in the 1930s.

The Archa transformation was repeated on a smaller scale in the total reconstruction of the Fidlovačka Theatre in an outlying Prague district. The theatre, originally built in 1921, had been the home of operetta productions and occasional plays, but it had fallen into disuse and total disrepair by the 1970s. A few enterprising Prague theatre people, also drawing on Miroslav Melena's design and technical skills, had it rebuilt in 1997. It has since housed hit productions of *Fiddler on the Roof* and *Man of La Mancha*, as well as Shakespeare's *Twelfth Night*.

The profiles of some other Prague theatres in the 1990s (e.g., the Vinohrady, Drama Club, Ypsilon, and former S. K. Neumann theatres) are more notable for their basic continuity than for radical changes or distinctive innovations.

After Jaroslav Vostrý departed from direct involvement with the theatre in the early 1990s, the actor-centered Drama Club was headed from 1993 to 1998 by Slovak director Vladimír Strnisko (b. 1938), who had guest-directed there in previous years. His productions in the 1990s indicated a turn toward classics such as Molière's *Miser* (1992), Sartre's *No Exit* (1993), an adaptation of Wedekind's *Lulu* plays (1994), and Chekhov's *Three Sisters* (1997), all of which displayed Strnisko's finely tuned balance between intellectual insight and dynamic stage business. Playwright and director Ladislav Smoček, who founded the theatre in 1965 and still directs in it, staged Pirandello's *To Clothe the Naked* (1993) in a characteristically vigorous, colorful production that exploited the farce as well as the pain intrinsic to the piece. In 1996 he revived his *Cosmic Spring*, arguably the last major play by a Czech to have been written since the 1968 invasion. Smoček updated some elements of the play's ecological themes to make it as relevant in the 1990s as it had been in the 1970s. Smoček has also guest-directed at the National Theatre, the Vinohrady Theatre, and the theatre in Pilsen. As effective as they have been, the repertoire and production level of the Drama Club have not surpassed its work of the 1980s, much less that of the 1960s.

The Vinohrady Theatre, traditionally the rival of the National Theatre, is currently under the artistic leadership of former actress Jiřína Jirásková (b. 1931) and now includes Vladimír Strnisko as staff director. It has a corps of Prague's most seasoned actors, headed by probably the best actor in Prague, Viktor Preiss (b. 1947). His range encompasses the heroic, the classically farcical, and the subtly complex, as was evident in a half-dozen productions such as Molière's *Miser* (1991), Pavel Kohout's *Poor Murderer* (1992), and Oldřich Daněk's *How Easy It Is to Rule* (1993), an ironic, Dürrenmatt-like study of Bohemia's King Charles. *Poor Murderer* was masterfully directed by Luboš Pistorius, whose career dated back to the immediate postwar era and included notable work at a number of Prague theatres, including the Vinohrady, the Realistic, and the National, where he was represented after the Velvet Revolution by an effective production of Pirandello's *Right You Are* (1993). Pistorius died in 1997. The Vinohrady has probably had the most consistently well attended productions of major Prague theatres in the 1990s, which is attributable to its solid professional work and its repertoire, a blend of old and modern classics rather than anything startling or new.

After a period of internal dissension following the Velvet Revolution, the Ypsilon Theatre regrouped and consolidated its strengths under its founder and ongoing head, Jan Schmid. The core performers have remained remarkably constant, as has its style — a blend of amiable, semi-improvised foolery and serious social comment, interwoven by the musical talents of its ensemble. Its good-natured undermining of traditional patterns of theatre presentation is a form of casual postmodernism with social overtones that dates back some thirty years. The theatre has retained its audience-friendly informality, with performers shifting easily from onstage involvement to Brechtian detached comment to casual byplay with the spectators. In addition to its own adaptations of *Romeo and Juliet* (1993), I. A. L. Diamond's *Some Like it Hot* (1993), Grabbe's *Jest, Satire, Irony, and Deeper Meaning* (1994), or its own collectively created quasi-documentaries like *Mozart in Prague* (1991), it occasionally also presents relatively straightforward grotesque comedies such as Boris Vian's *The Head of Medusa* (1996) or loosely structured

Jan Schmid's Ypsilon production of Grabbe's Jest, Satire, Irony, and Deeper Meaning, *1994. Actors as musicians have been a hallmark of Ypsilon productions for three decades. Photo by Josef Ptáček.*

variety programs of chat, song, and talk-show repartee, generically titled *Evenings in the Lamplight.*

The one major change in its recent operations has been a positive one: in 1996, with corporate support, it finished construction of a larger, better-equipped performance space with a fixed stage at one end in the same building it has been using for years, while still retaining its older, smaller space with flexible seating arrangements for more intimate productions. Two very successful new works, which sustain Ypsilon's tradition of probing and reexamining the nature of the Czech character and temperament, opened in the new space: humorously idiosyncratic adaptations of Smetana's *The Bartered Bride* (1996) and *Everything for the Com-*

[208] MODERN CZECH THEATRE

pany (Vše pro firmu) in 1997, a 1920s novel that satirizes the encounter between high-powered Western business practices and the more easygoing ways of the Czechs, a pointed theme for Czech audiences today. Its author, Karel Poláček (1892–1944), was a Jew who died in Auschwitz. Both works drew heavily on Ypsilon's composer-in-residence, Miroslav Kořínek (b. 1943), and the unusual musical abilities of Ypsilon's ensemble, particularly with folk and jazz material. One of Ypsilon's most recent productions, *The Holy Family* (1998), a Hungarian play by Gyorgy Schwajda, continues a probing of relevant issues today. It is unusual for Ypsilon in being an essentially straightforward, even serious work depicting contemporary problems of aging, loneliness, and alien values among ordinary people, yet even here the Ypsilon treatment could not be completely denied: several elderly women's roles were played by Ypsilon's veteran male actors.

The S. K. Neumann Theatre (which had sheltered Krejča and Grossman in the 1970s and 1980s, respectively) was successfully transformed into the Theatre under the Palm (Divadlo pod Palmovkou) by the forceful, enterprising efforts of its young artistic director, Petr Kracik (b. 1958), who joined it as a director in 1991 before becoming artistic head in 1992. His strategy involved tightly organized, economic operations in support of an eclectic repertoire calculated to assure audience support: well-known works with strong story lines requiring relatively young actors — *Hamlet* (1992), *Of Mice and Men* (1992), *Peer Gynt* (1993), Peter Shaffer's *Black Comedy* (1993), and one or two Czech works. It is essentially a traditional repertory approach, but implemented by a youthful, enthusiastic company committed to the program and its emphasis on text and actor rather than elaborate staging. In 1994, feeling more secure with his audiences, Kracik began to phase in somewhat more problematic texts: Georg Büchner's *Wozzek*, Dostoyevsky's *The Idiot*, Pinter's *Homecoming* (1994), and Janusz Głowacki's *Antigone in New York* (1994). Subsequent well-received productions have included Lorca's *The House of Bernarda Alba* (1995), Pedro Barca de Calderón's *Life Is a Dream* (1996), Strindberg's *Miss Julie* (1997), and Gorky's *Summerfolk* (1999).

Ongoing traditional repertory practices are rightfully associated with the National Theatre, and yet even here several new approaches and operations have been tested in the 1990s. Its operations became modified because of certain changes in its production venues, such as the completion in 1991 of major reconstruction and technical modernization of what had been the Tyl Theatre. In reopening, it reverted to its earlier name, the Estates Theatre (Stavovské divadlo),[7] and resumed its function as the second stage of the National Theatre, specializing in smaller-scale dramas and operas (above all, those of Mozart). Such works had been performed in the New Stage during the reconstruction work on the Tyl. The New Stage, a separate theatre building next to the historic National Theatre, had opened in 1983, just as reconstruction began on the Tyl Theatre. With production shifting back to the rechristened Estates Theatre in 1991, the sole tenant of the New Stage became the Laterna Magika ensemble.

Another significant development relating to the operations of the National Theatre was the opening in 1992 of an intimate nonproscenium stage in the attic of the Kolowrat Palace, a building adjacent to the Estates Theatre. The Kolowrat building had also been reconstructed as part of the Tyl restoration, and it now serves as the administrative headquarters of the National Theatre drama operations. The Kolowrat Theatre has become the venue for the small-scale chamber work of the National Theatre, in effect its first permanent studio theatre.[8] Recent well-done productions there have included a bill of Pinter one-acts (*The Lover* and *Ashes to Ashes*), directed by Karel Kříž, and Beckett's *Happy Days*, directed by Michal Dočekal (b. 1965), both in 1998.

Primarily responsible for the creation of the Kolowrat Theatre, Ivan Rajmont has also directed most often in it. During his tenure as head of drama at the National Theatre from 1990 to 1997, the drama ensemble maintained a good though not outstanding overall level of performance, with an eclectic repertoire of classics and some contemporary works that fundamentally upheld traditional features of repertoire selection and staging practice. Undoubtedly the most celebrated National Theatre production of the post-1989 era was a dramatic adaptation of a nineteenth-century novel by the brothers Mrštík, *A Year in the Country*. The production, directed by Miroslav Krobot (b. 1951), presented a powerful communal drama woven from greater and lesser social interactions, passions, and ceremonies of village life, with skillfully orchestrated staging reinforced by offstage choral song, tapping the rich cultural associations of village life for most Czechs. It had the cumulative force of a broad river or other elemental embodiment of nature, and it won the Alfred Radok prize for best production of 1993.

Another of Miroslav Krobot's National Theatre successes was a spirited revival of Gogol's *Marriage* (1994). Among Rajmont's own most satisfying productions were Euripides' *Medea* in the Kolowrat (1993) and Dostoyevsky's *The Possessed* (1997). Jan Kačer, the National Theatre's senior resident director, continued his solid, carefully prepared work in productions such as Josef Topol's previously unstaged 1980s play, *Farewell, Socrates* (1991), *Peer Gynt* (1994), and *Midsummer Night's Dream* (1997), with Radovan Lukavský, the Hamlet of the 1960s, playing Puck in a colorful but otherwise orthodox production.

In the fall of 1997 the National Theatre experienced a major change of artistic leadership, which I shall discuss later.

Two other established theatres that experienced transformations of identity in the years following the Velvet Revolution, the Realistic and the Balustrade, each also became associated with striking new talents and some of the most innovative, often controversial staging of the 1990s.

Under the leadership of Karel Kříž, the Realistic Theatre became instrumental in the buildup to the November 1989 Velvet Revolution, as described in a previous section. In response to the new, free regime, the theatre changed its name and its identity in 1991, becoming known as the Labyrinth Theatre, adding a studio branch deep in medieval vaults adjacent to the theatre proper, and launching an ambitious program to create a cultural center for theatre and other art forms. Almost simultaneously, however, it ran into real estate problems symptomatic of the new economy: the previous private owners of the property took measures to evict the reconstituted theatre in order to generate more income from the property. Consequently, high anxiety prevailed at the Labyrinth for several years, until the theatre came under the control of Prague municipal authorities in 1997. In the administrative shakeup that followed, Kříž resigned as managing director in 1997, while staying on as artistic director, but the entire company was dissolved in the spring of 1998, the third long-established theatre group to expire since 1989. Concurrently, the municipal authorities announced plans to build an entirely new theatre on the site where the Švanda Theatre began its long life in 1881. A major controversy over the decision to raze this Prague theatrical landmark had not been settled at century's end.

In the meantime, Kříž and his ensemble had been presenting two main lines of productions: larger-scale work in the main theatre and more intimate, experimental work in the subterranean, stone-arched studio. His own most striking full-scale production at the Labyrinth was a tetralogy of Euripidean tragedies centering on Troy (1994), but, somewhat like Rajmont in the National, Kříž seemed to favor more intimate production work in his studio, where he directed two highly physicalized and musical montages of nondramatic material: *Opera Dada* (1992), a lively revue of Dada materials, and *The Oar and the Rose* (Veslo a růže; 1993), a study of political and religious issues in tenth-century Bohemia.

Just as it was at the cutting edge in theatre-related events leading to the Velvet Revolution in Prague, the Labyrinth was also the host for the first professional productions in Prague of two young directors who had been attracting increasing attention during the late 1980s in amateur and regional professional theatres: Hana Burešová and Petr Lébl. Both directed productions at the Labyrinth in 1992 and clearly established the presence of a new creative generation associated with the postmodernist wave.

Prior to her work at the Labyrinth, Hana Burešová (b. 1959) had worked as a director for five years in professional regional theatres, developing her inventive

A scene from Hana Burešová's production of The Barber of Seville *at the Labyrinth Theatre, 1992. Photo by Oldřich Pernica.*

and freshly theatrical methods before coming to the Labyrinth. Her first production there, in September 1992, took advantage of the ancient vaulted space of the cellar studio to provide an atmospheric background for Grabbe's *Don Juan and Faust*. Often regarded as unstageable, the play was so successful in her theatricalized embodiment of Grabbe's grotesque tragi-comic mixture of romantic ideals and all too human folly that it won the first Alfred Radok award for best production of 1992 and was still being performed in 1999, though no longer at the Labyrinth.

In November 1992, in the main theatre, Burešová went on to stage *The Barber of Seville*, which revealed her talent for employing the *commedia dell'arte* tradition of conscious theatricality, bright, inventive stage business, and sharp character treatment. Her flair for incorporating music, mime, and masks both respected and parodied the Beaumarchais-Rossini material. The production brought to mind the work of the Ypsilon Theatre, but Burešová's staging was more formally structured and controlled; moreover, it did not stress the musicianship of the cast, and it had almost no interplay with the audience.

Burešová closed the year, in December, with a double bill of nineteenth-century Czech farces by F. F. Šamberk — *Boucharon* and *I'm Having a Benefit* (Mám příjem) — that cheerily spoofed the Czech Sokol movement and provincial Czech theatre itself, respectively.[9] As in *Barber of Seville*, she showed a finely tuned feeling for a blend of farce and human vulnerability; the humor in these productions was never merely mechanically effective, nor was the comedic treatment of period details and manners without affection.

Burešová's two other productions at the Labyrinth extended her directorial reach: T. S. Eliot's *Murder in the Cathedral* (1993) and a 1930s Czech comedy by J. Žák, *School, Life's Foundation* (Škola základ života; 1994). Burešová presented an essentially orthodox rendition of Eliot's religious verse drama, but enhanced its theatrical vitality with expressive lighting, sound, and choreography. The school play, a generic, comedic depiction of classroom confrontations among high school students and teachers, became in Burešová's staging a lively farce with interpolated music, while not losing sight of the work's serious overtones. It was to be Burešová's last production at the Labyrinth: internal disagreements on administrative and policy matters led to her ending her work there in 1995.

Meanwhile, Petr Lébl (b. 1965) had been primarily associated with amateur theatre in Prague before joining the Labyrinth. Working in a Prague cultural house with his own ensemble, Jelo, he had produced some dozen works, including his own subjective, poetic, playfully bizarre texts and scenarios as well as equally unconventional adaptations of others' work, such as his 1985 dramatization of Kurt Vonnegut's *Slapstick*, which Lébl translated as *Grotesque*. His first production at the Labyrinth, in February 1992, was an original Czech play by a younger colleague (Egon Tobiáš, b. 1971). *Vojcev* is an enigmatic, precocious spoof centering on a young author who finally seems to turn into a dog. In what was still the essentially conservative theatre world of Prague, the production created a furor. Many praised it for its provocative challenge to habitual theatre practice; equally many condemned it as a self-indulgent flouting of intelligible, coherent stage action.

The following November, a few days before Burešová's *Barber*, Lébl staged Tankred Dorst's *Fernando Krapp Wrote Me a Letter* in the Labyrinth studio. A dramatization of a novel by Miguel de Unamuno, the production was a landmark demonstration of Lébl's consciously parodistic, highly subjective, and wittily stylized theatrical vision of a more conventional stage source. It also placed second, after Burešová's *Don Juan and Faust*, in the Radok competition for best production of the year 1992. *Fernando Krapp* was an almost operatic presentation of an inherently painful marital drama; every production element, including Lébl's own scenography, was orchestrated to create a disciplined, unified, high-camp version of what had originally been a serious work. Both *Vojcev* and *Fernando Krapp* enhanced Lébl's reputation for singular, provocative staging that fundamentally rejected familiar patterns of interpretation and performance, even transcending those usually considered avant-garde. It was not surprising that he intensely irritated many observers even while prompting enthusiasm in others. He left the Labyrinth in 1993, for an offer he couldn't refuse, as I shall describe shortly.

The Balustrade Theatre, which had come under Jan Grossman's leadership once again in 1990, also experienced stressful times before entering its present phase. Conflicts of repertoire policy developed between artistic director Grossman and several of his key actors in 1991, ending in the actors' departure. Grossman went on to direct an outstanding production of Havel's *Temptation* (Pokoušení, 1991) and Alan Bennett's *Kafka's Dick* (1993) before his untimely death in early 1993. His passing marked the loss of a second major director from the 1960s to occur after the Velvet Revolution, the first being Miroslav Macháček of the National Theatre, in 1991. In a larger sense, Grossman's death closed the twentieth-century era of the Balustrade, for Grossman's successor — no less than Petr Lébl — was distinctly of a new generation and sensibility that pointed to the next century.

In the fall of 1992 Grossman invited Lébl, whose *Vojcev* he had seen at the Labyrinth, to stage a production in the Balustrade Theatre later that season. Lébl turned to the work of a slightly older Czech contemporary, J. A. Pitínský's eccentric original play *The Little Room* (Pokojíček). The premiere was in the spring of 1993, a few months after Grossman's death. Lébl then successfully competed for the position of artistic head of the Balustrade Theatre and was appointed in the summer of 1993, at the age of twenty-eight. Since then, Lébl has continued to polarize audiences as well as critics while indelibly imprinting the Balustrade with his highly theatrical and highly stylized staging.

In quick succession at the Balustrade, Lébl radically adapted and staged Genet's *The Maids* in 1993; the nineteenth-century Czech classic by L. Stroupežnický, *Our Swaggerers* (Naší furianti) in 1994; and a highly controversial rendition of Chekhov's *The Sea Gull* in 1994, which was later awarded the Radok prize for the best production of that year. Still another award designated the Balustrade as Theatre of the Year 1994. Lébl's productions since then have been somewhat tamer but still provoked disputes: Gogol's *Revizor*, J. M. Synge's *Playboy of the Western World*, and Joe Masteroff, Fred Ebb, and John Kander's *Cabaret*, all in 1995; and Chekhov's *Ivanov* in 1997, which won a second Radok prize for Lébl, and the Balustrade was again chosen as Theatre of the Year.

Rather than create his own scenarios from nondramatic sources, as is done by some of his colleagues, Lébl prefers to work with regular plays, which he uses as armatures for his striking, offbeat, personalized, and carefully wrought embellishments in staging. Some continued to dismiss his work as perverse, egoistic exhibitionism, while others saw in it the theatre of the twenty-first century. In any case, the Balustrade Theatre was no longer simply the house of Havel and Grossman (and Evald Schorm in the late 1970s). It became the house of Lébl as well.

During his tenure at the Balustrade, Lébl has also brought in other, relatively young directors with similarly innovative, even radical methods. One was Hana Burešová, Lébl's onetime colleague at the Labyrinth. In the course of her breakup with the Labyrinth, Burešová had two creditable but not exceptional guest productions at the National Theatre in 1995: Calderón's *Miraculous Magician* and Verdi's opera *Rigoletto*. In 1996, in response to Lébl's invitation, she staged an adaptation of Molière's "doctor" comedies at the Balustrade, *The Flying Physician* (Létavý lékař), which exploited her zest for *commedia* farce, masks, and exuberant stage imagery.

In July 1996, two months after the Molière production, Burešová became artistic head of her own ensemble, situated in a relatively small proscenium house, the Longstreet Theatre (Divadlo v Dlouhé), which had been occupied by various ensembles under different names for fifty years. Here the shifting circumstances of Prague theatre life led to her ensemble (several of whose members had been with her since her pre-Labyrinth days) being joined with another young group of actors, recent graduates from DAMU, who had formed the core of the suburban Dejvické Theatre a few years earlier. The two ensembles became one, with a guiding triumvirate of Burešová, her dramaturg husband Stepan Otčenášek (b. 1954), and Jan Born (b. 1960), the former head of the Dejvické ensemble. Each group retained some of its previous repertoire, but the first fully integrated production was a successful revival of Josef Topol's *The End of Carnival* (1997), in which Burešová theatrically amplified the play's use of masks and shifted the emphasis from the older to the younger generation of characters. In the spring of 1998, in her own theatre, she directed a well-received production of Fernand Crommelynck's *Magnificent Cuckold* in a strikingly expressionistic manner, echoing her penchant for plays with strong elements of the bizarre and grotesque, such as her earlier *Don Juan and Faust*.

Of greater consequence than Burešová's guest production of Molière at the Balustrade was Lébl's earlier invitation, in 1993, to Jan Antonín Pitínský (b. 1959),[10] to join him as director and dramaturg at the Balustrade. Pitínský has staged five plays there: in 1993, *She's Strong in Zoology* (Silná v zoologii), an odd, obscure play prefiguring aspects of the feminist movement, written in 1912 by Stanislav

Hana Burešová directing Josef Topol's The End of Carnival, *1997. Carnival masks and costumes lined the stage space. Photo by Jaroslav Prokop.*

Mráz (1864–1918); in 1994, an adaptation of Graham Greene's *The Heart of the Matter*; in 1996, Thomas Bernhard's *Ritter, Dene, Voss*; in 1997, *Tanya, Tanya*, by Olga Mukhina, a contemporary young Russian writer; and in 1999, Bernhard's *Histrionics* (Der Theatermacher).[11]

Pitínský won two consecutive Radok awards, for 1995 and 1996, and a third for

J. A. Pitínský's *production of Stanislav Mráz's* She's Strong in Zoology *at the Balustrade Theatre, 1993. The singer and musicians in the background are Pitínský's addition to the original play. Photo from the Balustrade Theatre.*

1998. Somewhat older than either Burešová or Lébl, he has been a nomadic director associated with a variety of theatres throughout the country, and he seems to have equally strong, more varied talents. Unlike Burešová and Lébl, who are products of urban Prague, Pitínský was born and raised in less cosmopolitan areas of Moravia, which he still considers his home and where he has done most of his work. Like Lébl, he developed from amateur roots, particularly with Brno's Amateur Circle (Ochotnický kroužek), which he helped establish. But he also worked as a writer and director with the Goose on a String and HaDivadlo companies of Brno. Much of his early directorial work consisted of staging his own scenarios of poetry and prose, which evolved into occasionally expressionistic collages orchestrating elements of text, music, and choreographed mime.

While both Burešová and Lébl studied at DAMU, the Prague theatre academy (Burešová completed the program, but Lébl had only brief, intermittent exposure to it), Pitínský never had formal theatre training. His formal training was as a librarian. (Lébl's most sustained higher education was in graphics design, which is evident in his designing of his own productions and sometimes those of others.)

Lébl and Burešová were talented actors, whereas Pitínský is an experienced playwright with many productions to his credit. His plays exhibit a mixture of neo-naturalistic characters and dialogue, Kafkaesque or Strindbergian situations as if adapted by Ionesco, surrealistic stage imagery, and flashes of dark humor lacing generally painful, even violent relationships and disagreeable events: e.g., *The Pineapple* (Ananas; 1987); *The Mother* (Matka; 1988); *The Park* (1991); *Bulldoggery* (Buldočina; 1992); and *The Little Room* (1993).

The Mother is especially strong medicine, a depiction of a lowbrow proletarian family (with a maid!) dominated by the title character, a woman who is an instinctively ruthless guardian of what she considers traditional domestic, familial values to the extent that she is indirectly responsible for the destruction of her family and an innocent outsider. At the end, alone but imbued with a strange sense of power, she forms a disturbing, ambiguous alliance with a stereotypical Communist labor organizer. Pitínský referred to the work as "a sad, painful oratorio of anger and impotence against those who steal our lives and who wasted and unfortunately even literally bludgeoned so many other promising human lives. And they don't want to cease doing it. I told myself that this would be the last Socialist Realist play, that I would take all of it, the filth, and bury it into this *Mother* of mine."[12] The sense of aversion to oppressive family values, as well as to any ideology, is conveyed not only by the action but by Pitínský's unique blend of colloquial, often coarse Czech dialects, which he occasionally lifts to near poetry.

The Little Room is similar in its nuclear familial action, which again results in a senseless, inadvertent destruction of three adult children by their parents, who, although tediously exhibiting a sense of petty bourgeois normalcy, are actually calloused, indifferent beings. The play prompts thoughts of Strindberg's *The Pelican*, but with an incongruous sense of absurdist humor jarring with the deaths of the three children, who reappear as ghostlike figures while the oblivious parents carry on with their complacent lives. Lébl's staging of the play at the Balustrade in 1993 took the inherently grotesque action several surrealistic steps further with the interpolation of bizarre props and business, such as a motorcycle lowered from the flies, which the parents mount as they prepare for a vacation in South America at play's end. Although striking and disturbing, his plays thus far lack broad appeal.

Although other young Czech directors have also shown distinctive talents,[13] it is the trio of Burešová, Lébl, and Pitínský — especially the last two — who are considered the most important new artists of Czech theatre of the 1990s. All three have strong theatrical imaginations, relying heavily on music and expressive, coherent visual imagery in their productions. What sets them apart from their contemporaries and older colleagues most distinctly, however, is that their radical breaking down of inherited conventions of staging is not randomly capricious or merely intended to shock, although it may seem so at times. More often than not, their creations also possess perceptive insights and an overall mature command in shaping their material. Little seems haphazard or irrelevant to a total design.

Of the three gradually aging *enfants terribles*, Burešová is the least *terrible*. Indeed, her works are often good-natured, cheerful farces, and she does not appear to be in her element with darker or tragic material. It seems symptomatic that Lébl and Pitínský have each staged several Kafka works, while Burešová has not done any, although her work with Grabbe and, indeed, Crommelynck should not be ignored. She also seems most at home within mainstream theatre operations, which may relate to her structured, formal theatre training and subsequent progression within the professional repertory system, in which she has been a bright, imaginative, intuitively theatrical presence. Burešová is also more inclined to work with fidelity to playwrights' fully developed scripts, whereas Pitínský and Lébl lean toward substantial adaptations of given plays, and, as noted, Pitínský in particular has often created his own scenarios from nondramatic sources. In this and some other respects Pitínský and Lébl seem to be in the E. F. Burian or Alfred Radok tradition, while Burešová seems more akin to Jiří Frejka in his early poetistic, *commedia dell'arte*–based work.

Though Pitínský and Lébl are similar in many respects, Pitínský seems to be more economical and selective in his conceits, and perhaps more responsive to the core humanity and social implications within his plays, whereas Lébl leans toward a prodigality of effects, often at the expense of characterization. Some have also made a distinction between Pitínský's lyrical talents as a director and Lébl's inherently more dynamic, dramatic bent.

A Lébl production is identifiable by his stylized blend of expressionism, surrealism, camp, and a tongue-in-cheek playing with his own conceits. He himself has said that his source is always within himself and that his prime motive is to satisfy himself. Redeeming his work from self-indulgence are the sheer range and inventiveness of his theatricalized imagination, the precision and artistry of his effects, their overall unity of tone and form, and certain moments when a seemingly perverse stage sequence suddenly suggests a fresh, valid insight into traditional materials. For example, in the last act of his *The Sea Gull*, the arbitrarily white costumes of the older characters and the white fabrics that cover most surfaces suggested an institutionalized, moribund society, perhaps even the lined interior of a coffin, effects that were superimposed on Chekhov's text yet arguably

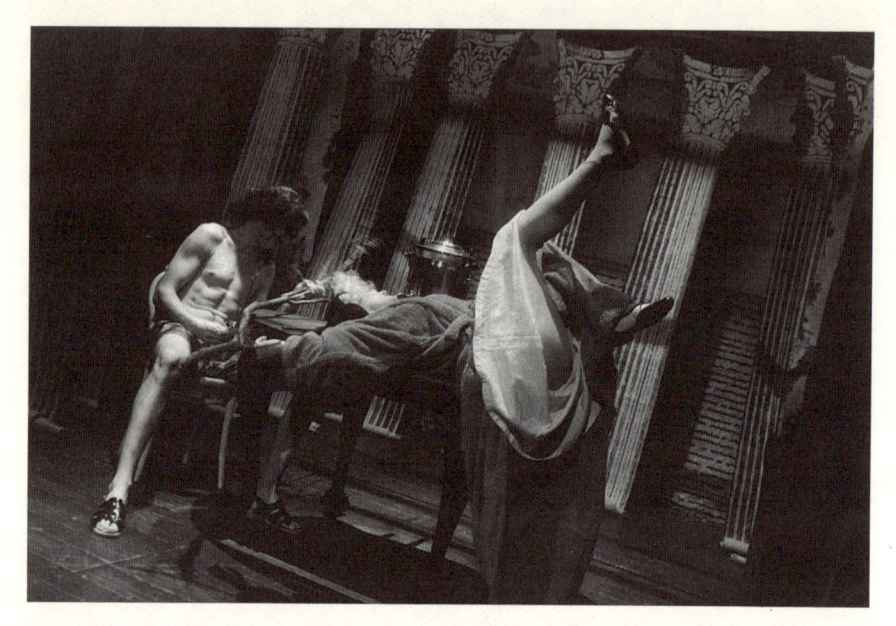

A scene between Trigorin and Masha in Petr Lébl's production of Chekhov's The Sea Gull *at the Balustrade Theatre, 1994. Masha is drinking cognac straight from the samovar spigot. Photo by Josef Ptáček.*

provided a defensible metaphoric comment on the world that callously rejects a Nina and Treplev. On the other hand, many similar effects do not yield so positive a resonance and often impede the flow and tempo of the performance, such as elaborate visual gags parodying silent film melodramas in *The Sea Gull*. A sense of proportion is something that Lébl is still in the process of developing; even his most inventive stage images and dynamic activity often reach a point of surfeit and lose their impact. After reaching an apex of supercharged theatrical effects in *Revizor* and *Cabaret*, however, he seemed relatively more sober in his staging of *Ivanov* at the Balustrade. The relation between character insight and attention to theme vis-à-vis near-extravagant stage business was more nearly balanced than is usual for him.

In the fall of 1997 Petr Lébl extended his career to the National Theatre itself as guest director of Smetana's opera *The Brandenburgs in Bohemia*. In the tradition-drenched "Golden Chapel on the Vltava," he imbued the historical action with the qualities of childlike myth, legend, and folktales, almost as if it were a marionette play, as some critics saw it. It was a treatment that predictably raised the hackles of many while delighting some others. Back in his own Balustrade Theatre in the spring of 1998, his attempt to transfer Stanislaw Wyspianski's *The Wedding* (Wesele), a play rooted in Polish cultural allusions and values, to a Czech milieu did not seem a success to most viewers, even though Lébl's choice of this play with its very skeptical look at romanticized revolutionary ideals that come to nothing seemed relevant to many aspects of life in the post–Velvet Revolution Czech Republic.

In December 1998, to celebrate the 40th anniversary of the first production at the Balustrade (*If a Thousand Clarinets*), Lébl staged a contemporary Bulgarian play by Christo Bojcev, *Colonel Bird*, an uneven satiric farce involving inmates of a mental asylum in the ruins of an abandoned monastery in a remote mountainous region of the Balkans. The full satire develops when crates of NATO military supplies meant for Bosnia are mistakenly air-dropped to the monastery. Under the guidance of one of the patients, a former colonel, the patients become transformed into a disciplined military unit and decide not only to join NATO but to seek entry into the European Parliament in Strasbourg. Although the primary effect is one of rampant farce, Lébl's staging exploits the script's ridiculing of the military mentality, the pretentiousness of upstart new states, the mistreatment of Romanies (gypsies) in Europe, and the enormous contrast of values inherent in the frescos of the monastery and the present. The play as written sags in the second half, but Lébl's creative fancy is as fresh as ever.

It is especially Pitínský who has been enhancing his reputation as a director in the 1990s, both in his choice of texts and in his staging, as witnessed by his Radok awards for best productions of 1995, 1996, and 1998. The first was for *Sister Anxiety* (Sestra úzkost), produced by the youthful Dejvické group in 1995 (before their union with Burešová's ensemble). It was based on his own scenario drawn from folk and mytho-religious motifs in the writings of two early-twentieth-century Czech writers, Jan Čep (1902–1974) and Jakub Deml (1878–1961). Somewhat in the vein of the National Theatre's 1993 award-winning *A Year in the Country* with its focus on the rituals, games, and passions of village life during the cycle of seasons, *Sister Anxiety*, as shaped by Pitínský, became a creation of impressionistic, fanciful stage poetry formed from text, mime, dance, and song rather than a staging of epic prose. His second Radok award was for his direction of *Job*, a "dramatic oratorio" by composer Martin Dohnal (b. 1959) drawn from a novel by Austrian author Joseph Roth. Produced by the HaDivadlo group in Brno in 1996, it updated the biblical story to the twentieth century and the tribulations of a Jewish immigrant in America. As in *Sister Anxiety*, Pitínský demonstrated a masterful theatrical orchestration involving not only text, acting, and scenography, but also an even more substantial musical component that equaled in significance the realistically slanted human story. The two works evoked memories of Burian's highly orchestrated work with folk and musical material more than a half-century ago.

Pitínský has also worked very successfully in large theatres as well as small. His

J. A. Pitínský's award-winning production of Sister Anxiety, *at the Dejvické Theatre in 1995. Photo from the Longstreet Theatre.*

stage adaptation of Federico Fellini's 8 1/2 (1995) and his version of Gabriela Preissová's *Her Stepdaughter* (1996) were done in the spacious auditorium of the theatre in Zlín, Moravia. On the other hand, in more intimate, chamber productions such as Thomas Bernhard's *Ritter, Dene, Voss* (1996) or Mukhina's *Tanya Tanya* (1997), both at the Balustrade Theatre, Pitínský also proved that he could subordinate his own metaphoric expressiveness and creative fantasy to serve the playwright's script with sensitive attention to its layered details, their shaping and timing, while still interpolating small bits of business or props as his signature.[14] In *Tanya Tanya*, Pitínský was able to merge his musical bent with his choreographing skills: much of the dialogue occurs as the characters are dancing. Pitínský's achievement in the Bernhard play was highly praised by critics, who voted this production second only to Pitínský's own production of *Job* as the Radok production of the year 1996.

Pitínský tackled two monumental projects in the 1997–1998 season. As guest director at Burešová's Longstreet Theatre in the fall of 1997 he staged a dramatization of Thomas Mann's *The Magic Mountain* and at the National Theatre in the spring of 1998 a dramatization of Jaroslav Durych's (1886–1962) 1929 novelistic trilogy, *Going Astray* (Bloudění), which traces events of the Thirty Years War and the impact on the Czechs of their defeat by the Habsburgs. Instrumental in adapting both works himself, he staged them with respect for their inherent compo-

[222] MODERN CZECH THEATRE

nents of language, theme, and action while shaping their complex stories with an eye for theatrical values. His own staged prologue for *Going Astray* was characteristic: a depiction of the execution of the Czech nobles in the Old Town Square after their defeat at the battle of White Mountain in 1620. Under glaring light, anachronistically dressed in 1950 civilian suits, they deliver their final words into an upstage microphone as their freshly slain comrades fall into the black orchestra pit one by one. It is a scene that must have reminded many in the audience of the Communist show trials of the 1950s with their extorted public confessions. The sheer scale and length of the productions was daunting, but while most critics had various reservations they agreed that Pitínský's directorial talents were as vital as ever, especially and more successfully in *The Magic Mountain*.

Pitínský won his third Radok award for his staging of Purcell's opera *Dido and Aeneas* in Pilsen's J. K. Tyl Theatre in the spring of 1998. The highly artificial nature of the piece lent itself to Pitínský's stylized approach in decor, costumes, and choreographed staging and also his playful introduction of elements from English afternoon teas and readings from *Alice in Wonderland*. Such touches recalled his *mis-en-scène* for *Sister Anxiety*, especially in the use of almost totally white costuming and stage dressing, even though the high artifice of Baroque opera was perhaps more organically suited to Pitínský's approach than were the folk sources of *Sister Anxiety*. In Pitínský's hands, *Dido and Aeneas* became a feast for the eye and a stimulus of fancy while never losing grace or lightness of touch.

The production was followed by Sophocles' *Oedipus Rex* in the HaDivadlo in Brno in the late fall of 1998. I saw it in the spring of 1999 when it visited the Archa Theatre in Prague, where the action was contained by an audience on three sides. Once again Pitínský drew on folk elements (here Moravian) in costuming, music, and movement patterns, all in an effort to deemphasize the literary component in favor of more elemental, ritual elements underlying it. It seemed to me that Pitínský's processing of the source material resulted in surface embroidery more than in any revelation or intensification of the tragic power inherent in Sophocles' work.

Pitínský's two most recent productions strongly contrasted. *Histrionics*, the published English title of the original German *Der Theatermacher* (in Czech, *Divadelník*), another play by Thomas Bernhard, opened in February 1999 in the Balustrade Theatre. The play has been taken as a darkly comic portrayal of charismatic dictators, national or domestic, of actors, perhaps of theatre as a whole. It is a virtual monologue by a megalomaniacal actor-director-playwright, Bruscon, who, with his touring mini-ensemble of wife, son, and daughter, winds up in a long unused peformance hall adjoining a tavern and pigpens in a small provincial town. It is Bruscon's own epic drama they are to perform, with characters ranging

Petr Lébl in the mid-1990s. Photo by Ondřej Němec.

from Napoleon to Schopenhauer, Madame Curie, Einstein, Stalin, and the Winston Churchills, to name perhaps half of those alluded to in the dialogue preceding the performance, which never takes place. Bernhard's play lives or falls by the acting of its protagonist, who in this instance was played by Martin Huba, a Slovak actor of enormous talent who dominated and sustained the action with his infinite variety and vitality. Such guest-acting performances are relatively rare in Czech theatre, but not unprecedented. Pitínský himself, in the earlier *Ritter, Dene, Voss* at the Balustrade, used Slovak actress Emilie Vášáryová in the role of Ritter. Both Slovak performers spoke Slovak, while the others spoke Czech, a seeming inconsistency that bothered no one because of the star performers' strength of stage personality.

Most recently, Pitínský staged a dramatization of a short 1970s novel by Peter Handke, *A Special Woman* (Zvlaštní žena), in Prague's Komedie Theatre in April 1999. It is a thin play, which fails to generate enough interest in its title character, a contemporary independent woman, to warrant audience interest or involvement. In relation to Pitínský's other more recent work, it seemed a pointless exercise of his inventive theatrical skills, which were evident in his ingenious decor (clear plastic walls and furniture) and in his choreographed, musically accompanied movement for the actors.

What has set the work of these young directors, especially that of Lébl and Pitínský, apart from similar "irregular" or "alternative" approaches found in many of the post-1968 studio theatres is perhaps related to their having grown up during the Normalization era of the Communist regime and being therefore distinctly averse to explicit political issues as well as most forms of uniformity or traditional authority, with little sense of obligation to most rules, traditional patterns, or routine conventions of theatre. They have felt completely free to create as they wish

*Jan Antonín Pitínský in the mid 1990s.
Photo by Jaroslav Prokop.*

with any source materials. As Lébl said to me in 1994, he was primarily reacting against being bored by anything that one would consider traditional. The result, in comparison with their immediate predecessors, has been a more complete release of imagination and fancy, an unburdened, often consciously playful theatricality without the sense of a cultural, sociopolitical mission that was so striking in the Ypsilon, Theatre Goose on a String, HaDivadlo, and others. Indeed, one would have to return to the heady days of the First Republic in the 1920s, still riding the exhilarating crest of the postwar wave of independence, to find parallels in Czech theatre, specifically in the early work of Honzl, Frejka, E. F. Burian, or Voskovec and Werich before fascism became a threat. Moreover, the new Czech generation has had many foreign models more celebrated for subjective experimentation with forms and metaphors than for socially relevant depictions of character or speculative explorations of human destiny (e.g., the theatres of Robert Wilson, Peter Sellars, Peter Zadek, Frank Castorf, or Pina Bausch). In a broader sense, the work of all these new *auteur*-directors could also be viewed as *fin de siècle* variations of the prototypal visions and practices of Edward Gordon Craig and Vsevolod Meyerhold, who saw the director as a sovereign artist — the prime creator of autonomous works of theatre art.

In the late spring of 1994, at the invitation of president Václav Havel, some twelve Czech writers, critics, directors, and dramaturgs participated in a roundtable discussion of the present state of Czech theatre (that is, since the Velvet Revolution). Among the topics were two that seem particularly apt in any consideration of Czech theatre of the 1990s. Several of the participants noted the conditions of emptiness and aloneness they felt once the oppressions of the previous decades had been eliminated. Havel said he had half-jestingly asked himself, "Wasn't I in fact happier under Communism, because I constantly had a certain horizon, a certain perspective, something to struggle with, something to fight for?"[15] (Havel also cited Beckett as one who had superbly dramatized such states of being, and then added that perhaps what their theatre was waiting for was a Czech Beckett.)

Other observations at the roundtable related to the problematics of postmodernism in contemporary Czech staging. Some viewed it as a self-indulgent aberration which rejects sense or meaning. With regard to directors who used dramatic scripts as mere raw material for their own visions or whims, one speaker observed, "Once again a playwright serves someone else's purpose and is simultaneously robbed of his most essential meaning."[16] Nevertheless, others suggested that postmodernism in the Czech context was really a defense against any form of totalitarian thought and that some of postmodernism's seemingly willful manifestations were also well conceived and executed compositions, which most audiences were not yet equipped to access or decipher. Certainly the work of Lébl and Pitínský would seem to support both sides of the dispute.

From another point of view, if they and others have been responding primarily to their own inner creative urges more strongly than to broader social or political realities, they may be doing so because social and political conditions have not crystallized or assumed the form of clearly definable threats or targets. Virtually all the work of these directors has sufficient wit, imagination, and force to have been a worthy opponent to the threats or repressiveness faced by their major predecessors. Indeed, some of their pre-1989 productions could be taken as veiled reactions to the deformations and stultification of the late Normalization era.[17] In other words, it is not the fault of today's new directors or playwrights that they lack adequately defined targets such as fascism, the Nazis, or Soviet communism. For the time being they must still make do, ironically, with an excess of freedom and a corresponding shortage of fuller social resonance.

In its own way, nevertheless, their work in the mid- and later 1990s began to reflect more of the issues affecting contemporary Czech society in what is still a transitional period: ethical choices in a context of increasingly materialistic, commercial values; a sense of anxiety and alienation in the midst of seeming material security. Even Lébl, probably the most provocative of these talented young directors, began introducing less capricious motifs and tones in his 1995 production of *Cabaret* (cynicism, decadence, fascism) that reflect not simply pre-Hitler Germany but aspects of Czech life today. And in *The Wedding* as well as *Colonel Bird* he certainly dealt with a number of contemporary political-humanitarian phenomena applicable to the Czech Republic, even though farcically in the latter. Burešová's *End of Carnival* still has a certain retro relevance today, and most of Pitínský's productions, though sometimes coming close to playing with forms, confront more universal issues of human interaction. It is as though, having given rein to sheer play and personal expression, these artists now seem to be testing the possibilities of theatre that assumes a certain responsibility to their new society.

Other developments suggest that the two worlds of contemporary Czech theatre embodied in the essentially traditional productions of the National Theatre in contrast with the audaciously contra-traditional staging of the newcomers might be in the process of being bridged, if not fused. Strong evidence of such potential cross-fertilization was inherent in 1997 in the new leadership of the National Theatre and its repertory plans.

Ivan Rajmont's successor as head of drama at the National Theatre starting in the fall of 1997 was Josef Kovalčuk, the twenty-fifth person to occupy that position, which originated in 1911 during the Kvapil era. Kovalčuk was for years a dramaturg, the close collaborator of playwright-director Arnošt Goldflam in the significant HaDivadlo studio theatre of Brno. Kovalčuk's appointment was only one sign of the increased significance of Brno as a major theatre center, containing as it does the HaDivadlo, the Theatre Goose on a String, the State Theatre of Brno, the important Amateur Circle, and the strong theatre division of the Janácek Academy of Performing Arts, in which Kovalčuk served as dean, 1990–1996.[18]

Given his core affiliation with the HaDivadlo, Kovalčuk's appointment also reaffirmed the significance of the studio theatre concept during the last decades of Czech theatre, which Rajmont himself actively endorsed in his own work and that of others, especially in the National Theatre's Kolowrat studio. More to the immediate point, Kovalčuk's decisive repertoire and directing choices for the 1997–1998 season included bringing into the National Theatre a number of directors of the new generation, those who did their first important work in the 1980s and thereafter: Ivo Krobot (b. 1948) to direct a dramatization of *Romance for a Cornet* (Romance pro křídlovku), a narrative poem by František Hrubín; Petr Kracik (artistic head of the Palm Theatre) to direct a Czech classic by J. K. Tyl, *Arsonist's Daughter*; and — most significant — J. A. Pitínský to direct Jaroslav Durych's *Going Astray*, as noted earlier. The drawing together of the "two worlds" was to be strengthened even more by the inclusion of Petr Lébl to direct a production of Smetana's opera *The Brandenburgs in Bohemia* for the National Theatre's opera company. At the other end of the balance beam, of course, were Krejča and his *Faust*, as well as some productions retained from the present repertoire. It promised to be one of the more interesting National Theatre seasons in decades.

Not surprisingly, all the works assigned to the new directors were Czech, for one of the fundamental mandates of the National Theatre is to provide a sustained showcase for Czech works. But with the Czechs again under foreign pressures (e.g., Updike's relatively benign "sleek brigades") the strong turn to Czech plays also suggested an urge toward critical self-examination as well as a reaffirmation of identity. The National Theatre, the flagship of Czech theatre, the nation's "gift to itself," continued to fulfill its traditional mission as a source of cultural enlightenment and as the nation's conscience.

It also seemed clear that part of Kovalčuk's vision was a strengthening of that tradition by the infusion of fresh directorial approaches. In several respects it was reminiscent of the Krejča era of the late 1950s and early 1960s, when the National Theatre was doing the most exciting work in all of Czech theatre, primarily because the leadership (Krejča) had a new vision of theatre's potential as well as a dedication to Czech drama. Kovalčuk also planned a workshop for new playwrights, which would be an echo of Krejča's workshop productions of Hrubín, Topol, and Kundera forty years earlier. (At century's end the shortage of viable new Czech plays is disturbing, as one revealing statistic makes clear: of the twenty-four productions directed by Pitínský, Lébl, and Burešová since 1995, only six have been written by Czechs.) At the very least, the plans projected in 1997 suggested that Czech theatre was moving toward the twenty-first century with a consolidation of its most vital, productive forces and with balanced respect for tradition and innovation.

Most critics and audiences agreed that the bringing together of untested scripts and young directors (however talented) was an experiment that must be undertaken if a theatre is to stay alive. Moreover, time would be required for any such experiment to produce desired results, especially in a theatre of the size and sheer inertia of the National. In the event, not unexpectedly, the productions had mixed results. I have already touched on Pitínský's *Going Astray* and Lébl's *The Brandenburgs in Bohemia*, both with positive elements but not successful as a whole. Ivo Krobot's *Romance for a Cornet* was even more problematic; most critics found it inadequate in dramatizing Hrubín's poetic text. On the other hand, Petr Kracik's straightforward production of Tyl's *The Arsonist's Daughter* was an unexpected hit of the season despite critics' reservations concerning the simplistic sentimentality of Tyl's play; the Czech classics are apparently alive and well for Czech audiences when done with adequate freshness and dynamics. The play incorporates much of nineteenth-century Czech culture in its scenes of both village and urban life, even the Czechs' belief of what a successful Czech-American would be like upon his return to his homeland. I saw one other new Czech play in the National Theatre in the spring of 1999, Antonín Přidal's (b. 1935) *The Night After* (Noc potom), directed by Ivo Krobot. It is a melodrama about five mature women whose private lives intertwined with the larger social and political stresses of the Communist era. Although many of the issues were of interest, the play seemed overwritten and overly complicated in weaving together a number of strands.

Regardless of its shortage of clearly positive results thus far, Kovalčuk's attempt to revitalize a great tradition in the National Theatre has been a step in the right direction and has recalled those of Rajmont, Krejča, and Hilar before him. And as provocative outsiders like Lébl and Pitínský challenged traditional approaches to staging, so too had others: the Ypsilon, Goose on a String, and HaDivadlo of the previous generation; the Balustrade and Drama Club a decade before them; Radok, Burian, v + w, Frejka, and Honzl in even earlier years; and the initial innovators, Kvapil and Hilar. This heritage, a never quite extinguished flame of creativity, remains a hallmark of twentieth-century Czech theatre.

Another hallmark noted throughout this book has been the alternation between times of creative expansion and contraction in response to external social and political realities. Paradoxically, periods of creative expansion often occurred in the face of adversity, as in the 1930s, the late 1950s, and the 1980s. On the other hand, the creatively expanding years of the 1990s, like the 1920s (and the brief interlude of 1945–1948), followed a significant liberation. The 1920s witnessed the blossoming of the Czech avant-garde in an age when the Czech theatre had no particular duty or obligation to its society; in the 1990s, in similar circumstances, we have seen comparable fresh, imaginative work from people like Burešová, Lébl, and Pitínský. Awaiting the Czech avant-garde of the 1920s were the crises of the 1930s and the terrors of the wartime 1940s. What awaits the Czech neo-avant-garde in the first decades of the new millennium is unclear. In what circumstances will it be maturing, ripening? Will it be able to maintain its identity and integrity in the face of a steadily increasing flood of film, television, and electronic media entertainment?

If the past is any indication, one thing seems clear: peak eras of theatre are the product of many forces in fortuitous combination — gifted playwrights, remarkable individual artists, substantial subsidies, well-organized infrastructures, and special historical moments. Two or even three of these are probably insufficient; all of them must intersect. Czech theatre at present is marking time, in process, with varied signs of vitality and distinction. Whether, when, or how a fruitful synthesis will occur is unforeseeable. Given the Czech theatre's past, however, I take this as an occasion for hope and expectation rather than resignation or despair.[19]

NOTES

INTRODUCTION

1. Kenneth Tynan, "The Theatre Abroad: Prague," *New Yorker* (1 April 1967), p. 99.
2. Stanley Buchholz Kimball, *Czech Nationalism: A Study of the National Theatre Movement, 1845–83*, p. 76.

1. 1780–1900:
SOME EXPOSITION BEFORE THE MAIN ACTION

1. Marionette theatre has enormous importance to the Czechs, in great part due to its contributions to the cause of their language, culture, and theatre. Long before regular Czech theatre performance became an established phenomenon in the nineteenth century (and even then only in major cities), itinerant marionette performances in Czech had been crisscrossing the countryside publicly sustaining the Czech language, history, legends, and other traditions for highly receptive semiliterate audiences. The most celebrated master was Matěj Kopecký (1775–1847).
2. In the meantime, other cultural landmarks of the National Revival movement included the establishment of the Czech Society for Sciences in 1784 and a chair of Czech Language and Literature at the otherwise German-dominated Charles University in 1791; Josef Dobrovský's *History of the Czech Language and Literature* (1792); the founding of what became the National Museum in Prague in 1818; the establishment of a Foundation for Czech Language and Literature (Matice česká) in 1830; Josef Jungmann's five-volume *Czech-German Dictionary* (1834–1839); and František Palácký's five-volume *History of the Czech Nation in Bohemia and Moravia* (volume 1 in 1836). Ironically but symptomatically, Dobrovský's volume and Palácký's history were still published first in German. Czech poets also contributed powerfully to the revitalization of the Czech language. Outstanding among them were Jan Kollar (1793–1852), František Ladislav Čelakovský (1799–1852), Karel Hynek Mácha (1810–1836), regarded as the greatest of them all, and Karel Jaromír Erben (1811–1870). An outstanding source of information on Czech cultural history of this and other eras up to the 1960s is Derek Sayer, *The Coasts of Bohemia*.

3. *Dějiny českého divadla* (History of the Czech Theatre), ed. František Černý, vol. 2, *Národní obrození* (The National Revival), p. 39.

4. Ibid., p. 314.

5. Kimball, *Czech Nationalism*, p. 114. Kimball remains the most authoritative source in English on the campaign for the Czech National Theatre.

6. His full name was Pavel Švanda ze Semčic.

7. She was born Hana Kubešová, but has been remembered as Kvapilová since her marriage in the mid-1890s to Jaroslav Kvapil, the first great Czech director of the twentieth century.

8. See Kimball, *Czech Nationalism*, pp. 136ff.

2. 1900–1938: FROM THE TURN OF THE CENTURY TO MUNICH

1. Eduard Kohout, *Divadlo aneb Snář* (Theatre, or a Book of Dreams), p. 52.

2. K. H. Hilar, *Boje proti včerejšku* (Battles against the Past), pp. 280–281.

3. Ibid., pp. 281–282.

4. Ibid., pp. 282–283.

5. Ibid., pp. 58–59.

6. Josef Träger, "Hilarova osobnost ve vyvoji novodobého českého divadla" (Hilar's Creative Presence in the Development of Modern Czech Theatre) in *K. H. Hilar*, ed. Jiří Hilmera, p. 9.

7. Josef Träger, *O Hilarovi* (Prague: Umělecká Beseda, 1945), p. 12.

8. *The Jews of Czechoslovakia*, 2 vols. (New York: Society for the History of Czechoslovak Jews, 1968), vol. 1, p. 485.

9. *The Jews of Czechoslovakia*, vol. 2, p. 552.

10. For a more detailed account of the Red Seven, see Vladimír Just, "Červená sedma," *Divadelní revue* 4 (1991): 91ff.

11. The following section draws in part on my article "High Points of Theatre in the First Czechoslovak Republic," *Modern Drama* 27:1 (March 1984): 98–111.

12. Langer (1888–1965) became known, even abroad, for his contemporary plays with colorful character types from different classes. An M.D. and a habitué of Prague cabarets, he was co-author of some sketches with Jaroslav Hašek as early as 1912. His first real stage success was *A Camel through the Needle's Eye* (Velbloud uchem jehly) in 1923 at the Švanda Theatre. His most successful work, *Fringe Area* (Periferie, 1925), presented a lively slice of Prague semi-low life embodying a Dostoyevskian theme of crime and punishment. Critics consider *Mounted Patrol* (Jízdní hlídka, 1935) his most accomplished drama. It deals with a tragic episode in the lives of Czech legionnaires caught up in the battle between the Red and White armies in the not yet stabilized Soviet Union following World War I. Among numerous other interwar Czech playwrights to achieve more than fleeting recognition were Edmond Konrad (1889–1957), Karel Čapek's wife and National Theatre ac-

tress Olga Scheinpflugová (1902–1968), and Frank Tetauer (1903–1954). All managed to capture various facets of contemporary Czech life with some success.

13. Čapek's trilogy of novels in the early 1930s is most highly regarded and made him a serious contender for the Nobel Prize in the late 1930s: *Hordubal, The Meteor* (Povětron), and *An Ordinary Life* (Obyčejný život).

14. One product of their association was Čapek's three-volume study, *Conversations with T. G. Masaryk* (1928–1935).

15. Honzl's Czech translation of Alexander Tairov's *Notes of a Director* was a source of inspiration to many in Czech theatre of the interwar years. Two of Honzl's own important theoretical studies, "Dynamics of the Sign in the Theatre" (Pohyb divadelního znaku) and "The Hierarchy of Dramatic Devices" (Hierarchie divadelních prostředků), appear in English in *Semiotics of Art*, ed. Ladislav Matejka and Irwin R. Titunik (Cambridge, Mass.: MIT Press, 1986), pp. 74–93 and 118–127, respectively.

16. Josef Čapek wrote one earlier play on his own, *The Land of Many Names* (Země mnoha jmen), an unsuccessful work directed by Karel at the Vinohrady in 1923. It might almost be viewed as foreshadowing *Adam the Creator* in that humankind is presented with the opportunity to create an ideal society on a newly arisen continent; but all of the world's ills inevitably appear, and fortunately the continent is destroyed by an earthquake.

17. Burian's opera *Bubu of Montparnasse*, composed in 1929, languished for years, unproduced, until it was rediscovered in the Burian archive and staged with great success in the Prague State Opera in March 1999.

18. Both plays were designed by Hofman and directed by Karel Dostal (1884–1966), Leopolda Dostalová's older brother, who in his youth had worked under Reinhardt in Germany before joining the National Theatre in 1922 as both actor and director, becoming chief director in 1935. He is primarily associated with plays of intellectual challenge requiring skilled, finished performances, such as Greek tragedy and works by G. B. Shaw and Luigi Pirandello.

19. Several other Czech directors of the interwar years deserve mention. While a student in Germany, Jan Bor (1886–1943) had become familiar with Reinhardt's work and studied with František Zavřel in Munich. Bor first attracted attention as a strong director of works by Strindberg, Dostoyevsky, and Wedekind as well as Aristophanes and František Langer in the Švanda Theatre between 1919 and 1924. His best work, however, was done at the Vinohrady Theatre (1924–1939), where he became Kvapil's successor as artistic director. From 1939 until his death, he served as head of drama at the National Theatre and was highly regarded for his productions of emotive psychological dramas, such as adaptations of Dostoyevsky and some Czech works, including his own play, *Suzaňa Vojířová*. Viktor Šulc (1897–1945?), another German-trained Czech artist, studied with both Reinhardt and Leopold Jessner in the 1920s. Hilar invited him to work in the National Theatre, where he directed from 1924 to the early 1930s before moving to Bratislava, where he headed the Czech drama section of the Slovak National Theatre until 1938. A Communist-oriented artist, he is primarily associated with his bent toward German expressionism, which had passed its heyday by the time he sought to apply it. As an offspring of an old Czech-Jewish

family, he was sent to Auschwitz in 1942, where he was killed shortly before the end of the war. Oldřich Stibor (1901–1943) was another dedicated Communist artist who, like E. F. Burian, worked toward a poetic synthesis of theatre elements. His chief work occurred in Olomouc in the 1930s, where he staged numerous modern international classics and, in 1935, the first production of Vsevolod Vishnevsky's *Optimistic Tragedy* outside the Soviet Union. Stibor's inclination toward Soviet and leftist theatre was intensified by two trips to the Soviet Union to observe their theatre, particularly Tairov's. Although he admired Burian's work, he publicly criticized Burian's inconsistent stance vis-à-vis a united (leftist) artistic front in 1938.

3. THEATRE DURING THE OCCUPATION AND WAR YEARS

1. For example, *A Truly National Theatre* (Divadlo vskutku Národní), 1939; *Laughter and the Theatre Mask* (Smích a divadelní maska), 1942; *Stage Speech and the Verse of Tragedy* (Jevištní řeč a verš tragedie), 1944.

2. Vladimír Just, "Divadlo satiry," in *Theatre of the New Age* (Divadlo nové doby) (Prague: Panorama, 1989), p. 182.

3. Bořivoj Srba, "Theatre behind Bars" (Divadlo za mřížemi), *Divadelní revue* 1 (January 1995): 21. In addition to Srba, my main sources for the comments on theatre in Terezín and other camps were Eva Šormová, *Theatre in Terezín 1941/1945* (Divadlo v Terezíně) (Ústí nad Labem: Severočeské nákladatelství, 1973); Šormová, "The Problematics of Theatre in Terezín 1941–1945" (K problematice divadla v Terezíně 1941–1945), *Divadelní revue* 2 (April 1995): 65–72; and *Theater-Divadlo*, ed. František Černý (Prague: Orbis, 1965). Many plays and films have attempted to recreate the experience of Terezín, but the greatest of such attempts is the film *A Distant Journey* (Daleká cesta), directed by Alfred Radok in 1948, which I shall touch upon in the next chapter.

4. THE POSTWAR YEARS AND THE 1950S

1. Ota Ornest, *Hraje váš tatínek ještě na housle?* (Does Your Dad Still Play the Violin?), pp. 228f. Ornest (b. 1913) spent the war years in London and then returned and joined the newly formed Realistic Theatre as an actor and director. His most productive years were at the Municipal Theatres, which he headed (while also directing) for over twenty years, starting in 1950.

2. The material in this chapter is partly drawn from my article "The Dark Era in Modern Czech Theatre: 1948–1950," *Theatre History Studies* 15 (1995): 41–66.

3. A tribute to Josef Stalin on his seventieth birthday, two years after the Communist takeover, conveys much about the tenor of the time: its values, attitudes, and sheer rhetoric. The greetings appeared in a major theatre journal: "We thank Stalin for the very existence of our theatre culture, as we thank him for the very existence of our nation and our

freedom.... We thank Stalin for the very possibility of helping to create socialism in our country. Stalin — creator of the principles of Socialist Realism, the art of recreating life.... We thank Stalin, genius of socialist society, for the themes of our most beautiful productions. The noblest assignment of any of our actors is the embodiment of the greatest heroic figure of contemporary world drama, the figure of Josef Vissarionovic Stalin" ("70 J.V.S.," *Divadlo* 1:4 [December 1949]: 105).

4. Tynan, "The Theatre Abroad," pp. 99–123.

5. Personal interview with Milan Lukeš, fall 1993, Prague. Lukeš (b. 1933) was an important editor and professor of theatre in the 1960s and 1970s, respectively. He became head of drama at the National Theatre in the 1980s and minister of culture, 1989–1993, after which he returned as a faculty member to the Department of Theatre and Film at Charles University.

6. Jaroslav Pokorný, "Jindřich Honzl," *Divadlo* 5:7 (July 1954): 648.

7. The other members were director Karel Dostal and actor Jaroslav Průcha (1898–1963).

8. In the prewar era Frejka wrote, "Theatre is not the servant of politics just as it isn't the servant of literature. It has its own role in a given time, like electrotechnology or architecture, and, like them, seeks its contemporary form" (Jiří Frejka, *Živé divadlo* [Living Theatre], p. 24).

9. Symptomatic of the paranoia about machinations and threats from the West was the disturbance caused when a high-placed official threatened to cancel the production of Shaw's *Saint Joan* when he heard Dunois' lines from scene 3: "Blue bird, blue bird, since I am friend to thee, change thou the wind for me.... will you grudge me a west wind?" The speech was taken to be a provocative, treasonable reference to Western superiority.

10. To be precise, he did apply for formal membership, but it is not clear that he ever obtained the final technical approval. In any case, he seemed to consider himself a Communist by 1948.

11. This information was conveyed to me in conversation by Antonín Dvořák (1920–1997), author of *Trojice nejodvážnějších* (A Trio of the Bravest), a book dealing with Honzl, Burian, and Frejka. The Frejka collection of the Theatre Section of the National Museum contains a document that supplements that information. Dated April 21, 1948, it is a statement of understanding between Frejka and Otomar Krejča regarding Frejka's matching the salary offered to Krejča by the National Theatre. The document, moreover, states that the roles of Othello, Faust, and Hamlet are to be Krejča's in future seasons. Just which other actors were promised Hamlet by Frejka was not clear.

12. This information is in Dvořák, *Trojice nejodvážnějších*, pp. 229f. Frejka had continued his work as professor in the theatre division of the State Conservatory and was also instrumental in establishing the Academy of Performing Arts (AMU) in 1945.

13. Miroslav Kouřil, onetime designer and technical head of Burian's D theatre and a highly placed functionary in postwar Czech theatre circles, ultimately became part of the culture section of the Central Committee of the Communist Party. Vladimír Šmeral (1903–1982), an actor at the Vinohrady, was one of Frejka's chief opponents there (he may well have been one of the others expecting to play Hamlet). Valtr Feldstein was head of the

arts section of the Ministry of Education. František Vnouček (1903–1960) was a politically committed actor in Burian's postwar ensemble. "All honor to labor!" was an honorific, universally voiced slogan of the Communists. The note is in the Frejka collection of the Theatre Section of the National Museum.

14. A full account of the production and its reception is in Eva Šormová, "E. F. Burian: Pařeniště," *Divadelní revue* 2 (1993): 40–52.

15. Adolf Scherl, *Emil František Burian*, p. 39.

16. Books tracing the development of postwar playwriting in Czechoslovakia include Marketa Goetz-Stankiewicz, *The Silenced Theatre*; and Paul Trensky, *Czech Drama since World War II*.

17. Adolf Scherl, personal interview, spring 1994, Prague.

18. Bosley Crowther called it "the most brilliant, the most powerful and horrifying film on the Nazis' persecution of the Jews that this reviewer has yet seen" (*New York Times*, August 28, 1960).

19. Many productions by Krejča, Radok, and Honzl mentioned in this article are described and illustrated in my monograph *The Scenography of Josef Svoboda*.

20. The whole episode is described in Zdeněk Hedbávný, "Alfred Radok: Chodská nevěsta," *Divadelní revue* 3 (1992): 29–38.

21. Needless to say, these directors were not alone in resisting the deadening system with greater or lesser theatrical successes, nor were they alone in experiencing the stresses of artistic and personal survival in the 1945–1960 era. Other directors (not previously mentioned) who warrant attention would include Miloš Hynšt (b. 1921) in Brno and elsewhere; Milan Pásek (b. 1920) in Brno and elsewhere; Luboš Pistorius (1924–1997) in several Prague theatres; and Evžen Sokolovský (1925–1998) in Brno.

5. THE DYNAMIC 1960S, PART ONE: SIGNIFICANT NEW PLAYS

1. The material in this chapter is based on my article "Post-War Drama in Czechoslovakia," *Educational Theatre Journal* 25:3 (October 1973): 299–317.

2. For a critical survey of the postwar plays, see Goetz-Stankiewicz, *The Silenced Theatre*; and Trensky, *Czech Drama since World War II*.

3. Less subtle and complex but equally interesting in its focus on personal relationships presented within a contemporary context of social institutions was an earlier play, *That Sort of Love* (Taková láska, 1957) by Pavel Kohout, who had been an enthusiastic supporter of the new Communist order in earlier years. Dealing with the suicide of a young woman and employing several distancing techniques, it is in effect a Brechtian treatment of a thoroughly un-Brechtian scenario: a romantic, at times melodramatic love story with sociopolitical overtones arising from the implication that the society itself may have contributed indirectly to the girl's despair.

4. Smoček chose American GIs in the Pacific because of his close and positive contact with the Americans who liberated Pilsen, his home, in April 1945.

5. The most pointed of the critical novels were Ludvík Vaculík's *The Axe* (Sekyra) in 1966 and Milan Kundera's *The Joke* (Žert) in 1967.

6. Especially notable were Miloš Forman's *Loves of a Blonde* (1965) and *The Firemen's Ball* (1967); Ivan Passer's *Intimate Lighting* (1965); Evald Schorm's *Courage for Every Day* (1964), *The Return of the Prodigal Son* (1966), and *Pastor's End* (1968); Jan Němec's *The Party and Its Guests* (1966); and Jaromil Jireš's *The Joke* (1968), an adaptation of Milan Kundera's novel.

7. The Resolution of the Central Committee of the Czechoslovak Writers' Union in 1967 said: "A society for which the center of attention and chief measure is not the citizen and the status of his rights and responsibilities, in which man is but the object of manipulation, such a society does not need culture. Even a man who has become reconciled to manipulation . . . does not need culture; in fact he fears it; it becomes uncomfortable to him even to the point of hatefulness" (*Fourth Congress of the Union of Czechoslovak Writers* [IV. Sjezd Svazu československých spisovatelů] [Prague, 1968], p. 13).

8. Quoted in *Winter in Prague*, ed. Robin Alison Remington, p. 7.

9. Of the realities to which Havel's play alludes, a Czech scholar has written: "Bureaucratic politics envelop even simple processes and acts . . . with a strange politico-economic mysticism while transforming concrete objects and concrete persons into bureaucratic symbols and hieroglyphics. . . . Human qualities are replaced by an ideological and political scheme which is manipulated to maintain the appearance of orderliness" (Jiří Cvekl, quoted in Vladimír V. Kusin, *The Intellectual Origins of the Prague Spring*, p. 41).

10. Václav Havel, *Disturbing the Peace*, p. 54.

11. Tad Szulc, *Czechoslovakia since World War II*, p. 13.

12. In his address to the Fourth Congress of the Writers' Union in 1967, Ludvík Vaculík said, "The first law of power is that it tries to maintain itself by reproducing itself more and more precisely. Secondly, it becomes more and more homogenous, purging everything foreign to it until each part is a replica of the whole and all parts are mutually interchangeable" (quoted in *Winter in Prague*, p. 5).

13. Quoted in *Fourth Congress*, p. 41.

14. Václav Havel, in "Ještě jednou obrození?" (Yet Another [National] Revival?) *Divadlo* 20:1 (January 1969): 32.

6. THE DYNAMIC 1960S, PART TWO: KEY PRODUCTIONS IN NEW STUDIO THEATRES AND ELSEWHERE

1. This chapter develops material in my article "Art and Relevance: The Small Theatres of Prague, 1958–1970," *Educational Theatre Journal* 25:3 (May 1977): 229–257.

2. The urge toward smaller, cabaret-type literary entertainment in the late 1950s was not

restricted to Prague, as the history of Kladivadlo illustrates. Kladivadlo, a pun on the Czech words for hammer (*kladivo*) and theatre (*divadlo*), headed by Pavel Fiala (b. 1937), began in 1958 in the east Bohemian town of Broumov as an amateur cabaret devoted primarily to poetry. It continued in this vein until it moved to Ústí nad Labem in 1965 and turned professional as a branch of the State Theatre in that north Bohemian city. During its peak years as an author-centered ensemble it often appeared in guest performances at Prague's Balustrade Theatre. Kladivadlo lasted until 1971, by which time it no longer had the freshness and inventiveness of its earlier years. See Vladimír Just, "Kladivadlo," *Divadelní revue*, 4 (1994): 48f.

3. Eva Kozlanská, "Theatres That Test the Times" (Divadla, která si podrobuje čas), *Divadlo* 21:3 (March 1970): 3.

4. Alena Urbanová, "They Had to Come (Museli přijít)," *Divadlo* 20:10 (December 1969): 29. The concept and the words are a remarkable echo of similar statements describing v + w's theatre in its early phase.

5. Quoted in Jan Císař, *Theatres Which Found Their Time* (Divadla která našla svou dobu), p. 30.

6. Havel also had stagehand experience in Jan Werich's ABC Theatre in the 1959–1960 season. Subsequently, Havel had the good fortune to work as Alfred Radok's directorial assistant on two productions at the Municipal Theatres in the 1961–1962 season. Both experiences left a lasting impression on Havel's perception of theatre and its potential impact on audiences. See Jarka Burian, "Václav Havel's Notable Encounters in His Early Theatrical Career," *Slavic and East European Performance* 16:2 (Spring 1996): 13–29.

7. Jan Grossman, "The World of a Small Theatre" (Svět malého divadla), *Divadlo* 14:7 (September 1963): 18.

8. Jan Grossman, "An Obsolete Invention?" (Zastaralý vynález?), *Divadlo* 18:1 (January 1967): 57.

9. Ibid.

10. Karel Kraus, "The Balustrade as a Type" (Zábradlí jako typ), *Divadlo* 14:7 (September 1963): 41.

11. Jan Grossman, "Presenting *The Garden Party*" (Uvedení Zahradní slavnosti), in *The Garden Party* (Zahradní slavnost), p. 80.

12. Grossman, "An Obsolete Invention?" p. 59.

13. Ibid.

14. *Král Ubu*, ed. Jan Grossman (Prague: Divadelní ústav, 1966), p. 106.

15. Grossman, "Presenting *The Garden Party*," p. 78.

16. Jaroslav Vostrý, "Theses on a Theatre-Club" (Téze o divadle-klubu), *Divadelní noviny* 12:13 (March 1969): 4.

17. Vostrý, quoted in Zdeněk Hořínek, "Činoherní klub 1965–66," *Divadlo* 17:7 (September 1966): 11.

18. Alena Vostrá and Jaroslav Vostrý, "Dramaturgic Notes" (Dramaturgické poznámky), *Divadlo* 18:1 (January 1967): 81.

19. Ibid., p. 82.

2. Material from two of my articles formed the basis of this chapter: "Václav Havel: From Playwright to President: Notes and Recollections," *Soviet and East European Performance* 9:2–3 (Fall 1989): 12–19; and "Havel and the Velvet Revolution," *American Theatre* 6:12 (March 1990): 38–40.

3. The production, its context, and its repercussions are described by Petr Oslzlý, "On Stage with the Velvet Revolution," *Drama Review* 34:3 (Fall 1990): 97–108.

4. Ibid., p. 106.

5. Miloslav Klíma, *Scéna* 24 (December 20, 1989): 1.

6. Václav Havel, "New Year's Address," in *Open Letters* (London: Faber and Faber, 1991), p. 392.

10. LIBERATION AND ITS PAINS: THE FIRST YEAR AFTER THE NOVEMBER REVOLUTION

1. My account was originally published as "The Not So Velvet Fallout of Czechoslovakia's Velvet Revolution," *Theatre Three*, 10:11 (1991): 65–75.

2. Lída Engelová, director, during an interview in the fall of 1990.

3. Havel, "New Year's Address," p. 395.

4. Václav Havel, "The Velvet Hangover," *Harper's Magazine* (October 1990): 18–21.

5. For a fuller account of Krejča between 1976 and 1991, see Jarka Burian, "Notes from Abroad: Krejča's Voice Is Heard Again in Prague," *American Theatre* (June 1991): 36–37.

6. Jan Dušek, stage designer and, at the time, dean of the Theatre Academy (DAMU), during an interview in the fall of 1990. A detailed account of one theatre's efforts to adapt to post–Velvet Revolution conditions is Dennis C. Beck, "Divadlo Husa na Provázku and the 'Absence' of Czech Community," *Theatre Journal*, 48:4 (December 1996): 419–441.

11. CZECH THEATRE OF THE 1990S

1. Parts of this chapter are drawn from two articles I wrote in 1994: "Cloudy Forecast for New Prague Spring," *American Theatre* (December 1994): 76–77; and "Prague Theatre Four Years after the Velvet Revolution," *Slavic and East European Performance* 15:1 (Spring 1995): 14–26.

2. John Updike, "Prague Again," *Ontario Review* 46 (Spring–Summer 1997): 72.

3. Recent information indicates that with regard to standard of living, the Czech Republic has moved from 39th to 36th on the world scale in the past year and that it is second only to Slovenia among former members of the Communist bloc. The same source also indicates, however, that the Communist Party is now favored by 17.8 percent of potential voters, second among all parties. See Jaroslav Nový, "Does a Resurrection of Communism Threaten the Czechs?" (Hrozí Česku Vzkříšení Kommunismu?) *Americké Listy* 10:15 (July 29, 1999): 1.

4. It is true that commercialism in one guise or another has entered into many aspects of repertoire selection, advertising, ticket sales, and other promotional activities. New theatres (especially in Prague) devoted primarily if not entirely to turning a profit have emerged to cater to a public craving Western popular entertainment, especially musicals: *Hair*, *Jesus Christ Superstar*, and *Evita* are among the most notable examples of nonrepertory productions by private entrepreneurs. Free enterprise is also evident in the mushrooming of small self-supporting theatre groups doing only one or two productions targeting specific, mainly tourist, audiences, as well as in the ongoing *agentura* system of packaged, small-cast productions booked into restaurants, hotels, social centers, and occasionally even regular provincial theatres. Such activities have modified but not substantively altered the essential profile of Czech theatre today.

5. Established in honor of the great mid-century director, the Alfred Radok awards are bestowed each spring for the best work of the previous calendar year. The winners of the best production award have been Christian Dietrich Grabbe's *Don Juan and Faust* in 1992 (Realistic Theatre, dir. Hana Burešová); a dramatization of a Czech novel by the Mrštík brothers, *A Year in the Country* (Rok na vsi) in 1993 (National Theatre, dir. Miroslav Krobot); Chekhov's *The Sea Gull* in 1994 (Balustrade Theatre, dir. Petr Lébl); a scenario based on Czech prose and poetry, *Sister Anxiety* (Sestra úzkost) in 1995 (Dejvické Theatre, dir. J. A. Pitínský); a dramatized scenario of an Austrian novel by Joseph Roth, *Job*, in 1996 (HaDivadlo, Brno, dir. J. A. Pitínský); Chekhov's *Ivanov* in 1997 (Balustrade Theatre, dir. Petr Lébl); and Henry Purcell's *Dido and Aeneas* in 1998 (J. K. Tyl Theatre, Pilsen, dir. J. A. Pitínský).

6. Goldflam's other plays in the 1990s have included *A Small Pogrom* (Malý pogrom; 1992); *Day of Love* (Lásky den; 1994); and *A Few Stories* (Několik historek; 1995). Although he ended full-time affiliation with the HaDivadlo Theatre in 1993, he has continued to direct there occasionally, as well as in Prague's Ypsilon, Balustrade, and Longstreet theatres and in the Brno theatre academy (JAMU), where he has been on the faculty. His latest project is the direction of his own recent play, *The Agreement* (Smlouva), a contemporary treatment of the Abraham and Isaac story. It is scheduled to open on the Kolowrat stage of the National Theatre in October 1999.

7. For a history of the Estates Theatre and its reconstructions, see J. Burian, "Prague's Stavovské Theatre: Its Background and Renovation," *Theatre Design and Technology* 31:3 (Summer 1995): 36–46.

8. Previous studio theatre operations in the National Theatre were only temporary: Jiří Frejka's few semi-improvised productions in the early 1930s, and Jindřich Honzl's more developed project in 1945–1948.

9. Analogous to the German Turnverein, the Sokol was a nineteenth-century Czech organization stressing Czech culture and organized gymnastic activity as a source of national pride and moral uplift. Suppressed during the Communist era, it is once again active today.

10. Pitínský was born Zdeněk Petrželka. He took the name Jan Antonín Pitínský after a 1980 encounter with police in Brno stemming from his outdoor, traffic-obstructing "Hap-

European cultural identity." In the 1990s Oslzlý became managing director of Goose on a String as well as its dramaturg, while Peter Scherhaufer and Eva Tálská remained its chief directors. In the spring of 1999 Tálská created the scenario and directed a well-received production of *With Me, Death and a Horse* (Se mnou smrt a kůň), a tragicomic, nonverbal depiction of life and backstage relations in a circus milieu. Also in 1999, the theatre experienced a great loss in Scherhaufer's untimely death. In the meantime, HaDivadlo had merged with the former Amateur Circle to form the Cabinet of the Muses, an administrative entity allowing both theatres to use the same new but limited quarters in Brno.

19. Contemporary Czech theatre suffered a grievous loss with the sudden death of Petr Lebl in Prague on December 12, 1999. The news reached me as this book was in its page proof stage.

SELECTED BIBLIOGRAPHY

Blackwell, Věra. "Literature and Drama." *Survey* 59 (April 1966): 41–47.
Boháč, Ladislav. *Tisíc a jeden život* [A Thousand and One Lives]. Prague: Odeon, 1981. Memoir by an actor-director in the National Theatre from 1928 to 1973, a colleague of Hilar, Frejka, Honzl, and Krejča.
Burian, Emil František. *O nové divadlo* [The New Theatre]. 1940. Prague: Ústav pro učebné pomůcky, 1946. Collection of his writings and lectures in the 1930s.
Burian, Jarka. "Theatre in Czechoslovakia." *Drama Survey* 6:1 (Spring–Summer 1967): 93–104.
———. "European Newsletters: Prague." *Plays and Players* 16:6 (March 1969): 45–46; 16:8 (May 1969): 58–59; 16:11 (August 1969): 61–62; 18:2 (September 1971): 60.
———. *The Scenography of Josef Svoboda*. Middletown, Conn.: Wesleyan University Press, 1971.
———. "Otomar Krejča's Use of the Mask." *Drama Review* 16:3 (September 1972): 48–56.
———. "A Scenographer's Work: Josef Svoboda's Designs, 1971–1975." *Theatre Design and Technology* 12:2 (Summer 1976): 11–34.
———. "The Scenography of Ladislav Vychodil." *Theatre Design and Technology* 15:2 (Summer 1979): 8–17.
———. *Svoboda: Wagner*. Middletown, Conn.: Wesleyan University Press, 1983.
———. "Designing for the 90s." *Cue International* 62 (November/December 1989): 32–37. About Czech designers Jaroslav Malina and Jan Dušek.
———. "Josef Svoboda and Laterna Magika's Latest Productions." *Theatre Design and Technology* 24:4 (Winter 1989): 17–27.
———. "Ciller and Žídek: Two Expressive Minimalists." *Theatre Design and Technology* 28:2 (Spring 1992): 33–38.
———. "Grossman, Macháček, Schorm: The Loss of Three Major Czech Directors of the Late Twentieth Century." *Slavic and East European Performance* 13:3 (Fall 1993): 27–30.
———. "Two Women and Their Contribution to Contemporary Czech Scenography." *Theatre Design and Technology* 32:5 (Fall 1996): 19–29. On Marta Rozkopfová and Jana Zbořilová.

———. *Pražská dramaturgie*. Prague: Sfinx Janda, 1930. Hilar's later essays.

Holzknecht, Václav. *Jaroslav Ježek a Osvobozené divadlo* [Jaroslav Ježek and the Liberated Theatre]. Prague: Státní nákladatelství krásné literatury, 1957. Focuses on v + w's theatre.

Judson, Horace. "The Czech Stage: Freedom's Last Barricade." *Time* (July 25, 1969): 50–51.

Just, Vladimír. *Proměny malých scén* [Changes in the Small Theatres]. Prague: Mladá fronta, 1984. Survey of cabaret-type studio theatres from the early years of the century.

K. H. Hilar. Ed. Jiří Hilmera. Prague: Narodní muzeum, 1968. First formal attempt at rehabilitating Hilar in the Communist era.

K. H. Hilar. Ed. Miroslav Rutte. Prague: Československy dramatický svaz a družstevní prace, 1936.

Kimball, Stanley Buchholz. *Czech Nationalism: A Study of the National Theatre Movement, 1845–83*. Urbana: University of Illinois Press, 1964.

Kohout, Eduard. *Divadlo aneb Snář* [Theatre, or a Book of Dreams]. Prague: Odeon, 1975. Autobiography of a major Kvapil and Hilar actor whose career extended into the 1960s.

Kronika armádního uměleckého divadla [Chronicle of the Army Art Theatre]. Prague: Naše vojsko, 1955. Solid documentation on Burian's theatre from its pre-origin to his death.

Kusin, Vladimír V. *The Intellectual Origins of the Prague Spring*. London: Cambridge University Press, 1971.

Liehm, Antonín. "Theatre in Czechoslovakia." *Theatre Quarterly* 2:6 (April–June 1972): 72–80.

———. "Alfred Radok." *International Journal of Politics* 3:1–2 (Spring–Summer 1973): 23–39.

Narodní divadlo a jeho předchůdci [The National Theatre and Its Predecessors]. Ed. Vladimír Procházka. Prague: Akademia, 1988. Encyclopedia of National Theatre artists.

Nekolný, Bohumil. *Studiové divadla a jeho české cesty* [Studio Theatres and Their Czech Pathways]. Prague: Scéna, 1991. Very detailed focus on post-1970 studio theatres.

Nová česka scéna [The New Czech Stage]. Prague: Umělecká beseda, 1937. Well-illustrated commentary on contemporary Czech staging.

Nové české divadlo 1918–1926 [The New Czech Theatre]. Ed. Miroslav Rutte and Josef Kodiček. Prague: Aventinum, 1927. The first of an informative, well-illustrated series of four volumes devoted to contemporary Czech theatre between 1918 and 1932. The same editors and publisher produced *Nové české divadlo 1927* and *Nové české divadlo 1928–29*, in 1927 and 1929, respectively. The series ended with *Nové české divadlo 1930–32*, ed. Miroslav Rutte and František Götz, in 1932.

Obst, Milan, and Adolf Scherl. *K dejinám české divadelní avantgardy* [Toward a History of the Czech Theatre Avant-garde]. Prague: Československá akademie věd, 1962. Definitive work on prewar Honzl and Burian.

O Divadle 1 [About Theatre]. Ed. Karel Kraus. Prague: Lidové noviny, 1990. Valuable collection of samizdat essays on Czech theatre during the Normalization era.

Ornest, Ota. *Hraje váš tatínek ještě na housle?* [Does Your Dad Still Play the Violin?]. Prague: Primus, 1993. Detailed account of Ornest's career in post–World War II Czech theatre.

Oslzlý, Petr. "On Stage with the Velvet Revolution." *Drama Review* 34:3 (Fall 1990): 97–108.

Pešek, Ladislav. *Tvář bez masky* [Face without a Mask]. Prague: Odeon, 1977. Informative autobiography of an actor who spanned generations from Hilar to Krejča.

Piša, A. M. *Divadelní avantgarda* [Theatre Avant-garde]. Prague: Divadelní ústav, 1978. Collection of Pisa's reviews and commentaries on leading avant-garde ensembles from 1926 to 1941.

Prolegomena scénografické encyklopedie [Prolegomenon to a Scenographic Encyclopedia]. Ed. Miroslav Kouřil. 20 vols. Prague: Scénograficky ústav, 1970–1973. Well-documented articles on theatre history, theory, architecture, directing, and scenography.

Ptáčková, Věra. *Ceska scénografie XX. stoleti* [Czech Scenography of the Twentieth Century]. Prague: Odeon, 1982. Definitive study of modern Czech stage design; exceptionally well illustrated.

Rutte, Miroslav, and František Bartoš. *The Modern Czech Scene*. Prague: Vladimír Žikeš, 1938.

Sayer, Derek. *The Coasts of Bohemia: A Czech History*. Princeton, N.J.: Princeton University Press, 1998. Thorough, scholarly, readable account of Czech social and cultural history to the 1950s.

Scherl, Adolf. *Emil František Burian*. Berlin: Henschelverlag, 1966.

Schneider, Alan. "Behind the [Iron] Theater Curtain." *Evergreen Review* 79 (June 1970): 91–94. Compare with Kenneth Tynan article (below).

Srba, Bořivoj. *E. F. Burian a jeho program poetického divadla* [E. F. Burian and His Program for a Poetic Theatre]. Prague: Divadelní ústav, 1981. Collection of Burian's writings and extended essay by Srba.

Svět a divadlo [World and Theatre]. Ed. Karel Král. Critical journal published six times a year since 1990 under the auspices of the Theatre Institute (brief English resumes of articles), which often includes texts of plays; some illustrations.

Svoboda, Josef. *The Secret of Theatrical Space*. Trans. J. Burian. New York: Applause Theatre Books, 1993. The master scenographer's career autobiography.

Szulc, Tad. *Czechoslovakia since World War II*. New York: Viking, 1971.

Trensky, Paul I. *Czech Drama since World War II*. White Plains, New York: M. E. Sharpe, 1978.

Tynan, Kenneth. "The Theatre Abroad: Prague." *New Yorker* (April 1, 1967): 99–124.

Unruh, Delbert. "Action Design." *Theatre Design and Technology* 23:1 (Spring 1987): 6–13. "Practical Problems of Space." *TD&T* 26:2 (Summer 1990): 33–40. "Philosophical Problems of Space." *TD&T* 26:4 (Fall 1990): 25–32. "The Problem of Costumes."

Bohemia, 3, 7, 29, 55
Bojcev, Christo: *Colonel Bird*, 221, 226
Böll, Heinrich: *Clown, The*, 146
Bolshevism, 36
Bor, Jan, 61, 233n 19; productions: *Zuzaná Vojířová*, 58
Born, Jan, 215
Brahm, Otto, 19, 22
"Bratislava Ladder," 74
Bread and Puppet Theatre, 205
Brecht, Bertolt, 31, 44, 45, 57, 83, 84; *Threepenny Opera*, 45
Breton, André, 53
Brezhnev, Leonid, 141, 145
Brno, 3, 14, 44, 69, 164
Brook, Peter, 204
Brussels Expo, 87, 88
Büchner, Georg: *Wozzek*, 209
Bunraku, 205
Burešová, Hana, 211–213, 215, 216, 217, 218, 219, 226, 229; productions: *Barber of Seville, The*, 212; *Boucharon*, 213; *Don Juan and Faust*, 212; *End of Carnival, The*, 215, 226; *Flying Physician, The*, 215; *I'm Having a Benefit*, 213; *Magnificent Cuckold, The*, 215; *Miraculous Magician*, 215; *Murder in the Cathedral*, 213; *Rigoletto*, 215; *School, Life's Foundation*, 213
Burian, Emil František, 3, 5, 35, 40, 45, 46, 49, 53, 54, 55, 59, 60, 61, 62, 70, 75, 76, 77, 78, 79, 81–85, 88, 89, 152, 153, 219, 229; acting school, 59; Army Art Theatre, 83; in Communist Party, 43, 55; death (1959), 85; D34 (theatre), 45, 53–55, 65, 84, 86, 161; D39 and D40, 59; D46, 81; post–World War II theatre, 70, 72, 75, 195; productions: 45, *Barber of Seville, The*, 55; *Bedbug, The*, 84; *Before Sunrise* (opera), 43; *Bubu of Montparnasse* (opera), 233n 17; *Eugene Onegin*, 54; *Grinder Karhan's Team*, 82; *Hamlet III*, 55; *Hotbed, The*, 82, 83; *Life in Our Days*, 45; *Loretka*, 59; *Manon Lescaut*, 58; *Maryša*, 59; *Merchant of Venice, The*, 45; *Midnight Wind*, 84; *Miser, The*, 45; *Old Story, An*, 59; *Romeo and Juliet, The Dream of a Prisoner*, 82, 85; *Spring's Awakening*, 54; *Threepenny Opera, The*, 45; *War*, 45; *Werther*, 55; *Winter Battle, The*, 83, 84; *Theatergraph*, 54, 87; *Yegor Bulychov*, 45; theatre of synthesis, 54; Voiceband recitals, 43, 62
Burian, Vlasta ("King of Comics"), 31, 36, 42, 50, 60, 70, 80

Cabaret Bum, 36
cabarets, 29–31, 32, 36, 42, 65, 115, 116, 152, 161, 163, 237n 2
Cabinet of the Muses, 244n 18
Calábek, Milan: *Czech Christmas Mass, The*, 142–143
Camus, Albert, 94
Čapek, Joseph, 5, 34, 37, 61, 62; *Adam the Creator*, 40; *Fateful Play of Love, The*, 49, 64; *Insect Comedy, The*, 38–39, 40, 77, 112, 114, 197; *Land of Many Names*, 233n 16
Čapek, Karel, 5, 31, 32, 33–34, 36, 39, 52, 61, 108, 184; *Adam the Creator*, 40, 52; *Brigand, The*, 37; *Fateful Play of Love, The*, 37, 49; *Insect Comedy, The*, 38–39, 40, 77, 112, 114, 197; *Makropulos Affair, The*, 39, 40, 52; *Mother, The*, 52–53; proscribed writer no longer, 101–102; *RUR (Rossum's Universal Robots)*, 36, 37–38, 40, 52; *White Disease, The*, 51, 52, 141
Carousel (theatre), 174
Carroll, Lewis, 169
Catsplay (Hungarian work), 150
Cellar (theatre), 174
censorship, 15, 55, 102, 140, 145
Center for Experimental Theatre, 243n 18
Čep, Jan, 221
Černý, František, 182

Červený, Jiří, 30
Chaplin, Charlie, 31
Charles IV (Holy Roman emperor), 18
Chekhov, Anton, 22, 23, 95, 147; *Bear, The,* 14; *Cherry Orchard, The,* 127, 193; *Ivanov,* 180, 214; one-acts, 64; *Platonov,* 150; *Sea Gull, The,* 89, 149(photo), 214, 219–220; *Three Sisters, The,* 132–133, 206
činohra, 6
Civic Forum, 186, 187
Claudel, Paul, 23
Club of Czech and German Theatre Workers, 45
Cocteau, Jean: *Human Voice, The,* 64; *Orphée,* 43; *Wedding on the Eiffel Tower,* 43
commedia dell'arte, 26, 42, 59, 152, 212
commedia zannis, 175
communism: breakdown in Eastern Europe, 154, 183. *See also under* Czech theatre
concentration camp theatre performances, 62–66
Concert for Mr. Masaryk, A, 143–144
constructivism, 32
Copeau, Jacques, 29, 31
Corneille, Pierre: *Cid, The,* 27
Craig, Gordon, 22, 26, 29
Cramp (theatre), 174
Crommelynck, Fernand: *Magnificent Cuckold, The,* 215
cybernetic machine, 120
Czech avant-garde, 32, 36, 43, 85, 229
Czech communist regime (1948–1989), 1, 5, 68, 69, 70–76, 83, 84, 93, 97, 105, 181, 187–188
Czech lands. *See* Bohemia; Moravia
Czech language, 2, 9, 10, 29–30
Czech Republic (1993), 199–200, 203, 221, 226, 240n 3 (ch. 11)
Czech theatre, 6; and communism, 1, 35, 45, 147, 148–149; eighteenth to nineteenth centuries, 2, 9–19; export to West, 87–88, 113–114; government subsidies, 3; homogenous culture, 3; Jewish presence, 30, 172; as moral and educational force, 2, 12, 15–16; lines of descent, 3; and national identity, 2, 10, 15, 31; nationalized, 69, 70; late 1950s thawing, 75, 85, 86, 91–92; 1960s creative surge, 93, 111; 1975–1985, 153–155; 1980s thawing, 155–169; and plays of contemporary life, 10–11, 17, 19, 28, 94–96, 150–160; post–World War I, 31–33, 36, 40, 44–45, 51, 55–56; repertory system, 3–4; strike, 186; suspension of (1944–1945), 58; after Warsaw Pact armies invasion, 138–152. *See also* actors; designers; directors; playwrights; specific theatres
Czechoslovak Writers' Union, 94, 102
Czechoslovakia: Communist Party, 36, 73, 78, 79, 80, 93, 94, 95, 102, 145–146, 150, 181, 190–191, 240n 3 (ch. 11); geographical influence, 1–3, 31; German occupation (1938–1945), 2, 55, 57–66; German population, 68; independence/Republic of Czechoslovakia/First Republic (1918), 1, 2, 20–21, 31–32, 55; invasion by Warsaw Pact armies (1968), 93, 137. *See also* Czech communist regime; Czech Republic; Habsburg Empire

dada, 32, 43
DAMU. *See* Academy of Performing Arts, Theatre Academy
Daněk, Oldřich: *How Easy It Is to Rule,* 207; *You Are Jan,* 156–158, 178
De Ghelderode, Michel: *Masquers of Ostende,* 131
Deml, Jakub, 221
de Musset, Alfred: *Lorenzaccio,* 132, 133–135
designers, 3, 23; in post–World War I theatre, 32, 34, 36, 38–39, 46; in post–

Hašler, Karel, 61
Hauptmann, Gerhardt, 17; *Beaver Coat, The*, 62
Havel, Václav, 5, 33, 104, 119–120, 145, 149, 154–155, 182, 186, 225–226, 238n 6; Czech Republic president (1990), 1, 187, 190; on theatre, 110; *Garden Party, The*, 102–103, 104, 119, 120, 129, 185; *Increased Difficulty of Concentration, The*, 104, 123; *Largo Desolata*, 193–194; *Memorandum, The*, 103–104, 119, 120, 143; *Temptation*, 214; *Tomorrow We'll Start It Up*, 183; *Urban Renewal*, 184
Hellman, Lillian: *Autumn Garden*, 88; *Little Foxes, The*, 87
Henlein, Konrad, 44, 51
Heydrich, Reinhard, 58, 61
Heythum, Antonín, 36; stage set: *Cirkus Dandin* (photo), 42
Hilar, Karel Hugo, 3, 5, 20, 21, 24–28, 34–35, 38, 40, 49–50, 229; and the grotesque, 26, 27, 28; histrionic, hyperexpressive sense, 26, 34; on Kvapil, 25; at National Theatre, 25, 34–35, 38, 49–50; productions: *Adam the Creator*, 40; *Antony and Cleopatra*, 27; *Cid, The*, 27; *Coriolanus*, 38; *Dance of Death, The*, 27; *Dawns, The*, 28; *Doctor in Spite of Himself, The*, 38; *Don Juan*, 27; *Georges Daudin*, 26; *Hamlet*, 40; *Hussites, The*, 28; *Insect Comedy, The*, 38; *Medea*, 38; *Merchant Schippel*, 26; *Mourning Becomes Electra*, 49; *Oedipus*, 49, 50(photo); *Pan*, 28; *Penthesilea*, 27; *Romeo and Juliet*, 40; *School for Scandal, The*, 27; *Snob, The*, 27; *Undivine Comedy, The*, 28; at Vinohrady Theatre, 21, 24; on Zavřel, 26–27
Hilbert, Jaroslav: *Falkenštejn*, 53; *Guilt*, 18
historical drama, 12, 15–16, 18, 21, 142, 156–159, 164, 166

Hitler, Adolf, 32, 44, 55; theatre caricature, 46
Hoffmeister, Adolf: *Brundibár*, 65
Hofman, Vlastislav, 34, 36; stage design: *Hamlet*, 40, 41(photo); *Mourning Becomes Electra*, 49; *Oedipus*, 49, 50(photo)
Holocaust, 68. *See also* Terezín
Honzl, Jindřich, 35–36, 39–40, 42–43, 46, 47, 48(photo), 49, 53, 59, 60, 70, 75, 76–77, 78, 89, 229; and National Theatre, 49, 70, 76–77; productions: *Alchemist*, 49; *Ass and Shadow*, 46; *Blood Wedding*, 77; *Breasts of Tiresias, The*, 43; *Fist in the Eye, A*, 51; *Golem, The*, 46; *Great Smelting, The*, 77; *Heavy Barbara*, 51; *Insect Comedy, The*, 77; *Jan Hus*, 77; *Juliette* (opera), 53; *Maryša*, 77; *Moscow Character*, 77; *Mute Canary, The*, 43; *Orphée*, 43; *Revizor*, 77; *Ubu Roi*, 43, 63
Horáková, Milada, 82
Horníček, Miroslav, 85
Hrab, Ondřej, 205, 206
Hradčany Castle (Prague), 15, 55
Hrubín, František: *Oldrich and Bozena*, 142; *Romance for a Cornet*, 227; *Sunday in August, A*, 89, 95–96
Huba, Martin, 224
Hubalek, Claus: *No More Heroes in Thebes*, 129
Hübnerová, Marie, 18, 23
Hudeček, Václav, 156–158
Hus, Jan, 156
Husák, Gustav, 145, 187
Hynšt, Miloš, 149, 154, 236n 21

Ibsen, Henrik, 14, 17, 19, 21, 22, 23; *Doll's House*, 14; influence of, 18; *Peer Gynt*, 209, 210
Ionesco, Eugene, 94; *Bald Soprano*, 119; *Lesson, The*, 119; *Rhinoceros*, 105; 141

"irregular theatre," 165
Ivanov, V. V.: *Armored Train, The*, 78

JAMU. *See* Academy of Performing Arts
Janáček, Leoš: *Jenufa* (opera), 17; *Makropulos Affair, The*, 39
Jára (da) Cimrman Theatre collective, 173–174, 239n 4
Jarry, Alfred: *Ubu Roi*, 43, 60, 105, 119
jazz, 31
"Jazz Revues": *Fata Morgána*, 46; *Golem, The*, 46
Jelínek, Miki, 173
Jelinková-Švandová, Ema, 21, 33, 50; roles, 26, 36
Jessner, Leopold, 29
Jews, 30, 57, 61, 62–65, 68, 172. *See also* Terezín
Ježek, Jaroslav, 46, 48(photo)
Jirásek, Alois, 17, 18, 22; *Lantern*, 57; *Vojnarka*, 17
Jirásková, Jiřína, 207
Jirsíková, Nina, 62
Joseph II (Habsburg emperor), 9, 10

Kabuki, 205
Kačer, Jan, 124, 149, 154, 159, 184, 194, 210, 239n 5; productions: *Farewell, Socrates*, 184, 210; *Midsummer Night's Dream*, 210; *Peer Gynt*, 210; *Urmefisto*, 158–159(photo); *Voices of the Birds*, 184; *When Your Number Comes Up*, 126
Kafka, Franz, 30, 105; *Trial, The*, 122–123
Káňa, Vašek: *Grinder Karhan's Team*, 82
Karafiat, Jan: *Bugs, The*, 64, 65
Kašlík, Václav, 72
Kästner, Erich: *Life in Our Days*, 45
Keaton, Buster, 31
Kien, Peter: *Puppets*, 64
Kierkegaard, Søren, 94
Kladivadlo, 237n 2

Klicpera, Václav Kliment, 11, 12, 15; *Comedy on the Bridge*, 11; *Evil Stag*, 59; *Hadrian*, 11
Klíma, Ivan, 102, 149, 154; *Castle, The*, 105–106; *Jury, The*, 146
Klíma, Ladislav: *Honest Mathew*, 163
Kohout, Eduard, 25; roles, 40, 49
Kohout, Jára, 50, 51, 149
Kohout, Pavel, 102, 154; *August, August, August*, 106; *Poor Murderer*, 207; *That Sort of Love*, 236n 3; *Trifles and Troubles*, 195
Kolár, Josef Jiří, 13
Kolowrat Theatre, 210, 227
Komedie Theatre, 224, 242n 13
Kopecký, Jan: *Play of the Martyrdom and Glorious Resurrection of Our Lord and Savior Jesus Christ, A*, 101; *Play of the Star, A*, 101
Kořínek, Miroslav, 209
Kouřil, Miroslav, 53, 69, 81, 235–236n 13
Kovalčuk, Josef, 170, 227, 228, 229
Kracik, Petr, 209, 227, 239n 5; productions: *Arsonist's Daughter, The*, 227; *Black Comedy*, 209; *Hamlet*, 209; *Of Mice and Men*, 209; *Peer Gynt*, 209
Kras, Hans: *Brundibár*, 65
Krasiński, Z.: *Undivine Comedy, The*, 28
Kraus, Karel, 88, 89, 120, 128, 202, 203
Krejča, Otomar, 3, 5, 61, 75, 79, 88–91, 147, 148(photo), 149, 153, 154, 182, 184, 227, 229, 235n 11, 242–243n 13; on art and life, 135; directing style, 89, 91, 130–132; at National Theatre, 88, 89, 91, 107, 116; at Neumann Theatre, 150–51; productions: *Bagpiper from Strakonice, The*, 89; *Cat on the Rails*, 98; *Cherry Orchard*, 193, 202; *Drahomira and Her Sons*, 89; *End of Carnival*, 107, 111; *Faust*, 203–204, 227; *Garden Party, The*, 102–103, 129; *Green Cockatoo, The*, 131,

O'Neill, Eugene, 45; *Mourning Becomes Electra*, 49
opera, 15, 17, 28, 39, 43, 59, 72, 86, 141; children's, 64–65; surrealist, 53
Ornest, Ota, 67, 75, 112, 194–195, 234n 1 (ch. 4)
Osborne, John: *Entertainer, The*, 88
Oslzlý, Petr, 164, 165, 166, 182, 243–244n 18
Ostrovsky, Alexander, 17
Otčenášek, Stepan, 215

Palach, Jan, 139
Palácký, František, 12, 14, 15, 231n 2 (ch. 2)
Pallenberg, Max, 45
Pásek, Milan, 236n 21
Patriotic Theatre, 10, 11
Patton, George, 68
Pavlíček, František, 149, 154; *Heavenly Ascension of Saška Christ, The*, 107–108
Pešek, Ladislav, 59
Pilsen, 14, 150, 223
Pinter, Harold: *Ashes to Ashes*, 210; *Birthday Party, The*, 128; *Homecoming, The*, 209; *Lover, The*, 210
Pirandello, Luigi: *Mountain Giants, The*, 202–203; *To Clothe the Naked*, 207
Piscator, Erwin, 31, 45
Pistorius, Luboš, 207, 236n 21; productions: *Poor Murderer*, 207; *Right You Are*, 207
Pitínský, Jan Antonín, 201, 215–218, 219, 221, 225(photo); plays written: *Bulldoggery*, 218; *Little Room, The*, 214, 218; *Mother, The*, 218, 227, 229, 241n 10, 241n 12, 243n 14; *Park, The*, 218; *Pineapple, The*, 218; plays directed: *Dido and Aeneas*, 223; *8 1/2*, 222; *Going Astray*, 222–223; *Heart of the Matter, The*, 216; *Her Stepdaughter*, 222; *Histrionics*, 223–224; *Job*, 222; *Magic Mountain, The*, 222, 223; *Oedipus Rex*, 223; *Ritter, Dene, Voss*, 216; *She's Strong in Zoology*, 215, 217(photo);
Sister Anxiety, 221, 222(photo); *Special Woman, A*, 224; *Tanya, Tanya*, 216
Plautus, Titus: *Pseudolos*, 58
playwrights, 6–7, 124, 125, 200–201; eighteenth-century, 10–11; Jewish, 57, 172; 1990s, 201; nineteenth-century, 11, 12, 15, 17, 18; post-1968, 170, 174; in post–World War I theatre, 32, 232n 12; twentieth-century, 31, 91–105; women, 17, 124. *See also* dramaturg
Pleskot, Jaromír, 88, 149, 154, 195; production: *Hamlet*, 88
poetism, 32
poetry, 18, 39, 43, 58, 116, 117, 152, 169, 173, 217, 231n 2 (ch. 1), 237n 2
Poláček, Karel: *Everything for the Company*, 208–209
Polekran (multiscreen projection system), 96, 97(photo)
political trials, 82–83
Polívka, Boleslav, 164
popular theatre. *See* cabarets
Pospíšil, Zdeněk, 164
postmodernism, 86, 152, 202, 226
Potužil, Zdeněk, 173
power motif, 105–106, 143, 167
Prague Conservatory, 40
Prague Five, 174
Prague Spring (1968), 2, 75, 93, 137
Preiss, Viktor, 159(photo), 207
Preissová, Gabriela, 17; *Her Stepdaughter*, 17, 222; *Household Woman*, 17, 19
Přidal, Antonín: *Night After, The*, 228
prompter/*souffleur*, 4
Protelkult, 40
Provisional Theatre, 10, 13, 14, 29; 1939, 57, 58
Průcha, Jaroslav, 77
Prussians, 29
Purcell, Henry: *Dido and Aeneas*, 223
Pushkin, Alexander: *Eugene Onegin*, 54

[260] INDEX

Radok, Alfred, 3, 5, 61, 71, 72, 75, 80, 85–92, 87(photo), 139, 149, 123, 153, 154, 182, 184, 219, 229; and Burian, 85, 89; and Krejča, 75, 85–86, 88–91; directing style, 90–91; films, 86–87; and Honzl, 89; and Laterna Magika, 87, 88, 112, 113; at Municipal Theatres of Prague, 88, 91, 112; at National Theatre, 86, 87–88, 89, 113; productions: *Atlantida*, 88; *Autumn Garden*, 88; *Bride from Chod, The*, 87, 89; *Clown, The*, 146; *Devil's Circle, The*, 88; *Distant Journey, A* (film), 86; *Eleventh Commandment, The*, 87; *Entertainer, The*, 88; *Golden Carriage*, 88; *Last Ones, The*, 113, 114(photo); *Little Foxes, The*, 87; *Marriage*, 112; *Merry Widow?, The*, 86; *Opening of the Springs, The* (cantata), 88; *Pagliacci*, 86; *Play of Love and Death, The*, 91, 112–113(photo); *Rigoletto*, 86; *Scent of Flowers, A*, 139; *Tales of Hoffmann, The*, 86; *Village of Women*, 90; *Theatre of the Fifth of May*, 72, 86

Radok, Alfred, Award, 200, 210, 214, 216, 223, 241n 5

Radoková, Marie, 87(photo)

Rajmont, Ivan, 175–176, 184, 188, 196–197, 210, 229; productions: *Medea*, 210; *Neapolitan Disease*, 176; *Tatar Fair*, 176; *Possessed, The*, 210

Realism in theatre, 12, 14, 17, 19, 23, 40, 73, 77, 83, 85, 94, 98, 106, 127

Realistic Theatre, 72–73, 183–185, 210–211

Red Army, 68

Red Seven (cabaret), 30–31, 36, 152

Reduta (tavern), 116–117

Reiner, Karel, 65

Reinhardt, Max, 22, 26, 29, 30, 44

repertory system, 3–4; rejection of, 115–116

Revolutionary Stage, 36

Rieger, František, 12, 14

Říp, Mount, 13

Robemont-Dessaignes, George: *Mute Canary, The*, 43

Rolland, Romain: *Fourteenth of July, The*, 78; *Play of Love and Death, The*, 112–113

Romantic movement, 12, 16, 18

Rostand, Edmond: *Romantics, The*, 64

Rubín (cellar studio), 173

Rudolf (Habsburg crown prince), 15

Russian theatre, 2, 17

Sabina, Karel, 166, 173

Šamberk, F.: *Eleventh Commandment, The*, 87

šantány, 30

Sardou, Victorien, 18

Sartre, Jean-Paul, 94; *Dirty Hands*, 141; *Flies, The*, 141; *No Exit*, 206

satire, 11, 17, 26, 27, 31, 33, 34, 35, 41, 46, 51, 61, 84, 86, 94, 102–106, 115, 117–118, 120, 141, 147, 163–164, 178, 209, 221

Saunders, James: *Scent of Flowers, A*, 139

Saxe-Meiningen (duke), 22

scenography, 111–112. *See also* designers

Schacter, Rafael, 65

Scheinpflugová, Olga, 232–233n 12; *Killed, The*, 64

Scherhaufer, Peter, 164, 166–169, 243–244n 18; productions: *Betrayer and Betrayed*, 166–167; *Shakespearomania*, 167–169

Scherl, Adolf, 85

Schiller, Friedrich, 14, 17; *Maid of Orleans*, 58

Schmid, Jan, 161, 162, 163, 164, 207

Schnitzler, Arthur, 19; *Green Cockatoo, The*, 131

Schonová, Vlasta, 65

Schorm, Evald, 127, 150, 154, 160, 215, 237n 6; productions: *Brothers Karamazov*, 154; *Crime and Punishment*, 127,

Théâtre-Libre (Paris), 19
Theatre News, 147
Theatre of Anna Sedláčková, 60–61, 70
Theatre of Jára Kohout, 60
Theatre of Satire, 71–72, 73, 86
Theatre of the Absurd, 114, 121. *See also* absurdist theatre
Theatre of the Czech Army (Vinohrady Theatre), 80
Theatre of the Fifth of May, 72, 73, 86
Theatre of Vlasta Burian, 60, 70
Theatre of Work, 53–54
Theatre on a String (Brno), 5, 164–169, 180, 183, 185, 195, 227, 229, 243n 18
Theatre on the Balustrade, 5, 88, 114, 117–118, 119–123, 125, 129, 130, 131, 134, 143, 150, 151, 154, 161, 184, 188, 193, 194, 210–211, 214, 215, 220, 229, 238n 2
Theatre on the Flyline, 242n 11
Theatre on the Fringe, 172–173
Theatre under the Palm, 209
Thirty Years War (1618–1648), 9
Tobiáš, Egon: *Vojcev*, 213, 214
Tolstoy, Lev, 17
Tomášová, Marie, 111, 128, 193
Topol, Josef, 84, 89, 128, 149, 154; productions: *Cat on the Rails*, 98–99; *End of Carnival*, 107, 111, 215, 216(photo); *Farewell Socrates*, 184, 210; *Hour of Love*, 99; *Midnight Wind*, 84; *Nightingale for Supper*, 99; one-act plays, 98, 100; *Their Day*, 89, 96–97; *Two Nights with a Girl*, 147; *Voices of the Birds*, 184
Tříska, Jan, 111
Trojan, Alois, 12
Tröster, František, 3, 36, 53; set: *Julius Caesar*, 53, 54(photo)
Turgenev, Ivan: *Month in the Country, A*, 44
Tyl, Josef Kajetán, 11–12, 15–16; productions: *Arsonist's Daughter, The*, 12, 28, 228; *Bagpiper from Strakonice, The*, 12, 59, 64, 89; *Bloody Judgment, A*, 12; *Drahomira and Her Sons*, 89; *Folk Festival*, 12; *Hard-Headed Woman, The*, 12; *Jan Hus*, 12, 15, 49, 141
Tyl Theatre, 73, 138, 139, 209. *See also* Estates Theatre
Tynan, Kenneth, 1, 75

Uhde, Milan, 154: *King Vávra*, 105
Unamuno, Miguel de, 213
Union of Czech Theatre Artists, 139
Utopia, 39, 40

v + w. *See* Voskovec, Jiří; Werich, Jan
Vaculík, Ludvík, 102, 237n 5
Vakhtangov, Eugene, 31, 44
Vála, Svatopluk, 169
Van Lerberghe, C.: *Pan*, 28
Vančura, Vladislav, 61; *Alchemist*, 49
Vášaryová, Emilie, 224
Vedral, Jan: *Urmefisto*, 156, 158–159, 178
Vega, Lope de: *Fuente Ovejuna*, 53
Velvet Revolution (1989), 5, 15, 181, 185–188, 197–198
Verdi, Giuseppe: *Rigoletto*, 86, 215
Verhaeren, Emile: *Dawns, The*, 28
Vian, Boris: *Head of Medusa, The*, 207
Villon, François, 174
Vinohrady Theatre, 21, 24, 25, 26, 36–37, 39, 44, 70, 78–80, 90, 115, 156, 184, 195, 207; as Theatre of the Czech Army, 80
Vojan, Eduard, 14, 23, 24; as Hamlet, 23(photo)
Vonnegut, Kurt: *Slapstick*, 213
Voskovec, Jiří, 5, 35, 48(photo); exile in U.S., 58–59; partnership dissolved, 71; productions, *see under* Werich, Jan; as v + w, 35, 41, 43, 45, 46, 80, 151, 229; *see also* Liberated Theatre
Vostrá, Alena, 124, 125; *On Knife's Edge*, 143; *When Your Number Comes Up*, 99, 100(photo), 126, 127

Vostrý, Jaroslav, 124, 125, 126, 195, 196(photo)
Vrchlický, Jaroslav, 18; *Hippodamia*, 18; *Night at Karlstein, A*, 18
Vychodil, Ladislav, 91; *Marriage*, 112; *Play of Love and Death, The*, 112–113(photo)
Vydra, Václav, 40
Vyskočil, Ivan, 116, 117–118, 119, 120, 129, 135, 151

Wagner, Richard: *Gesamkunstwerk*, 54
Webster, Margaret: production: *Tempest, The*, 58
Wedekind, Frank, 30, 206; *Earth Spirit, The*, 26, 36; *Pandora's Box*, 36; *Spring's Awakening*, 54
Werich, Jan, 5, 35, 48(photo), 85, 238n 6; exile in U.S., 58–59; partnership dissolved, 71; productions, 141; *Ass and Shadow*, 46; *Caesar*, 46, 47(photo); *Executioner and Fool*, 47; *Fata Morgana*, 46; *Finian's Rainbow*, 71; *Fist in the Eye, A*, 51, 71; *Golem, The*, 46; *Heavy Barbara*, 51; "Jazz Revues," 46; *Vest Pocket Revue*, 41–42, 43; as v + w, 35, 41, 43, 45, 46, 80, 151, 229. *See also* Liberated Theatre
"Where Is My Home?" (Czech national anthem), 12

Wilson, Robert: *Dr. Faustus Lights the Lights*, 205
Windmill ensemble, 59–60, 71
Wolker, Jiří, 64
Workers' Dramatic Chorus, 39
World Theatre Season (Aldwych Theatre), 113
Writers' Manifesto (1917), 24
Wyspianski, Stanislaw: *Wedding, The*, 220–221

Yalta Conference (1944), 68
Yiddish performances, 30
Ypsilon Theatre. *See also* Studio Ypsilon

Žák, J.: *School, Life's Foundation*, 213
Zavřel, František, 26–27; productions: *Coming to Wisdom of Don Quixote, The*, 26; *Earth Spirit, The*, 26; *King Václav IV*, 26
Zelenka, František, 46, 61, 65; Terezin attic, 63(sketch)
Zeyer, Julius: *Old Story, An*, 59; *Radúz and Mahulena*, 18
Zhdanov, A. A., 73
Žídek, Ivo, 239n 5
Zinner, Hedda: *Devil's Circle, The*, 88
Zola, Emile, 14